Every Parent

Every Parent

A Positive Approach to Children's Behaviour

Matthew R. Sanders PhD

with illustrations by Mike Spoor

ADDISON-WESLEY PUBLISHING COMPANY
Sydney • Wokingham, England • Reading, Massachusetts
Menlo Park, California • New York • Don Mills, Ontario
Amsterdam • Bonn • Singapore • Tokyo • Madrid • San Juan

Editor: K. Andrew Semmens
Production Editor: Susan Lewis
Text design by Christie and Eckermann Art and Design Studio
Cover design by John Windus

Illustrations by Mike Spoor
Typeset by DOCUPRO, Sydney
Printed in Australia by Globe Press

National Library of Australia
Cataloguing-in-Publication

Sanders, Matthew R.
Every Parent: a positive approach to children's behaviour.

Includes index.
ISBN 0 201 53930 6.

1. Child psychology - Popular works.
2. Behaviour disorders in children - Treatment.
3. Child development.

I. Title

649.64

Preface

Concerns about their children's behaviour and how to cope with it are among the most common sources of stress for modern parents. This book is intended as a resource for parents who want practical information on how to foster healthy adjustment in their children and advice on how to deal with common behavioural and developmental problems. Most parents who have concerns or questions about their children's behaviour or development have to rely on common sense and perhaps on advice from their own parents or friends — advice that is often conflicting or confusing. This book provides information on how to deal with specific behavioural and developmental problems, as well as ideas on how to prevent, where possible, difficulties arising in the first place.

When problems arise with children, for example delinquency, drug and alcohol abuse, and teenage pregnancy, the community is only too willing to lay blame on the parents, but successful parenthood is rarely acknowledged and most parents complete their parenting careers with little thanks for their efforts, no matter how well they have tackled the task. Parents usually enter this phase of their lives without any specific training or preparation for what lies ahead, and an increasing number are forced to cope on their own after marital breakdown and divorce. The modern family undertakes what is probably the most important job in the community: raising the future generation, often under less than ideal circumstances, such as with a single parent, with financial stresses, in poor housing, in crowded neighbourhoods, and with little support or preparation.

It is estimated that during the first 12 years of life, as many as one in five children will experience behavioural or emotional difficulties severe enough to warrant professional assistance from psychologists, psychiatrists, social workers, or other mental health professionals. Only a small fraction of these children actually receive any assistance.

The ideas and suggestions in this book are presented in an understandable, easy-to-follow, step-by-step fashion. The book is divided into three parts: part I provides background information on the nature and causes of, as well as solutions to, common behavioural and developmental problems in children. Part II deals with a series of common concerns that parents have about their children's behaviour and development during infancy, toddlerhood, the preschool and primary school years. Each chapter contains practical information on how to tackle individual problems; commonly encountered difficulties in carrying out the suggested plan of action are also included. Part III shows parents how to put the ideas covered in previous chapters into practice in the home.

I hope that readers find this book useful in undertaking an important and potentially extremely rewarding job in our society: raising well-adjusted youngsters.

Acknowledgements

This book is dedicated to the many children and their parents who have participated in the Family Intervention Programme in the Department of Psychiatry at the University of Queensland, Brisbane, Australia. Many of the ideas and suggestions about parenting contained in *Every Parent* have evolved as a result of the experience and feedback provided by parents and children participating in research projects and therapy programmes at this centre.

Special thanks go to my wife Tricia whose ideas on parenthood have been invaluable, and to my children Emma and Ben who have each contributed important suggestions about ways of making family life enjoyable for both parents and children. I would also like to express my gratitude to my colleague Dr Mark Dadds and to the many graduate students at the University of Queensland who have influenced my thinking and research on ways of assisting families experiencing difficulties with their children.

The material on incidental teaching and 'ask, say, do' on pages 55-62 and elsewhere draws heavily on the work of Professor Todd Risley and his colleagues at the Universities of Kansas and Alaska. 'Pause, prompt, praise' on page 195 was developed by Dr McNaughton, Dr Glynn and Dr Robinson from the Universities of Auckland and Otago.

Thanks are also due to Kathy Begg for her patient assistance with manuscript preparation.

Notes to the Practitioner

This book was written primarily for parents seeking information and practical advice on the management of common behavioural and developmental problems in preadolescent children. Professional therapists may also find the book useful as an adjunct to individual or group work with parents of behaviourally and emotionally disturbed children, or as a resource book for parents of normal children. The material is likely to be of interest to any professional group that works with parents. Much of the parenting information contained in the book has also been set out step-by-step fashion in a separate series of parenting guides for different problems. Most of the advice included has been tested with families seeking treatment from the Family Intervention Programme at the University of Queensland, and has been published in scientific journals.

These materials have been found to be most useful when used as part of a comprehensive assessment and therapeutic approach that aims to develop parents' competency in managing a wide variety of common difficulties. A companion therapist's manual detailing the conceptual and practical clinical basis of our approach to family intervention is being prepared. In routine clinical work, *Every Parent* can be used as a reading assignment to consolidate concepts or strategies introduced in therapy. It also provides effective management advice that parents can implement with their children. The materials are particularly useful with families who have children with oppositional disorders and conduct disorders. However, we have also used selected materials covered in the book with depressed, withdrawn, anxious, hyperactive, and learning-disabled children.

We have found that a very active teaching approach is useful with many parents of children with severe behavioural disorders to complement use of written materials. Typically, this involves providing specific guidance and instructions regarding which problems to tackle and in what order, demonstrations and modelling of skills through role plays, feedback, and coaching for parents as they practise the skills while the therapist observes the family interaction. Feedback and support, particularly in the early stages of tackling a problem, seem to be necessary with many families. With other parents, brief advice, guidance, and the written guidelines have proven to be sufficient to successfully resolve the problem. Obviously the intensity of the intervention in any family will depend on the characteristics of the presenting case, clinical assessment, and therapeutic judgement.

Contents

Tables and Figures

Tables

Figures

*Figures reproduced in Appendix 3 in reusable form.

PART I

Positive Parenting: An Overview

CHAPTER I

Challenges of Parenthood: Coping With Children's Behaviour

*'I have always desperately loved my child. I
have now learned to like him as well'*
(A parent tackling the task of changing her parenting.)

The Challenge

Being a parent is difficult. It is a demanding, challenging, and, at times, frustrating experience. It can also be tremendously rewarding. It is a full-time, lifelong, unpaid, and expensive endeavour. Most parents enter their parenting careers unprepared for what lies ahead and most complete their task with little recognition or thanks for their efforts. However, there is no occupation that is more important than raising the next generation. We are expected by society and by our own families to nurture and care for our children in a way that promotes their development and emotional well-being. This basic task of raising children is a complex one. In the process of growing up, children need to develop a sense of their own personal worth and to achieve self-discipline. They also need to learn a great many skills and behaviours that will enable them to become responsible, independent, and well-adjusted human beings. The fundamental challenge for parents is to raise healthy, emotionally stable children who have the necessary skills and resources to enter adult life.

What can parents do to achieve these goals and meet this challenge? In many ways the task revolves around understanding the normal processes of human development, including what influences children's behaviour. It involves learning practical ways of promoting healthy development, including how to encourage desirable behaviour and how to deal effectively with misbehaviour. Every parent is forced to confront the issue of discipline, usually well before their child's second birthday, and most find that there are no simple answers to this problem.

Most parents ask themselves these questions: 'Is it OK to smack my kids when they are naughty?' 'What is the best way to toilet train my 2-year-old?' 'How do I get my child to stay in his own bed at night?' 'What should I do if my child hits or bites other children?' 'How can I encourage my child to feel good about herself?' These and many other issues are among the multitude of practical concerns of parents learning to raise children.

We all want our children to grow up into well-adjusted youngsters, free of emotional and behavioural problems, but few of us have training in child development, parenting, or how to use techniques of behaviour change to achieve our ends. We rely on our own common sense and judgement. Some parents read about children's development or get advice from their parents or from friends who have children. Most of us learn to parent on the job, through much trial and error.

Fortunately, many common behavioural and developmental problems in children can be prevented. That is why this book focuses on how to prevent common behavioural problems and manage developmental tasks in toddlers, preschool children, and school-aged children. Much of the parenting advice given here is quite specific. You will find an easy-to-follow, step-by-step guide on ways of dealing with problems as varied as handling crying and whining in toddlers, and helping children learn to solve problems for themselves.

The material in this book is based largely on my clinical experience in researching and treating problems raised by parents seeking help for their children and themselves, and on my experience in raising two children of my own. Hundreds of children and their families have used the parenting advice discussed in this book, with excellent results. Some of this work has been published in scientific journals but this is the first time the material has been made available to the general public.

How to use this book

Refer to the relevent section whenever you feel you would like ideas on dealing with particular problems or topics. Each problem discussed has a fully self-contained guide for overcoming it.

You may be tempted to turn immediately to part II, which deals with solutions to the specific problems you may be having with your child. However, you'll find these advice sections more helpful if you read the material in part I first. This section deals with different types of behaviour problems, the causes of these problems, and strategies that can be used to promote good family relationships and thereby prevent many problems from arising. Refer to the sections of particular interest to you after reading these chapters. If you decide you would like to try one or more of the suggested strategies for handling particular issues then refer to the final chapter which deals with putting your plan into action. It is also a good idea to prepare yourself by reading the sections relating to problems that may be encountered in your child's next developmental phase.

Some of you may have already sought help from a professional therapist. If so, then it's worth discussing your plans with your therapist to ensure that you are not working at cross-purposes.

Parent Traps

Do you frequently feel exasperated, ashamed, or embarrassed by your child's behaviour? Do you find that your child often irritates you or that you have to threaten and shout a lot to get any cooperation? Do you frequently argue with your partner about how to handle your child's behaviour? Do you criticise yourself for being a less than perfect parent? If the answer to some of these questions is yes, then you may have become caught in a parent trap.

Parenting traps add to the burden of stress that many parents experience, and make the job of raising children more difficult. Positive parenting is a way to avoid these parent traps. It involves learning to influence and guide children's behaviour without resorting to yelling. It involves learning how to motivate children positively through encouragement when they are behaving well. It involves working as a team with your partner on parenting issues. These are the most common parent traps. Later on in the book there is advice on how to deal with them.

The **criticism trap** involves becoming locked into frequent and usually unnecessary power struggles with your child. It typically involves the parent reacting to the child's misbehaviour, such as fighting and arguing, with criticism ('Robert, leave your brother alone.'); threats ('If you do that one more time you're in big trouble, my boy.'); yelling ('Robert! Leave him alone!'); or hitting. This type of discipline, in which the parent's anger escalates rapidly, often backfires and can lead to resentment and further hostility between parent and child. If these kinds of battles take place frequently, it's time to try a new way of handling the situation.

The **leave them alone trap** occurs in combination with the criticism trap and involves the parent ignoring the child when she is behaving well or playing cooperatively. If good behaviour is taken for granted and ignored, it will occur less often in the future. A basic principle of positive parenting involves attending to and encouraging the behaviour you would like to see more often.

The **for the sake of the children trap** involves parents in unhappy and high conflict marriages staying together 'for the sake of the children' rather than learning ways to resolve their marital conflict. The assumption is that children need two stable parents. This ideal is challenged by research that shows that children who live in families where there is a lot of conflict and stress between the marriage partners have more emotional and behavioural problems than those raised in stable one-parent families. Serious marital problems should not be ignored. Conflict over parenting causes inconsistency which in turn makes many behaviour problems worse.

The **perfect parent trap** is the result of our desire to be perfect rather than merely competent parents. Since there is no such thing as a perfect parent, aspiring to become one leads to disappointment, resentment, guilt, and feelings of inadequacy.

The **martyr trap** is the one where parents become so over-involved in parenting that they neglect their own needs for intimacy, companionship, recreation, privacy, and fun, only to find that their marital relationship suffers and they end up feeling dissatisfied and resentful. Quality parenting takes place when adults have their own lives in balance. Being a martyr does not produce quality parenting.

Common Parenting Problems

Let's look at some common behavioural and developmental prob-lems and the difficulties they create for families. If you recognise your child, don't despair. Remember that solutions are offered later.

The whiner

Whether we call it whining, whingeing, grizzling, or complaining, most parents are intimately acquainted with the problem. The tone in a child's voice that turns a request into a demand, especially when it occurs often, can drive a parent to distraction. Many parents report that from the first time he opened his mouth the whiner seemed to have a high-pitched nasal tone. They go on to give endless examples: apart from whining for food before the evening meal, he will whine if a brother or sister touches anything of his, he will whine on trips to the supermarket, on trips in the car, and especially when the family visits his grandparents. In fact, the whiner seems to be whining all the time. Many parents of whiners pride themselves on being very patient and tolerant. They try really hard not to get upset or angry, but the pressure of having a child who constantly whines takes its toll. The parents may be fuming inside, and begin to worry when they start to resent the time they devote to their children. Often this prompts them to seek professional help.

The tantrum thrower

Since perhaps the age of 18 months this child has thrown incredible temper tantrums. The tantrum thrower's behaviour may become so unacceptable that her mother is requested to take her away from kindergarten. When she throws a tantrum, and that can be up to eight times a day, she can be heard at the end of the street. Some tantrum throwers' neighbours have called the police, convinced the child is being physically abused. A tantrum for this child consists of throwing herself to the floor, screaming at the top of her voice, swearing, hitting her hands and legs against the floor, and, on occasions, holding her breath until she is blue in the face. The tantrums can last from 30 seconds to 30 minutes, and are used as a way of controlling others, to get her own way. For example, she might throw a tantrum if refused something she wants. Many parents of tantrum throwers have reached desperation point when they seek professional help. They feel they have tried everything: spanking, pleading, bribing, trying to distract the child, and even ignoring the behaviour. Nothing has worked.

The bed refuser

This child doesn't really have a bed, or so it would seem. She sleeps on the floor in front of the television until her parents are ready for bed. Then she sleeps snuggled happily between the two of them. She simply refuses to go to bed in her own room and her parents have long since given up trying to make her stay in her own bed. They have also given up on trying to put her to bed at anything like a reasonable hour. She usually decides when she goes to sleep. On most nights she falls asleep in front of the television somewhere between 9.30 and 10.30 p.m. She awakens when one of her parents picks her up to take her to bed. Unless she is put into her parents' bed, she screams at the top of her voice until her parents finally give in. She is capable of screaming continuously for over an hour. Children who refuse to go to bed, repeatedly get out of bed, or frequently wake during the night, can become a real handful for parents who are often exhausted themselves at the end of a day and are dying for a break.

The bad sport

This child hates to lose. Ever since his parents can remember, he has had a competitive streak. In the beginning, one or both parents might have secretly admired the fact that the boy had spirit, but he was not actively encouraged to view every game or activity as something you have to win. He became a sore loser. When the bad sport starts school, none of the other children may want to play with him. His teacher will often report that he tries to bully and dominate his classmates. This does not really surprise his parents, who will have witnessed a scene like the following often. Their child is playing 'Star Wars' with his neighbour. They play quite happily for about 10 minutes while the bad sport tells his friend exactly what to do and repeatedly shoots down his space ship. However, as soon as it is the other child's turn, the bad sport refuses to 'die'. After being shot he immediately gets up, throws his space ship to the ground, and storms off in a huff. Often he will then burst in the back door sobbing, telling his parents that his friend 'always shoots down my ship'. The bad sport's 'have to win' attitude and competitive behaviour are his great undoing. If something isn't done to help him cope more effectively with his peers, he will end up being rejected by them.

The fussy eater

Some children with behavioural problems are not as noisy as these first two. An attractive, friendly, and polite 6-year-old who is liked by just about everyone he meets might be a fussy eater. At the dinner table he constantly plays with his food, eats very slowly, and won't even try a wide range of foods. He also refuses to use utensils properly, leaves the table frequently, complains about not being hungry, and becomes quite upset if pressured to eat. However, within 30 minutes of leaving the table, usually with his evening meal barely touched, he often wants a snack, typically a sandwich. Parents of fussy eaters claim that they refuse to eat anything that is good for them, such as meat and vegetables. All they really want is bread, ice-cream, and sweets, a diet that is not designed to build strong, healthy bones and muscles. What, when, where, and how a child eats is a major worry for many parents of young children. Many parent–child conflicts are fought at the family dinner table. Some parents spend the whole meal prodding, threatening, or pleading with their child to eat a small portion of carrot or broccoli. Others spend their time hassling their children about table manners, or eating too slowly, or gulping food. As we will find out, many of these problems can be avoided completely if the mealtime is managed correctly.

Improving problem behaviour

The whiner, the tantrum thrower, the fussy eater, the bed refuser, and the bad sport all have one problem in common: their behaviour brings them into conflict with parents and, in some cases, with teachers and peers. Their parents often hope that the behaviour causing the trouble will just go away. Various people may have advised them that the problem is 'just a phase' and that the child will eventually grow out of it. In many cases, however, the opposite is true. The problem becomes worse.

Improvements will not begin until the parents take action. This action involves the parents learning positive alternative ways of reacting to the child's behaviour. It requires them to directly and honestly challenge and then change their usual way of handling the problem. For many parents the solution is straightforward: it simply requires a decision to try a different way of managing the behaviour. For a few parents, other important changes are also needed. For example, parents who are preoccupied with their own interests, careers, or other pursuits may neglect their children's needs for attention, affection, and adequate supervision. These parents may need to rearrange their priorities to allow more time for their child. For other parents, all that is required is very minor adjustment in the strategies or tactics they already use. The type and amount of change required depends partly on the kind of difficulty being experienced.

A question of values

Child rearing is strongly influenced by a parent's values and beliefs. What we see as being either acceptable or 'problem' behaviour is influenced by the values we consider important. For example, parents who view total obedience and parent power as important to family life will interpret children's challenges to adult authority, such as the times when children become argumentative, as a threat, and this may lead to confrontation. Another parent may see the same argumentative behaviour as the child learning to express an opinion, to stand up for himself, and to be assertive. The same behaviour, then, can be viewed either as a problem or as quite healthy, depending on our values.

This book emphasises helping children become responsible, self-reliant, and self-disciplined. It also focuses on helping children learn to become independent decision makers and problem solvers. At the same time, however, children need to become civilised and socially skilled human beings so that they can live in harmony with others. This involves children learning how to compromise and to respect the rights and opinions of others, including their parents. Self-discipline stems partly from having clear guidelines and ground rules. However, all parents ultimately have to decide what values are important to promote in their children.

Different types of behaviour problems

As children move from infancy to adolescence, they are capable of behaving in a variety of ways that cause concern to parents. Children's behaviour problems come in many shapes and forms. Some are shortlived and improve with age, while others are more persistent and can be related to the development of psychological disturbance in later life. Behaviour problems can be divided into two main categories: the common, everyday behaviour problems of normal children, and behaviours that are symptoms of more serious behavioural disturbance or psychopathology.

Everyday behaviour 'problems' of normal children

All children behave at times in irritating, disruptive ways that may produce conflict within the family, for example a child might make silly noises, or pull faces at the dinner table. While these kinds of behaviours are 'problems' in the sense that they may be a source of family friction or tension, they are quite normal and commonly observed in children of a similar age. These problems often decrease as the child matures, providing the parents deal with them sensibly. They occur in children who are not behaviourally or emotionally disturbed.

Examples of such behaviours in infants and preschool-age children include crying and fussing, whining and attention seeking, occasional fussy eating habits, bedtime problems, disobedience,

attention seeking, clingy dependent behaviour, fear of strangers, and thumbsucking. Other common problems include hassles in getting a child to cooperate with family routines such as getting dressed, having a bath, cleaning teeth, eating meals, going to bed at night, or going shopping. Effective handling of these normal family hassles can prevent more difficult problems from arising, while their mismanagement in young children can lead to the development of more serious problems in school-aged children. Table 1 on pages 14–15 lists the 20 most commonly reported behaviour problems of children between the ages of 6 and 12.

More severe behaviour problems

Some children develop more serious problems, where the child's behaviour pattern is clearly different from that of other children of the same age. For example, many children have occasional fights or disagreements with their brothers or sisters, but a behaviourally disturbed youngster may have many more such fights, both at home and at school, may lose her temper frequently in a rage of uncontrollable anger and break and destroy her siblings' belongings, and then experience little guilt or remorse. The troublesome behaviour pattern tends to occur frequently, persists over time, and may be associated with other symptoms of psychological disturbance.

The majority of children's behavioural and emotional problems

Table 1: Commonly reported behaviour problems in children

Problem	6 years	
	% of parents	
	Occurs somewhat	Certainly applies
Bullies other children	13.0	2.2
Has temper outbursts	26.2	5.7
Destroys own or others' belongings	10.6	2.3
Irritable, quick to fly off the handle	34.2	8.1
Disobedient	27.7	6.8
Tells lies	21.2	2.9
Steals	9.6	1.3
Frequently fights with other children	13.1	2.2
Restless, overactive	37.8	15.2
Excitable, impulsive	*	
Inattentive, easily distracted	*	
Constantly fidgeting	*	
Can't settle to anything	10.0	3.2
Always climbing	*	
Afraid of new things or situations	27.3	5.9
Shy with other children	*	
Often worried about things	36.7	9.3
Often appears miserable, unhappy	12.8	1.6
Not much liked by other children	3.4	0.6
Rather solitary	44.5	15.2
Number of children in sample	1115	

* Item not measured.

This information is based on a study of New Zealand school children followed from birth. Data was kindly supplied by Dr D. Fergusson, Department of Paediatrics, Christchurch Clinical School of Medicine, University of Otago, New Zealand, and reproduced with permission.

8 years % of parents		10 years % of parents		12 years % of parents	
Occurs somewhat	Certainly applies	Occurs somewhat	Certainly applies	Occurs somewhat	Certainly applies
13.6	2.8	14.7	2.9	13.6	1.9
30.0	7.6	29.1	7.6	31.0	7.1
7.4	1.9	4.3	0.7	5.0	1.1
27.8	6.9	27.0	5.2	34.7	5.5
16.0	4.3	21.5	3.7	29.8	2.2
15.8	3.1	17.3	2.2	25.8	3.6
5.4	1.3	5.9	1.0	7.5	2.2
6.6	1.6	10.9	1.2	8.5	1.0
27.5	10.7	24.4	7.7	24.7	8.1
32.6	11.9	29.3	10.9	31.6	7.9
30.1	11.5	33.6	13.3	35.9	12.2
24.4	10.3	21.4	8.1	21.6	7.3
11.5	3.7	10.2	2.6	8.7	2.5
18.8	9.9	13.0	6.7	7.5	3.3
26.0	5.2	25.7	5.7	33.1	7.5
16.1	2.1	12.7	1.4	14.9	2.2
23.5	6.0	25.3	5.5	31.1	4.8
10.1	2.0	12.3	2.4	14.0	2.3
3.2	0.4	6.4	0.9	9.2	1.6
53.1	20.1	42.7	15.7	49.1	14.5
1092		1067		1020	

For each age, the first set of figures shows the percentage of parents that indicated the behaviour occurs to some degree. The second set of figures give the percentage of parents reporting that the item certainly applies.

can be divided into two groups: externalising and internalising problems.

Externalising problems are generally problems of 'acting out' that bring the child into conflict with others. Examples include antisocial behaviours such as disobedience, stealing, aggression, showing off, truancy, bullying, lying, being cheeky and disruptive at school, demanding attention, being selfish, being rude, or throwing temper tantrums. These problems are often described as **conduct disturbances**. They range from mild to severe and occur much more often in boys than in girls. Mild conduct problems typically include such behaviours as whining, non-compliance, attention seeking, tantrums, and demanding behaviour.

More severe conduct problems are more likely to persist into adolescence and adulthood. These include aggressiveness, stealing, lying, threatening, destructive behaviour, and truancy. Serious conduct disturbances often start out as mild problems at preschool age and get worse as the child moves through primary schooling. Children with severe conduct problems often have poor peer relationships, are more likely to drop out of school, and are at risk of developing antisocial personalities, alcohol and drug addiction problems, criminal behaviour, or other psychopathology as adults. Conduct disorders are the most common reasons for referral to mental health clinics for children, and about a third of these children develop serious behavioural and emotional problems as adults.

Internalising problems tend to be distressing to the individual child who is often anxious and has low self-esteem. Other problems can include phobias (intense irrational fears), worrying, depression, sleep problems, stomachaches, headaches, nausea, shyness, social withdrawal, and recurring irrational and unwanted thoughts (obsessions). Some children experience both internalising and externalising problems. Internalising problems are more frequent in girls than in boys, and once again range from mild to severe.

Less than one-third of children with behavioural or emotional problems receive any professional help. This book looks at ways of helping both groups of children: those with common or normal behavioural problems, and those with more severe behavioural or emotional disturbances. In the next chapter some of the causes of behaviour problems are looked at more closely, because to solve a problem it is necessary to understand why children behave as they do.

CHAPTER 2

The Causes of Behaviour Problems

Why do children behave in particular ways? How is it that children from the same family can be so similar in some respects, yet so different in others? Why do some children develop behaviour problems while others do not? What is the role of heredity and that of the child's family in influencing children's behaviour? None of these questions has a complete answer. However, to understand how children's behaviour develops we need to consider three main factors. From the moment of conception, children's growth and development is influenced by their inherited **genetic make-up**, the **family environment** in which they are raised, and the **broader culture** in which the family lives. Heredity and environment play joint roles in shaping children's behaviour and development. Together they determine what particular behaviours, skills, attitudes, and abilities each child develops. They also influence whether the child develops behavioural or emotional problems.

The relative importance of genetic and environmental influences varies, depending on the type of behaviour problem being discussed. Nevertheless, the following factors have been shown to be related to the development of behaviour problems in children in general.

Heredity: the child's temperament

Each child inherits a unique genetic make-up from both parents; this gives him or her the biological equipment needed for survival and for all subsequent development. Children inherit many of their physical characteristics from their parents, including eye colour, skin colour, hair texture, certain physical diseases, and a tendency to develop others. Some researchers believe that some psychological and behavioural characteristics are also largely inherited. These include intelligence, basic temperament, and a vulnerability to psychological disturbance. The word **temperament** refers to a biologically based tendency to behave in certain ways. Three basic personality attributes emerge early in a child's life and appear to be both inherited and related to the development of behaviour problems. These are emotionality, activity level, and sociability.

Emotionality is measured by an infant's arousal in response to events in the environment. Highly emotional infants fuss and cry a lot and often show fearful or angry reactions to sudden changes in stimulation, such as being spoken to by an unfamiliar person. They often respond negatively to stimulation.

Activity level refers to energy expenditure and the amount of vigorous movement and activity that children display. Active infants who have begun crawling or walking are often very busy. They are excitement seekers, with high activity levels. They have lots of gross motor movement, explore their environment energetically, and like vigorous play. These children are often headstrong, persistent and difficult to control.

Sociability refers to infants' preference for interactions with people. Sociable infants show a marked interest in human faces. They like the attention of others, and are responsive to that attention. They often initiate contact with a wide range of people, not just their parents. If an infant is high on sociability but the mother is low, the mother may find the child's demands for attention irritating and exhausting. This in turn can affect the quality of the parent's interactions with her baby.

From very early in life, about 10 per cent of children appear to be particularly difficult to rear. These children appear to inherit a 'difficult' temperament that places them at risk for developing behaviour problems later on. As babies, they fuss and cry a lot, are difficult to settle as they often have sleeping and feeding disturbances, and are difficult to get into predictable routines. Such problems usually arise within the first six months. Difficult babies are difficult for most parents to handle. Parents who have been through the ordeal of trying to settle a baby who cries frequently and will not settle at night know the frustrations, tensions, and anxiety these children can create. In other words, some children, because of their own temperamental characteristics, are more likely than others to create parenting problems that in turn can lead to further behaviour and adjustment problems. Many physically abused children have difficult temperaments. However, not all temperamentally difficult infants develop behaviour or adjustment difficulties, and some 'easy to manage' infants go on to develop problems later in life. The outcome depends not only on the child's temperament but on how parents deal with their child's behaviour and on their general child-rearing patterns.

The family environment

No two children are raised in identical environments, even if they are in the same family. In the early years of a child's life, the family has the task of socialisation, but once the child enters kindergarten or school, peers and teachers also start to play an important role. Parents still have the main responsibility to help children learn the many skills and behaviours they need if they are to grow into well-adjusted and responsible members of the community. As parents, we play a major role in helping children learn a great many things: to walk, talk, use the potty or toilet correctly, to dress and undress, tie shoe laces, and respect the property of others. We help our children learn to follow directions, ask politely when making requests, and, of course, to deal with frustrations, successes, disappointments, and conflicts with others. Parents do influence what behaviours children learn.

Even with children whose temperament perhaps predisposes them to psychological problems, the way we handle them affects whether difficulties continue, worsen, or improve. Biology and genetics provide the boundaries within which development takes place, but the child's family and life experience help her or him develop into a social being.

A lot of attention should be focused on the role environment plays in influencing behaviour for one important reason: while you cannot change your child's genetic make-up, you can change the

environment. As parents we decide how our child is raised and therefore the kind of environment our child experiences, at least at home. This means there is usually something quite concrete and specific a parent can do to prevent or overcome many common behaviour problems.

The role of learning and experience

Research by behavioural scientists has shown that many common behaviour problems in children are concerned with **social interaction**. In other words, these are problems in how children relate to other people in their lives and how others relate to them. Many problems are learned in the process of interacting with others. Even if children are biologically predisposed to developing problems, they are not born knowing how to steal, lie, cheat, throw temper tantrums, or to be violent. These behaviours usually develop gradually over months or years, and may eventually become part of the child's general pattern of behaviour. Understanding how children learn is extremely useful in deciding how best to deal with problems. Figure 1 on page 22 summarises the various factors within family relationships that contribute to behaviour problems.

Let's begin by discussing the idea that problem behaviours produce **consequences** that help to maintain them.

Accidental rewards for misbehaviour

From the very beginning, a child's behaviour produces environmental consequences. For example, babies soon learn that crying is a very effective way of signalling that they are in distress. Parents quickly learn to change a wet nappy or to feed their infant when she cries. Hence, crying leads to the consequence of being fed. A smile often results in an adult smiling back, or cooing, or cuddling the baby. Children learn that their behaviour matters. They quickly learn that it can be an effective way of controlling the actions of others.

Both desirable and undesirable behaviour can be influenced by the consequences they produce. Careful observation of children's behaviour often shows that it has 'hidden payoffs'. The reactions of parents and siblings can accidentally reward misbehaviour, as the case study below illustrates.

Carl is 3½ years old. His parents, Mary and Robert, have had problems with him since he was about 8 months old. They both

Figure 1: Factors contributing to the development of behaviour problems in children

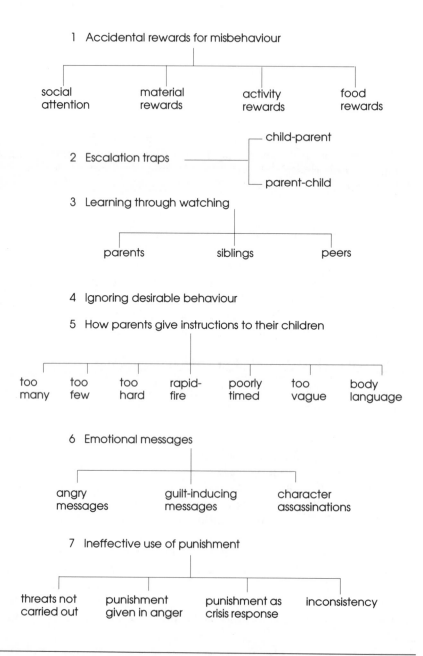

describe him as aggressive, disobedient, and constantly demanding their attention.

During an initial interview with this family, I was particularly interested in observing whether Carl would engage in any of the behaviours Mary had complained of and, if so, how the parents handled them. Carl, both parents, and I were in a large playroom equipped with a variety of appropriate toys and four chairs, one each for the adults and one for Carl if he wanted to be seated. From the moment our discussion started, Carl wanted his parents' attention. During the first 10 minutes of the interview, he interrupted his mother 12 times. An interruption usually consisted of his calling out, 'Mum, come and look at this,' or, 'I want you to play with me, *now*!' During this 10-minute period, Carl climbed on his mother's lap three times and poked his tongue out at her about 3 cm from her face. During this brief encounter, the mother gave Carl four instructions not to interrupt and the father gave three instructions to 'go and play'. After the twelfth interruption, Robert excused himself and attempted to 'settle' Carl down. Settling consisted of sitting down next to him on the floor and watching intently as Carl proudly showed his father how to work the crane on a large truck. For the next 20 minutes Carl was the perfect child. He had what he wanted, the complete and undivided attention of a grown-up. So long as he had it he was fine. However, problems arose immediately whenever he was required to play on his own.

Carl's behaviour in the playroom was fairly typical of his behaviour at home whenever the two parents attempted to talk to each other. It was also typical of his behaviour when he visited his grandparents or Mary's friends. In other words, his reaction was not an isolated response in an unusual clinical situation. Later observation of Carl, and his parents' reaction to him, showed a sequence of attention-gaining behaviour followed by adult attention that was played out many times each day.

Let us look closely at what happened and try to pinpoint some of the hidden payoffs for Carl. Firstly, it is quite clear that his interruptions and demands were very successful in gaining attention from his parents. To be sure, some of the attention was negative, but in terms of the sheer amount of reaction, Carl was clearly being overindulged by his parents. Secondly, Carl's behaviour was successful in temporarily interrupting the conversation of the adults in the room. Each time he whined for Mum to come and play, Mary paused and turned towards him, gave him eye contact, and then explained she was busy. Thirdly,

Carl's demanding eventually produced a very powerful consequence: Robert sat down and played with him just to 'shut him up'. Having what he wanted, Carl was quite happy and behaved himself for the rest of the session.

The hidden payoffs for misbehaviour are not always as obvious as they are in Carl's case, but careful observation of children's behaviour often reveals a pattern of social consequences that accidentally or unintentionally encourage misbehaviour. Four main types of consequences can reward difficult behaviour: social attention, material rewards, accidental activity rewards, and food rewards.

Social attention

Parents and children attend to each other in a variety of ways. They look, smile, hug, frown, grimace, talk, yell, threaten, spank, hit, and so on. Some children unfortunately learn that the surest way to get a 'bite' from their parents is to misbehave. When misbehaviour frequently results in social attention, the attention can reward the behaviour, as in Carl's case. Parental attention is the most common hidden payoff for bad behaviour. You might ask, 'What are we supposed to do? Simply ignore naughty behaviour?' Unfortunately, the answer is not as simple as this. Ignoring, as we will find out, does not always work.

Material rewards

Most parents occasionally have to deal with demands that they buy their child something, for example toys, sweets, or other items of interest. However there are dangers in giving in to demands like those illustrated in this case study.

> 'Mum, can you buy me this?' [*pointing to a toy in a department store*]
> 'No, Jamie, I said you weren't to ask for things in the store today.'
> 'Mum buy me this. I want it. *Pleeassse!*' [*getting agitated*]
> 'Jamie, don't carry on like that.'
> 'I want it. I want it. Buy it for me.'
> 'This is the last time. Don't you dare ask for anything else.' [*slightly irritated*]
> 'Gee, thanks Mum.'

Jamie is now much more likely to ask his parents to buy him things on future shopping trips. When demanding behaviour produces results, it is more likely to be repeated.

'Don't you dare ask for anything else'

Activity rewards

Another way parents can accidentally reward misbehaviour is to provide an activity the child likes as a consequence of misbehaviour. For example, many parents of young children use distraction to deal with conflicts over toys. If one toddler makes a direct line towards a toy truck another child is playing with, his mother might intervene just as he strikes and grabs the toy, saying, 'Darling, look at what mummy's got,' and holding up another toy. Often such distraction is followed by the parent giving the child a lot of attention while trying to interest him in the new toy or activity. One of the potential dangers of this approach is that the child is denied the opportunity to learn that you don't snatch other children's toys. Furthermore, the parent may have accidentally rewarded the behaviour by giving the child a lot of positive attention and an interesting alternative activity. Another example of an activity reward is a situation where a parent waits until a child is bored or whining and then, concerned that the child has been ignored, sits down and plays a game with her. Providing an activity reward for bored behaviour can cause problems, and it's better to deal with the whining first and then look for an opportunity to engage the child in a new activity.

Food rewards

Many parent–child conflicts are over food. Parents can very easily accidentally reward their child for bad behaviour such as complaining or demanding by giving him a drink or food. Unfortunately, not only does this action reward the child for complaining, it also rewards snacking between meals, with the consequence that the child may not eat properly at mealtime. He may also learn to rely on food as a way of reducing boredom or tension and therefore risk becoming overweight. Handling children's requests for food is a real problem for parents. It is important that parents respond predictably and immediately to a baby's hunger cries, but as a child develops (particularly by the age of 2) parents need to become more selective in responding to food requests. Children have to learn that meals are eaten at certain times and that unlimited access to food outside these times is not on. In essence, parents must change their way of dealing with food requests during infancy to avoid children using food as an escape.

Escalation traps

In an **escalation trap**, a child learns to 'turn up' or escalate the intensity of his or her behaviour to force the parent or another child to back down or give in. The child becomes more and more unpleasant until the adult either gives in or the adult threatens or actually carries out some punishment. Here is a typical example:

> 'Mum, can I go over to Tommy's house?'
> 'No, Jason, dinner will be ready in about ten minutes and I want you to tidy the mess in your room before dinner.'
> 'But I want to go out and play. I'm not hungry anyway [*in a whining voice*].'
> 'No. Dinner will be ready shortly. Come on. Go and do your room.'
> 'You're mean. I'm going anyway. Get out of my way.'
> 'Now listen, you. Just stop that noise. The whole neighbourhood can hear you carrying on. Well, I suppose

you can go for a little while but you must come back when
I call you. Not like last night when I had to come looking
for you.'
'Alright. 'Bye.'

You will notice that his mother's initial refusal to let Jason play
sparked off a counter-attack in which he became insistent and noisy.
At the point where his behaviour became quite unpleasant, his
mother backed down and let him have his own way. This parent has
just accidentally rewarded the child for escalating in the face of resistance. What Jason may have learnt is that when you don't get your
own way, all you have to do is to rant and rave and you'll get what
you want. He in fact received a double reward: his mother agreed to
his demands and he was allowed to play with Tommy.

Many parents find this kind of escalation hard to deal with,
particularly when it happens in public, but if children are rewarded
for escalating, they can become very difficult to manage.

Unfortunately, parents themselves are accidentally rewarded for
giving in to the child because the child *stops* the screaming or yelling,
at least for the moment. When both parent and child are being
rewarded, the pattern of interaction pays off and is likely to occur
again. Consider this situation:

'Paul, go and put away your bike and skateboard. Now,
please.'
'Dad, I'm watching my favourite show.'
'Go and do it now. Your mother can't get the car in the
garage with all that mess in the driveway.'
'No. Wait till the next ads.'
'Get moving lad or it's the belt for you [*reaching for his
leather belt*].'
'I'm going. I'm going. Why are you always yelling at me?'

Here we have another escalation trap. By complying, Paul has just
accidentally rewarded his father's threatening behaviour. Dad is now
more likely to threaten and yell when Paul disobeys. 'What's wrong
with that?' you might ask. 'After all, Paul did what he was told.' What
is wrong is that Paul will probably learn to comply only when he is
threatened, and will ignore requests that are put more calmly. There
are also some emotional side-effects to this kind of punishment, such
as the child becoming anxious, fearful, or angry. These will be
discussed later.

It is important to remember that both parents and children can *train* each other to escalate as a way of dealing with problems. Such escalation, particularly when it occurs often, is a very unpleasant form of family interaction. When parents find themselves continually having to escalate to get their child to cooperate, it is time to look for an alternative way of handling the problem. The child may be out of control. Aggressive children with more severe behaviour problems often show this pattern of escalation in their dealings with others.

Learning through watching

Children have a tremendous capacity to learn through observation. They will often try to imitate our actions and are delighted when they learn to do things just like Mum or Dad. Through observation, children learn many important things about their world.

Every day of a child's life, his or her parents provide a model of how to behave in certain situations. Because there is no such thing as a perfect parent, that modelling is sometimes of behaviours they do not wish their child to learn. For example, parents themselves may swear or use abusive language when annoyed about something. Many parents spank their child for being aggressive towards other children. When some parents see their child being violent towards others, they will say something like, 'I'll teach you to hit...', whack, whack. Children observe their parents closely at times like this. What they notice is that when something happens that Dad doesn't like, it is OK to yell, hit, and become angry. Rather than decreasing the child's hitting, this modelling may increase the chances that the child will hit in the future. Parents who hit often are likely to have children who hit a lot as well, particularly when they become parents themselves.

Many behaviour problems can be learned through modelling. Examples include foul language and swearing, cheating, lying, aggression, and disobedience. These behaviours can all be learned through observation, particularly if the child notices that the behaviour is successful in that the person gets his or her own way.

Children also model themselves on the behaviour of siblings, peers, and other high-status people such as rock stars and TV characters. This is well understood by the shocked parent who discovers her 6-year-old using words the child has never heard at home but picked up shortly after starting school or after a weekend visit from cousins. If older brothers and sisters are disruptive, noisy, or disobedient, younger siblings are more likely to try the same tactics.

Ignoring desirable behaviour

Some children develop behaviour problems because they rarely receive positive attention for good behaviour yet get jumped on every time they do something wrong. Feedback about the things we do right is important in developing a positive view of ourselves. One mother in our research project was observed interacting with her child at home on five different days for about 30 minutes each time. The child was causing considerable problems for her as he seemed to be withdrawn, sulked a lot, and would explode occasionally and lose his temper. Every 25 seconds, a trained observer noted what the child was doing and how the mother responded to him. The observer noted, for example, whether the parent praised, ignored, punished, threatened, asked the child a question, and so forth. The results of these observations were enlightening. They showed that 85 per cent of the total attention the child received followed some negative behaviour, for example whining, or sulking. Only 15 per cent of the attention he received was for positive behaviour. Yet the child was actually behaving appropriately about 52 per cent of the time. Not once over the five days was he praised for good behaviour. This parent was very surprised to learn that the child had been good for over half the time he was observed; she thought he had been naughty for about three-quarters of the time.

For this child there was little payoff for good behaviour. The message is clear: when you ignore good behaviour, don't be surprised if it disappears.

How parents give instructions to their children

All parents ask children to do things, and children learn to respond appropriately. Requests that require the child to initiate some action ('Come to the dinner table.' 'Begin your homework.' 'Put your toys away.' 'Wash your hands.') are called **initiating instructions**. **Terminating instructions** require the child to stop doing something ('Don't pull pussy's tail.') and are often followed by an initiating instruction ('Stroke pussy like this.').

Sometimes children simply refuse to comply with parental requests of either kind. Children who are very disobedient may be described by their parents as 'stubborn', 'headstrong', 'selfish', or 'determined', and a lot of conflict between parent and child can result. Every bath, mealtime, bedtime, family outing, shopping trip, or ride in the car turns into a battle of wills. Mum or Dad wants one thing, the child wants another. When such battle lines are drawn, the child often seems to win.

Some of these problems are related to how parents give instructions. Few stop to consider carefully how the timing, type of request, or the way it is made can affect children's behaviour. How to make your instructions and requests more effective is discussed in a later chapter, but for the moment let's look at some of the problems that can arise in giving instructions to children.

Giving too many instructions

There is a simple but basic rule relating to giving instructions to children. Every instruction we give or rule we make creates an opportunity for the child not to comply with it. The more instructions given, the more opportunities to disobey. During a 30-minute home observation, one parent in our research programme gave her 3-year-old 90 instructions, such as 'Don't do that.' 'Get down from there.' 'Leave it alone.' 'Don't whinge.' 'Come over here.' In 30 minutes the child had 90 opportunities to disobey. This could have been halved by halving the number of instructions. Apart from making the child feel picked on or 'got at', giving too many instructions is also exhausting for parents.

Giving too few instructions

Just as giving too many instructions can create problems, so too can the opposite. Children are more likely to learn what is expected of them and how to behave if their parents take the time to explain rules they would like to operate in specific situations. For example, some children develop poor table manners because no one has taken the time to give them proper instructions in the appropriate use of their knife and fork.

Instructions beyond the child's capabilities

What can reasonably be expected of children depends greatly on their age and developmental level. For example, a 9-year-old can reasonably be expected to make his own bed, however it is probably a task beyond most 4-year-olds, although the latter can be encouraged to help. Parents who expect too much too soon will experience resistance and sometimes resentment. For example, expecting a 3-year-old to tidy up a very messy room without any help is asking for problems. On the other hand, some parents don't ask their children to do enough for fear they will make a mess or not complete the task satisfactorily. Older children should be encouraged to take some responsibility around the home, including helping with dishes, tidying their bedrooms, helping with cleaning the yard, and so on. Families where both adults and children pitch in to complete necessary chores are best for children in the long run because with practice and encouragement they learn what to do and how to do it efficiently. It is simply not acceptable for 14- and 15-year-olds to expect their mothers to do everything around the house while they watch television or listen to music for hours on end.

Giving rapid-fire instructions

Sometimes the parent gives a string of instructions all at once, before the child has had a chance to comply with the first request. For example, they may say to a 9-year-old, 'I want you to finish your maths homework, rake up the leaves on the path, tidy your room, and then set the dinner table.' Children often feel bombarded with demands and would be much more likely to comply if each instruction had been given separately.

Poorly timed instructions

Sometimes poor timing on the parent's part leads to problems. If a child is doing something interesting, such as watching a favourite television show, a request that interferes with that is less likely to be obeyed. There needs to be some give and take here. Adults don't immediately jump to it if they are busy or already completing another task, and we need to take children's interests and activities into account before we ask them to do something else. You can avoid a storm by simply waiting until the TV programme has finished. However, it is important to recognise that some children will always say they are doing something interesting as a way of avoiding helping out at home. If this happens it is better to insist that the child complies anyway. Also, it is entirely reasonable to interrupt an activity and ask for something to be done, such as removing rollerblades from the stairs, if there is a risk or danger involved and it has already been requested anyway.

Giving vague instructions

Children are more likely to ignore requests that are expressed as questions than those that are clear, specific instructions. For example, a parent might say to a child, 'Would you like to have a bath now Jamie?' implying that the child has a choice. The choice is more apparent than real, however, because if the child doesn't respond the parent becomes insistent. Another example is the parent who wants to stop her 3-year-old who is monopolising a backyard swing and says, 'Why don't you want to let Mary have a turn now?' These kinds of 'questions' are instructions in disguise. If parents really want to give their children a choice they should be prepared for a response like 'No thanks, Mum' or 'No, I don't want to share'.

Other vague instructions

Some parents, when they see their child doing something inappropriate, will say 'Wayne ...', then pause and frown. If Wayne has just done three inappropriate things such as jumped on the couch, teased his sister, and hit his brother, it is unclear which behaviour the parent considers a problem or what is considered more acceptable. The parent should have said, 'Wayne don't jump on the couch. The couch is for sitting on.' Other examples of vague instructions include things like, 'Don't be silly,' 'For heaven's sake,' or 'Watch your step, boy.' In general, vague instructions are more likely to be disobeyed than clear, specific ones.

Instructions and body language

The effectiveness of a request depends not only on the words used but also on the accompanying body language such as our facial expression, whether we directly face the child, how close we are to the child, our posture, and tone of voice. Some parents learn quickly that before they ask their child to do something it is better to get within an arm's length, to get eye contact, and to avoid yelling out from some distance away. Long-distance instructions are easier for a child to ignore.

Emotional messages

Children's behaviour is affected by the emotional tone of what adults say to them. When children are difficult to handle, their behaviour often produces an emotional response that is conveyed to the child through the parents' words, actions, or body language. Some of the ways parents communicate their emotional reactions can create further problems for the child.

Frequent angry messages

All parents get angry with their children at times. As mentioned in 'Escalation traps' on page 26, children can accidentally reward parents for yelling and shouting by complying with the angry request. Unfortunately, such children may not learn to comply with calmly delivered, softly spoken requests. Instructions and other statements made when a parent is intensely angry ('You really are a horrible child sometimes!') can indicate that the parent is angry with the child rather than with the behaviour. An alternative is, 'I don't like that behaviour'. There is an important difference between the two messages. The first reflects on the child as a person, the second on what she or he is doing.

One of the parent's hardest tasks is to keep cool when disciplining or correcting a child. When we become extremely angry we lose our objectivity, over-react, and can punish the child unnecessarily severely. When a parent frequently becomes angry with a child it's often time to learn a new way of handling the problem.

Guilt-inducing messages

Some parents try to shame their child into cooperating. 'What would your teacher think of you now, if she could see you carrying on like that?' 'Why don't you think about someone other than yourself for once? I'm tired too but I still have to cook dinner.' 'I think you're being selfish and rude.' This is trying to control the child by making her feel guilty, ashamed, or embarrassed. However, the child may not understand specifically what she has done to cause problems for the parent. Parents who frequently moralise in order to manipulate their children into complying with their wishes can create much resentment and hostility. In many situations it simply doesn't work. Children may internalise these messages over time, start seeing themselves as mean, selfish, uncaring, and insensitive, and then act accordingly. Children who receive a lot of personal attacks like this can also become very self-critical and anxious. Some even become depressed.

If the child's behaviour is the problem, it is better to focus on it rather than on some underlying motive of the child's.

Character assassinations

Emotional and behavioural problems in children can also arise when their parents call them names. Children are often very sensitive to being called names such as 'stupid', 'dummy', 'dopey', 'idiot', 'lamebrain', 'egghead', 'bugger', 'bastard', or 'creep'. These words are sometimes used as part of a general character assassination of the child, but occasionally can be used in isolation. They may reflect the parent's exasperation with the child, but they usually make the situation worse rather than better.

Ineffective use of punishment

No topic creates more confusion and concern for parents than the issue of punishment. Here I am talking mainly about physical punishment or threats to use physical punishment as a way of disciplining a child. To smack or not to smack? Most parents answer this question well before the child's second birthday. On the one hand parents hear that to 'spare the rod is to spoil the child', on the other that corporal punishment is cruel and psychologically damaging. Experts disagree on the use of corporal punishment. Let me explain my view on the issue.

First of all there is little doubt that a firm hard smack on the bottom can be an effective deterrent, particularly when the child is doing something dangerous. However, this kind of punishment does not work for all behaviours, or for that matter for all parents. At best it works some of the time, with some behaviours, for some children. Even then it will only work if it is used correctly. People who advocate a 'damn good hiding' or a 'kick up the bum' as a solution to all of society's problems with children have a very limited understanding of children and their problems.

Secondly, many behaviour problems are directly related to the ineffective and inconsistent use of punishment, particularly corporal punishment. Many children referred to our programme have had

more hidings than hot dinners. Insufficient punishment is rarely a problem: how punishment is used frequently is. Punishment works best when it is applied immediately after the offending behaviour, every time the behaviour occurs, and in sufficient intensity to serve as a deterrent. Many parents, however, do not use spankings in this way. Here are some examples of how punishment can contribute to children's behaviour problems.

Punishment threatened but not carried out

'Andrew, if you do that to Robert one more time, you'll cop it.' 'Timothy, if I've told you once I've told you a thousand times, *don't* throw sand. One more time and that's it. It's the belt for you.' 'You wait until your father gets home.' When a child hears lots of threats but rarely receives any consequence, threatening punishment becomes an ineffective way of controlling behaviour. Sometimes threats of punishment can even serve as a dare to a child, who will then test the parent to the limit.

Punishment given in anger

Parents often use spankings and other punishments when they are angry with the child. When parents become extremely angry there is always a risk of losing control and really physically hurting the child. I have worked with children who have been so severely beaten that they have had to be hospitalised. Angry, out-of-control adults can inflict terrible, sometimes permanently damaging injuries on their children. Children have even been killed by their parents in a rage that has got out of control.

When a parent becomes angry it can signal to the child that the adult has lost control. As mentioned earlier, an angry parent will often criticise the child ('You horrible brat!') rather than the behaviour that is causing the problem. Such rage outbursts can make a child feel unloved, resentful, and insecure. Many parents who seek help for children with behaviour problems get into this trap of reacting to irritating behaviour with explosive outbursts. While feeling angry is normal, it is not always helpful to act in openly hostile ways when children misbehave.

Punishment as a crisis response

Problems can arise if punishment is used as a crisis reaction. I recall one parent in our programme who was constantly harassed with complaints and protests from her 10-year-old about where he wanted to spend a long weekend. Several times she had tried to reason with him and explain why it wasn't possible to do what he wanted (he wanted to go skiing and the family simply couldn't afford it). However, the child went on and on and on and on, with one complaint after another. Finally, the mother exploded, screamed at the boy, and sent him to his room. You may feel that you would do exactly the same, and that the parent's reaction was quite justified. However, this mother only punished the boy when his behaviour become absolutely intolerable to her. She was exhausted from the constant harassment, and when she finally broke she reacted in a fiercely emotional way. It might have been better to react earlier, and to use whatever discipline she felt appropriate *before* the boy's behaviour became intolerable.

We often lose our capacity to be objective in a crisis and end up over-reacting. In this case, after the explosion, the mother felt tremendously guilty and spent the next hour trying to calm her son down and to reassure him that she really did love him and was sorry. Part of this family's treatment involved teaching the mother to respond more quickly to difficult behaviour.

Inconsistent use of punishment

Many children learn to break rules and disobey instructions because they are not consistently enforced. Being consistent in our reactions to children is a difficult thing, because our mood, feelings, and behaviour are all influenced by a variety of other factors, such as our marriage, work pressure, and our health. These make being perfectly consistent almost impossible. However, when parents become very inconsistent in their use of punishment it is almost guaranteed to fail. If a child is punished for refusing to do chores on one day but not the next, she will not learn to complete her chores. Here is an example of the kind of thing I mean.

Shirley and Martin, both had full-time jobs in a city bank. Brad, their 7-year-old, was in Grade 2 at school, where he was polite and well behaved. At home it was a different story. According to Shirley, one of their main problems was that Brad used to swear and abuse both parents when he didn't get his own way. One clear difficulty the couple had was that they couldn't agree on how to deal with the problem. Shirley, who was on the receiving end of most of the outbursts, thought it was best to ignore the behaviour. Martin insisted that any swearing should be severely punished by whacking the child with his belt and sending him to his room where he would stay sulking, often for up to 2 hours. The parents' inability to agree meant that

Brad got away with swearing on some occasions, while on others he was severely punished. Such inconsistent use of punishment actually resulted in the behaviour getting worse over time.

Children cannot be expected to learn acceptable patterns of behaviour if their parents' reactions are unpredictable. The child gets a double message: sometimes swearing is OK, at other times it is not. This can be quite confusing to children.

The negative effects of punishment

While punishment can be made to work in managing children's behaviour, any parent who relies heavily on negative tactics to deal with misbehaviour should be aware of some of the dangers in this approach.

One of the most important side effects is that every time parents scream, shout, rave, or hit their child, they are modelling the very behaviour they want their child not to do. Children can easily learn that losing your cool and becoming aggressive is an acceptable way of dealing with frustration. Many abused children grow up to abuse their own children. In the long term, it is more useful to a child to learn alternative, successful, and non-violent means of dealing with conflict. Here, of course, parents can serve as positive models, teaching their children other ways of handling disagreements.

Children who are about to be punished often become anxious and fearful. A child who is sent to his bedroom to wait for his father to punish him often experiences negative emotions. He may cry, shake, or plead with his parents not to hit him. Good behaviour that is motivated solely by fear is unpleasant for children. When this fear happens often, the child may become excessively timid or with-drawn. He may also experience suppressed hostility and rage, and can become quite unmanageable when his parents are not around.

Children who are punished frequently may try to avoid or escape from the situation where punishment occurs. For example, many children who steal learn to lie to avoid punishment. Runaways have often experienced a lot of punishment at home. When I made a home visit to a family in our programme, I arrived at about 4.30 p.m. to witness a major battle taking place. The mother was chasing her 10-year-old boy around the house with a belt, trying desperately to catch him and to administer 'what he deserves'. Fortunately the child could run faster than the mother and finally disappeared down the street, yelling obscenities that I am sure could be heard several blocks away.

If punishment seems likely, it is a natural response for the child to escape. Something similar occurs when speeding motorists slow down if they see a police car. It also partly explains why criminals try to escape from prison. Many older children become runaways under just these circumstances.

One of the main difficulties of using punishment to control behaviour is that the effects are short-lived. Research has shown that punishment may lead to a temporary reduction in a problem behaviour, but it does not produce lasting change. One parent I can recall was a very strong advocate of the wooden spoon for her two boys when they were fighting. Every time they fought she would bring out the wooden spoon as a threat. Miraculously, she reported, they stopped every time. I asked the mother to keep a record of how often the boys fought and how often she threatened and actually used the wooden spoon. After one week the following results came back: fights 7; spoon threats 3, use of spoon 4. Clearly, her strategy had not led to a permanent reduction in the fighting. The boys had not learned to play cooperatively. The spoon only stopped the fight once it had started, and for lasting and meaningful behaviour change other strategies were needed.

While harsh punishment has disadvantages from the child's viewpoint, it has some problems for parents as well. First, parents can be accidentally rewarded for using punishment because it produces a *temporary reduction* in the misbehaviour. Unfortunately, parents may be more likely to use this approach in the future because of this payoff. Second, parents can easily be misled into thinking that the punishment has been effective. One way to check out whether your punishment technique is working is to count how often you have to use it. If from one week to the next you have to smack or threaten your child for the same behaviour at about the same rate, say twice a day, and this remains fairly constant, it is unlikely that the punishment is working. Effective punishment, and discipline in general, needs to be used less and less often because the child is learning the correct behaviour. Third, many parents find punishing an upset child a difficult, unpleasant chore and some feel extremely guilty and agitated after the event. For some parents, these emotional reactions can last long after the punishment is handed out.

When punishment is misused, used very inconsistently, or is excessively harsh, it can actually make a behaviour problem worse. One parent I interviewed claimed she lined each of her four children up every morning to give them a whack. She told them, 'That is for all the times you'll do something rotten today and I don't catch you.'

Marital problems

Common sense tells us that unhappy marriages can badly affect children. However, the connection between marital problems and difficulties with children is quite complex. The day-to-day demands of raising children can place a strain on any marriage, particularly when children are young, and some marital conflict can result from living with an extremely difficult child. However, with difficult children, couples' relationships can also be strained because each disagrees with the other on basic child rearing issues, such as what behaviours should be disciplined; what discipline should be used, how often, by whom; supervision of children; or how much time the parents spend with the child. Sometimes these conflicts are resolved in a straightforward way when both parents learn new parenting skills. When a couple can reach agreement on a basic workable strategy for dealing with the problem, the marital conflict often partially disappears.

When a couple's relationship is strained in a number of other areas and there is a lot of open hostility between the parents, children frequently suffer. Marriages where there are high levels of open conflict, for example arguments and shouting matches, appear to produce different effects on boys and girls. Boys may develop anti-social behaviours such as aggressiveness, whereas girls may become more anxious, withdrawn, and depressed.

Bad marriages affect children both directly and indirectly. Children are affected directly when they observe their parents engaged in conflict. This can be distressing to children who want their parents to be happy. Indirectly, they can be affected because the parent (typically the mother) worried about their marriage may become depressed, spend less time with the children, and become more inconsistent or irritable.

Children thrive in a positive, warm, loving family environment where the two parents work as a team in matters of child rearing. Where this is simply not possible, due to serious differences between parents, the couple need to seek marital counselling. Children who are quite emotionally unstable when the parents are together and there is a high level of open hostility often improve following a marital separation. Keeping together for the sake of the children can sometimes do more harm than good.

Peer and school influences

Children's behaviour is also influenced by factors outside the home. The two most important outside influences related to the development of behaviour problems are the child's relationships with other children and their academic progress at school. Children with behaviour problems are often unpopular. Aggressive and negative children are often rejected by their peers, who simply don't want to play with kids who bully, boss, or hurt other children. These children often have poor social skills and find it difficult to make new friends. Such rejection increases the chances that they will align themselves with other disruptive and difficult children. Once a child is part of a peer group or gang that encourages antisocial behaviour such as stealing, lying, and truancy, the difficult behaviour may deteriorate further, both at home and at school.

There is little doubt that a child's academic progress also has an important impact on behaviour and self-image. Children who are making slow progress at school, find the work difficult, have learning difficulties, or rarely receive any positive feedback or rewards, are at greater risk of dropping out of school. This in turn increases the chances that the child will come under the influence of a peer group consisting of other disillusioned youngsters. When children are unpopular, are failing at school, and are very disruptive, they are more likely to become involved in serious delinquent behaviours including drug and alcohol abuse.

The further down the path towards delinquency a child has progressed, the more difficult it is to reverse the process.

Parents' emotional problems

Most parents are aware that their moods affect the way they relate to their children. Our children's behaviour can also affect the way we feel about ourselves as parents and as people. It is not surprising therefore that a parent's emotional problems can affect a child's behaviour.

A parent's depression is the most common of the emotional problems that can affect children. It is estimated that up to 18 per cent of all adults will suffer from a bout of depression at some time in their lives. At any given time, up to 7 per cent of women are clinically depressed. While most adults experience occasional bad moods, perhaps following a disappointment or upsetting experience, most of these 'down' periods are shortlived, and will often respond to such simple solutions as a break from children, a chat with a close friend, or getting out of the house. Clinical depression is much more severe and persistent, affecting many aspects of a person's life including parenting. Symptoms of depression include feeling sad or miserable, loss of interest in usual activities, sleep disturbance (early morning wakening), weight loss, suicidal thoughts, feelings of helplessness and hopelessness, and of being unworthy. When parents are depressed, they often interact with their children less frequently, provide less supervision, and behave irritably and impatiently. This can lead to explosive outbursts over trivial things that normally wouldn't worry them. Depressed parents also find it hard to be consistent and positive with their children when they themselves are feeling miserable.

Families where one of the parents suffers from depression are more likely to have children with behavioural and emotional problems, particularly conduct disturbances. Exactly why this might be so is unclear. Some clinicians believe it is due to the child inheriting from the parent a vulnerability towards emotional disturbance; others believe it is because the parent's depression disrupts the parent–child relationship.

Whatever the causes, parents should consider seeking professional help to combat their depression so as to reduce the risks to their children. Many depressions respond well to modern treatment, and once the parent's depression has lifted somewhat, the children's problems can be tackled more effectively.

Stress and parenting

Modern parents are confronted with a variety of other day-to-day stresses, some of which may affect family relationships. These include financial, housing, or transport problems; work-related stress and pressure; problems with neighbours or interfering relatives; and stress associated with frequent moves, the death of a parent, lack of intimacy, divorce, and starting work again after having a baby. Most families cope with these stresses pretty well and their children are not adversely affected. However, anything that disrupts the normal family routines for a prolonged period can be upsetting to children, who like security and predictability. In such circumstances, children may become unsettled and more difficult to manage.

Parents' attitudes, beliefs and expectations

Parenting is a complex task. The way we raise our children is affected by our attitudes, beliefs, and expectations about children and child rearing. Parents' views are strongly influenced by the models their parents provided when they were children, their own experience with children, the opinions of marriage partners, and the media. Some of the beliefs parents commonly hold about children make the task of raising children difficult.

'It's just a phase.'

Parents sometimes explain away their children's behaviour, particularly misbehaviour, as a 'passing phase'. For example, parents of 2-year-olds who throw temper tantrums often comfort themselves by seeing the behaviour as part of a 'terrible twos' syndrome. It is important to remember that not all 2-year-olds throw tantrums, and that those who do, do not always grow out of it. While there are enormous differences between children of different ages, and parents' expectations of them need to be adjusted accordingly, many behaviour problems are not an inevitable and necessary part of normal development.

I can recall a parent at a playgroup meeting insisting that her 3-year-old's aggressive behaviour towards other children was 'just a phase' and therefore nothing to worry about. Unfortunately the other parents in the group were not quite as tolerant, and the child had become very unpopular with other children because of his aggression. This parent eventually sought help when her child was 5. His behaviour had become so difficult that the director of the kindergarten had asked her to remove him from the group. This child's behaviour was not a passing phase. His problem could have been dealt with much earlier if his mother had recognised that his behaviour was quite unacceptable and required modification.

'He's doing it deliberately, just to annoy me.'

I routinely ask parents requesting assistance with their children what they believe to be the cause of the problem. Some blame themselves, others believe that their children are motivated to upset, annoy, or irritate the parent deliberately. Sometimes a parent feels the child has some inbuilt personality flaw, an evil or a mean streak. Few children with behaviour problems are able to explain the reasons for their actions. Most simply do not know, and certainly all would have difficulty putting their reasons into words. Parents who are convinced that the problem is simply the result of a character flaw can often ignore important actions of their own that might contribute to the problem.

'It's all my fault.'

Other parents blame themselves for almost everything the child does. I have interviewed many guilt-ridden and worried parents. Often they become depressed, and in severe cases they may become immobilised and incapable of making even relatively minor changes to their daily routines. It is important to remember that some children are much more difficult to raise than others. Children who have feeding problems, cry excessively as infants, and have sleep difficulties are hard for almost all parents to deal with. In other words, the characteristics of the child, the child's peer group, the health of the child, and the degree of support parents can provide one another can all influence the way a child develops. It is simply not helpful for parents to blame themselves for everything that happens to their children. Feeling guilty and depressed only makes it harder to make the necessary adjustments and changes. Some things that happen to our children are out of our control anyway. We can't control what happens in the classroom or playground, the composition of a child's peer group, what television programmes are made for children, the advertising that is directed towards children, or the actions of our spouse towards the child. Self-blame is destructive and never solves anything.

Parents' expectations

The behaviour parents encourage, reward, or punish very much depends on what they consider normal for children at different ages. Some behaviour problems can arise because the parent expects too much too soon. For example, parents who try to toilet train infants of 6 to 8 months of age will often find the task more difficult than if they had waited until the child was 2 years old. By 2, children have sufficient physical maturity and understanding of language to learn to use a potty with little difficulty. Parents who expect their children to be perfect, for example always to be polite, well mannered, never to become angry and always tidy and helpful, are setting themselves up for a life of disappointment and constant battles. This is a particular problem for parents who are extremely house proud. Children need space to explore and to play. Children's games are often messy and apparently disorganised. Designating the child's own bedroom as the only place he can make a mess creates more problems than it solves. Some behaviour problems are the direct result of parents being overly fussy and rigid.

CHAPTER 3

Positive Parenting: Strategies for Fostering Improved Behaviour

Parenting is primarily concerned with the education and care of children. There are four fundamental goals that parents should aim to achieve if their children are to develop in a psychologically healthy way. These are:

- to create a caring family environment that encourages children to develop positive feelings about themselves and other family members
- to help children become socially competent in their interactions with others
- to help children master important developmental skills and tasks
- to help children learn to be responsible for their actions.

Parents who are successful in achieving these goals are more likely to produce happy, well-adjusted children.

Socialising children, that is, helping them to become more socially adept, is much easier when parents learn to interact with children in ways that promote behaviour change. This chapter discusses a variety of useful strategies for encouraging children to learn more acceptable, appropriate, and skilled ways of behaving and of interacting with others.

Many children who are difficult to manage, for example very aggressive or disobedient children, lack the social skills to deal with the situations they confront. Children who are aggressive, show off, boast, tease, or bully other children, often lack the social skills they need to make friends. Children who rudely demand attention when their parents have visitors often lack basic skills of being able to wait or ask politely for what they want. Other children have the skills but don't use them. For example, they know how to ask civilly if they want to borrow something from a sibling, but they simply don't do it very often, preferring to whine and complain to their mother instead. We need to know how to teach our children the skills they require in their dealings with others, and to motivate them to use those skills.

Most common behaviour problems can be solved by helping children to learn a more effective, skilled, or appropriate way of handling a situation. For example, when a mother tells her toddler who has just pulled her hair, 'No, don't pull hair. Stroke my hair like this,' she is demonstrating a correct alternative way of behaving.

The next two sections outline 18 strategies that can be used to promote healthy adjustment in children.

Strategies for promoting good relationships with children and for teaching desirable behaviour

This section deals with ways of encouraging good communication between parent and child, and provides ideas for helping children learn socially appropriate behaviours and important developmental skills and tasks. Table 2 summarises these positive parenting strategies. The approximate ages where different strategies are most useful are highlighted, but these should be used as a rough guide only.

Table 2: Summary of strategies for encouraging desirable behaviour

- spending quality time with your child
- tuning in to desirable behaviour
- giving plenty of physical affection
- conversing with children
- using incidental teaching
- setting a good example through modelling
- encouraging independence through 'ask, say, do'
- providing engaging activities for children

Spending quality time with your child

Recommended age range: children of all ages

One of the most important things you can give to your child is your time. Children of all ages need their parents' time and attention if they are to develop normally. This means more than simply being with your child and providing food, clothing, shelter, and supervision. It is possible for an adult to spend an entire week with a child, yet spend no quality time with him at all.

Children need to grow up feeling that they have a **caring relationship** with their parents. Ideally, both parents have to spend time with their children to accomplish this goal. The key to establishing an individual relationship with a child is to spend **frequent, small amounts of time** doing things the child likes to do. For example, children often want to show an adult something they have made, or talk to them about a discovery or experience. Your son might arrive home from preschool bursting to tell you about his trip to the fire station. This is the time to provide quality attention, when he is ready and interested in telling you about what happened. At that time, make yourself available. Interrupt what you are doing and give your child undivided attention for a short while. Often it takes only a few seconds.

Brief (30-second to 2-minute) periods of individual attention can do much to strengthen your relationship with your child. It is during these encounters that children learn that parents are accessible, approachable, interested, and caring. Quality parenting takes time. Listening patiently to a child's make-believe story, learning about what happened at preschool or school today, helping a child with a difficult toy, playing a game, and answering hundreds of questions

are all part of developing a child's sense of being cared for and loved. These activities can be tiring. Nevertheless, parents need to be accessible to children, whether they are babies or teenagers. Remember, *brief frequent encounters are generally better than longer but less frequent ones.*

Failure to show an interest in the child's day-to-day activities can make her feel that Mum or Dad doesn't care. Some parents get into the habit of frequently requiring the child to wait. 'I'm busy. I'll be there in a minute.' 'Wait until I've finished the washing up.' Requiring children to wait is sometimes both appropriate and necessary, for example if you are speaking on the telephone. However, when children *always* have to wait or are required to wait for too long, their parents miss out on the spontaneous joy and excitement at the point of discovery. Don't be surprised in this case if your child stops wanting to talk to you about things, or learns to demand very loudly to get your attention.

For older children, accessibility to parents is still important. Even though school-age children need less frequent attention from parents than toddlers and preschoolers, the crucial point is that parents are accessible when they are required. Parents can't provide guidance and support or function as a resource person for their child if they are inaccessible.

Tuning in to desirable behaviour

Recommended age range: children of all ages

Another important skill in developing good relationships with children involves giving positive attention or feedback when a child is behaving well. Attention can be a very powerful motivator. When your children are doing something you like, let them know you appreciate it. Catch your child being good and desirable behaviour will occur more often. Positive attention can be given in many different ways, for example a comment, touch, smile, wink, or hug. They all communicate to your child that you care, that you are interested in her, and that you approve of what she is doing. You will also be setting a good example for your child about how to relate positively to others. By encouraging good behaviour, you will help your child learn more quickly what is expected of her. Here are some guidelines.

Watch carefully.

Before you say anything, watch your child as she plays, moves around the house, or completes an activity. Identify anything she is doing that you would like to occur more often. In other words, ask yourself what **specific behaviour** of hers do you like.

Be clear.

Praise your child enthusiastically by *describing* the behaviour you like 'That's terrific Andy. You went to the bathroom all by yourself. Well done.' 'Thank you Mandy for taking out the rubbish today.' 'What a beautifully set table, Ben.' Describe the behaviour rather than the child. Rather than saying 'Kevin, you're wonderful,' say 'Kevin, that was very thoughtful the way you included Jamie in your game with Boris.' A specific description is more informative for the child.

Initially, respond immediately and often.

At first it is better to respond to the child's desirable behaviour as quickly as possible. For some children, particularly those who are disruptive, an immediate, quick response is necessary because the good behaviour may not occur very frequently. Initially praise your child often. Later on, when the new behaviour is occurring more often, the praise can be given less frequently. For example, you might decide you want to encourage your child to put her dirty school clothes in the washing basket at the end of each day. For the first week you praise her every time she remembers to put her clothes in the washing basket, but once she is putting her clothes in the right place each day, you will praise her only occasionally.

Take an interest in what your child is doing.

Watch with interest what your child is doing. Just knowing that a parent is watching a game or activity can serve as a powerful motivator. Children also want parents to watch when they have mastered a new skill, for example standing up on skates, catching a ball, or swimming the length of a pool.

Comment enthusiastically on your child's activity or game.

Describe your child's action or achievement warmly. With toddlers, comments such as the following can work well: 'That block tower is really terrific.' 'That puzzle has lots of pieces. How did you ever work that out?' 'That bulldozer looks as though it could easily push those blocks away.' Older children also like positive comments about their activities.

Comment on your child's toy.

Children love to share their toys with an interested adult. 'Hasn't dolly got beautiful yellow hair?' 'Has Teddy broken his leg? It must be very sore for him.'

Help out with difficult toys or games.

Offer help if your child is having difficulty with a toy. 'Peter, if you turn the blue one up the other way, the red one will fit on top.' 'If you turn the nut the other way it will go on.'

Be sincere.

Praise works best when you mean what you say and are genuinely interested in what the child is doing. This can be hard at times, particularly if you are tired or busy. However, praise that is given reluctantly, unenthusiastically, or in a flat, emotionless tone of voice is not as effective as sincere praise.

Use non-verbal attention.

Positive attention can include more than words. Sitting or standing near a child, touching, smiling, or simply joining in a game for a while all communicate your interest and show that you are pleased with what's going on.

Share your positive feelings.

When you praise your child, use 'I' statements such as, 'I am really pleased that you stayed close to me when we went shopping today.' 'I' statements communicate that your child's behaviour affects you positively. Other examples of 'I' statements include, 'I really think that was a tremendous effort to get your marks in maths up this term. Well done.' 'I really appreciate it when you offer to help wash up the dishes without being asked.'

Attend to small improvements.

In general, look for small and gradual improvements in behaviour rather than expecting your child to be perfect straight away. A child can be helped to learn a new skill if you attend to gradual improvements. For example, to teach a child to catch a ball, her parent could first stand really close and show her how to cup her hands, then gently throw the ball so it lands in the right place. If the child succeeds with her first 'catch', the parent could move slightly further back and repeat the action. Each catch can be praised. Over time, the throws can be harder and from further back. This kind of 'shaping' of a new skill is a very effective way of teaching children to do a variety of complex tasks.

Some cautions

Tuning in to desirable behaviour is a very effective way of changing behaviour. Children often feel good about themselves and respond with delight when parents are positive and encouraging. However, children who have received very little praise for good behaviour may at first react in an embarrassed or even silly way. Be prepared to persist if you get this kind of reaction from your child. It usually disappears once the child gets more experience in receiving praise. Sometimes, although not always, older children can become embarrassed by being praised in front of friends. With teenagers and older children it is better not to make too much of a fuss in front of peers. A quiet word in the child's ear works just as well. Praise can work with both younger and older children, providing it is genuine and done in such a way that the child feels comfortable.

Parents themselves may feel a bit awkward when they shift from reacting mainly to bad behaviour to responding to good behaviour. Some come from homes where they received very little positive attention themselves and they feel embarrassed or self-conscious when they start to relate to their child in a different way. Praising, like most skills, requires practice.

Giving your child plenty of physical affection

Recommended age range: children of all ages

Another way of communicating your interest in and caring for a child is to provide plenty of physical contact. Frequent holding, touching, cuddling, tickling, kissing, hugging, and so on are important if children are to grow up feeling cared for and comfortable with giving and receiving affection. Physical affection is very important in the first few years of a child's life if he is to form secure attachments with his parents. As a strategy for encouraging desired behaviour, physical affection is best provided either while the child is engaged in some desirable activity or immediately following it. Physical affection is not advised while the child is shrieking, crying, or throwing a tantrum. It may calm the child temporarily, but also may encourage these behaviours to occur more often.

Have plenty of physical contact.

Try to have some positive physical contact every day. If you want your child to be physically expressive, lots of practice helps.

Vary your contact.

Children enjoy variety as much as adults do. Holding hands, cuddles, kisses, tickles, hugs, pats, stroking, back rubs, and foot tickles are all ways of communicating affection and having fun with your child. Experiment. Find out what your child seems to like.

Be careful.

Avoid being rough. Accidents can easily happen when physical fun becomes too boisterous or the child gets over-excited, for example when parents throw their kids in the air.

Be spontaneous.

While most of the time it's OK to give your child physical contact when you feel like it, avoid doing so while the child is misbehaving, or as a way of calming an agitated child. Don't always expect your child to respond affectionately, particularly if she is absorbed in an activity.

Tell your child you care.

When you are close to your child, it's a good time to let kim know in words that you love him. Children need to hear that they are loved.

Do not force physical affection.

Some parents become upset because their child seems to reject physical affection. Children differ quite a lot in how much physical affection they seek from their parents. Not all babies like being cuddled. Some may even struggle and resist. As these infants get older, they may continue to resist or avoid physical contact with their parents. One way of helping such a child become more comfortable with physical contact is to start with the level of contact she feels comfortable with, and then to gradually increase the frequency and type of contact.

Begin with a pat or by touching the child lightly when you praise her, but don't expect her to do likewise. Let her first become comfortable with gentle, non-demonstrative contact. If the child seeks out contact, be prepared to reciprocate at the same level. For example, she may want to hold your hand as you walk down the street. Simply allow this to happen. Don't demand any more than the child is prepared to give. Gradually she will become used to more and more frequent contact and then other types of contact, such as a cuddle, may be possible. Forcing the child will not work, and may make the situation worse.

Conversing with children

Recommended age range: children of all ages

Children learn a great deal through conversations with adults. Showing an interest in what a child has to say is not only a way of giving positive attention for desirable behaviour, it also provides an opportunity for a child to practise conversational and other social skills, for example describing their experiences and events at school, or asking questions as a way of obtaining information. Conversational skills are important because it is through language that children learn to relate to others.

Wait until the child is engaged in an activity.

Take notice of when your child is busy and engaged in an activity. Approach him and move within conversational range.

Pause and observe the child's activity.

Find out what the child is doing. Take notice of the purpose of the child's activity. For example, sit on the couch and watch as your daughter tackles a new game on the family computer; sit next to your son as he works on his school science project.

Respond to your child's comments.

Make yourself available and ready to respond to any requests, questions, or comments that your child might make. 'Dad, look at how many battleships I have shot down!' Respond with an interested comment or answer. 'What's your highest score so far?'

Withdraw if there is a negative reaction.

Remove yourself if your child seems uncomfortable with your presence. If she becomes embarrassed, or in some way shows she would rather be alone, simply withdraw. There will be lots of other opportunities.

Offer an additional comment.

Give a brief, interested comment or question about the child's activity. 'That was a good kick.' 'How's your project coming along?' 'You've nearly finished that puzzle.' 'What's superman doing now?'

'Why did Mrs Smith become angry with Steven?' 'Can you show me how to play that later?'

Continue the conversation.

If the child responds or asks you another question, continue the discussion.

Share information.

Communication is a two-way process. Avoid getting trapped into asking a whole series of questions. Volunteer information about your experiences, the highlights of your day, ideas, opinions and feelings, so that a two-way discussion can occur. This kind of interaction fosters the child's conversational skills.

Keep the interactions relatively brief.

These sorts of interactions are best when they are fairly brief, say 30 to 60 seconds. Children can often converse better in short bursts. Their interest in discussing something can quickly change, particularly if another activity captures their attention.

Using incidental teaching

Recommended age range: 10 months to 9 years

There are tremendous learning opportunities in the home for children of all ages. Day-to-day interactions between children and parents provide a context for many exciting discoveries. Children, through their interactions with others, not only learn their native language, they learn important social skills and the many basic self-care skills such as brushing teeth, dressing, and toileting that are needed for independent living.

Many of these basic skills can be developed through a process of **incidental teaching**. This involves using interactions that children initiate as an opportunity for teaching a new skill. Good teachers have used incidental teaching for centuries.

When children initiate contacts with adults, they usually want help, want to show the adult something, want attention, or want information. Under these circumstances, they are often ready to learn. They are motivated to acquire new knowledge or skills because their attention is focused on the issue at hand and they are interested. In fact their request usually identifies the thing they want ('Can you show me how this works?'). The parent is now in a powerful teaching situation. He or she might simply answer the child's question or might invite the child to think of the answer herself ('See if you can figure it out. What do you think those screws are used for?'). In other words, the parent can delay giving the child what she wants so that she has the opportunity to solve the problem, think of the word, or practise the skill.

Incidental teaching occurs when the parent responds to the child's request ('Mum, can you tie my shoelaces?') by requesting a more advanced, sophisticated, or mature response ('Well, what's the first thing you have to do with the two laces?'). Incidental teaching can be used in many daily situations to develop a variety of new skills, such as when the child is getting dressed, during play, while talking to him about his day at school, while helping him with homework, while reading to him or hearing him read to you, or when he asks for help.

Incidental teaching works best when the parent has time to listen and is not rushed or hassled. It is important to be able to work out the topic the child is referring to. For example, when an 18-month-old points to an object but can't name it, the adult has to be able to work out the focus of the child's interest, such as whether he wants the cup or ball on the shelf. The child's topic or request should relate to something the parent is prepared and able to give, such as attention, permission, or help with a toy or activity, and the parent should be able to identify a potential learning goal for the child, for example to name the object she has just pointed to, to practise a skill, or to acquire some new knowledge. If you intend to refuse the request, then say no immediately and do not attempt to use incidental teaching. From the age of about 10 months, children make numerous approaches to their caregivers which present ideal opportunities for incidental teaching.

Set the scene.

Incidental teaching can be used anywhere that there are interesting and engaging things for the child to look at, touch, explore, or experience, or that are likely to promote conversation. Most homes have numerous objects or materials that can promote discussion.

Wait for the child to begin.

You should simply wait for the child to initiate conversation. Don't hover over him, just be accessible.

Respond to the initiation.

You should show an interest in what your child is saying by looking at her, smiling, and directing your full attention to what she is trying to communicate.

Check that you understand what the child is saying.

If you are not sure what your child means, check. 'What are you pointing to? Do you mean the fire engine?'

Ask the child to elaborate.

Ask the child to elaborate, expand, explain, or clarify. 'What colour is that car?' 'What do you want me to do with this train carriage?' 'Tell me where this one goes.' 'What happened when the settlers first arrived in this country?' When children are requested to elaborate on something they are interested in, it is an ideal time for them to acquire new knowledge and concepts about a topic. For example, when an 8-year-old is watching Dad check the tyres of the car before going on a long trip, the child might ask, 'Why are you doing that?' This is an excellent time to teach the child something about inflation of tyres for safe driving. If the child had not asked the question, she would have been far less receptive to Dad's explanation.

If necessary, prompt a better response.

If the child cannot or does not answer, the parent can prompt her. 'Remember how we made the pattern last time? One piece goes here and this piece goes . . .' 'Six times two equals twelve, so six times three equals . . .?'

Provide a model.

If the child still does not answer, or answers incorrectly, tell him the answer and ask him to repeat it. 'Six times three equals eighteen. What does it equal?' 'W-o-o-d spells wood. Can you spell that?'

Give positive feedback.

This involves confirming the answer given by the child so that she knows the answer is correct. 'Blue, that's right. The colour of your shirt is blue, the same colour as your bike.'

Incidental teaching is most effective when it is brief and enjoyable for both parent and child. If you feel angry or irritated during incidental teaching, stop the procedure immediately. As soon as the child indicates she has lost interest in the activity or game, do not persist.

Setting a good example through modelling

Recommended age range: 3 to 12 years

Children have a marvellous capacity for learning through observation. Modelling is a strategy parents can use in day-to-day dealings with children to encourage a wide variety of desirable behaviours and skills. At a general level, modelling is quite straightforward. It involves setting a good example for your child, showing your child through your own actions what is appropriate or desirable behaviour. Remember that while children learn a great deal through watching others, you are the most important model in your child's life. Here are some ideas on how modelling can be used to encourage desirable behaviour in children.

Identify the behaviours you wish to encourage.

The first step is to become aware of the behaviours you wish to encourage through modelling. Examples may include skills such as learning to use the toilet, setting the table, using a knife and fork, kicking a football, mowing the lawn (for older children), sewing, and needlework. Other things include how to take care of pets, make a bed, start a garden, use a hammer, iron clothes, and interact with family and friends. The particular skills a child can learn will depend largely on the age and interests of the child.

Let your child watch.

Children's natural curiosity will often lead to their observing your actions. Watch for signs of your child showing an interest in what you are doing.

Describe what you are doing.

Children learn a lot by having the adult explain or describe the steps involved in carrying out a task.

Answer your child's questions.

Using words the child understands, answer any questions he may have.

Allow the child to copy your actions.

If the activity is safe, encourage the child to try it for herself.

Help your child as necessary.

Children often need help when they try something for the first time. Offer assistance, then let him try again on his own.

Give positive feedback.

Praise your child's efforts by describing her accomplishments. 'That's great. You've sewn your first stitch.'

Avoid modelling undesirable behaviour.

Try to avoid setting a bad example, for example not wearing your seat belt, smoking, abuse of alcohol, using foul language, careless use or storage of power tools, not cleaning up after making a mess.

Do not force your child.

Don't force a child to copy a particular behaviour if he is not interested or is bored. Wait until he shows an interest.

Encouraging independence through 'ask, say, do'

Recommended age range: 3 to 7 years

Many parents try to encourage their children to do things for themselves as soon as possible. For example, children need to learn how to dress and undress themselves, how to play independently for short periods, how to wash themselves, clean their teeth, and use the toilet. Children should be encouraged to learn these skills as soon as they are ready.

Unfortunately, not all children seem motivated to learn these skills and our attempts to help them can be quite frustrating. They may demand that we dress them, or refuse to try to do things for themselves. As a result they can become overly dependent on their parents.

'Ask, say, do' is a way of helping children to become independent in self-care skills. It can easily be used in your daily dealings with children and can be used as soon as children have some basic understanding of language (from age 12 months).

Get everything ready.

Get everything you need, such as all items of clothing, toothbrush, and toothpaste ready in advance. This ensures that the child does not have to wait while you hunt around for missing items.

Gain your child's attention.

Look into your child's eyes, smile, and try to be cheerful and relaxed. If you are flustered or running late the child will sense this pressure. The whole idea is to make learning fun.

Ask.

Ask your child what is the first thing to be done. 'When we brush our teeth, what do we do first?' 'When we get undressed, what shall we take off first?' 'OK, we'll tidy up together. What should we pick up first?' The child has to think about the correct sequence of events and so feels in control of the task. Some parents feel that the child will not know, or will become uncooperative, but don't give up. Children eventually learn not only what to do but also the words related to the step.

If your child gives the correct answer, repeat it.

Repeating what the child says is a way of giving positive feedback and encouraging language development. 'Yes, that's right. You take off your shoes. Good boy.'

Say.

If the child does not give the correct answer, cheerfully tell him what to do. 'First you take off your shoes. You show me how to take off your shoes.'

If your child complies, offer praise for completing the task.

Remember that feedback for correct performance is important. 'Good girl. You did that all by yourself.'

Do.

If the child still does not perform the task, describe what's required by guiding him through the motions. For example, put your hands on his and guide his hands through the task. Use the smallest amount of physical pressure necessary to help him get started. Once the child has started, reduce the pressure so the rest can be completed independently.

Give positive feedback.

As the action is completed, speak up and praise the child by describing what's been accomplished. 'That's great. You took your shoes off all by yourself.'

Repeat the last six steps for each part of the task until it is completed.

For example, when teaching a child how to undress, go through these steps for the shoes, then the shirt, the pants, and so on.

Phase out your help.

Once your child has mastered all the steps involved, you can reduce the amount of help you give. One way of doing this is to require the child to perform several of the steps before giving praise and attention. Then wait until all the steps can be performed before giving attention.

Children will find it easier to learn a skill if the adult describes the actions involved. Don't expect your child to learn complex tasks all at once. It takes time and patience. Your child will not learn at all if you continue to do everything yourself for the sake of speed and convenience. If necessary, organise your morning routine to allow extra time with your child.

This basic strategy can be used for teaching children a wide variety of skills including tidying a bedroom, riding a bike, taking care of animals, learning to cook and sew, using a computer, and repairing a puncture on a bike.

Providing engaging activities for children

Recommended age range: all ages

Some children become difficult because they are bored and have very little to amuse themselves with other than watching television. The best activities for children are those where they can actively participate rather than passively observe. An environment that is rich in interesting things for children stimulates their curiosity as well as their language and intellectual development. It also keeps children active and busy and thereby reduces the likelihood of behaviour problems. Many parents soon discover that some of the most difficult times with children are when there is nothing for them to do, such as when visiting a grandparent who has lots of breakables on low tables, but no toys or other things of interest to children. Children quickly become bored, tired, and irritable in these situations.

Another important advantage of providing an interesting play environment is that incidental teaching becomes easier. Children will have more things to attract their attention and to talk about, which means more opportunities to initiate conversations with adults and therefore more opportunities for incidental teaching.

A play environment also needs to be a safe environment. Accidents in the home are a common source of injuries in children, and a particular problem with infants, toddlers and preschool children. Try to ensure that your home is as safe as possible. Some tips on safety-proofing the home are covered on pages 92–95 in chapter 4.

There is no need to spend a lot of money on expensive toys that often have a very limited life. There are some simple rules on selecting toys for children: they should be robust, capable of being used in a variety of ways, and able to be used by children of different ages. They should not have too many small moveable parts. These sorts of toys can easily be swallowed by young children, are hard to clean up, and have parts that can easily be lost.

Group activities for older children

Recommended age range: 7 to 12 years

Some of the best activities for children involve them in participating as a member of a group or team. Through such group contact, children can learn about being a team member, sportsmanship, how to relate to other children, how to take turns, how to win and lose gracefully, how to work together with other children, and, in sporting activities, how to improve coordination and learn rules.

Children in most modern communities have access to a wide variety of activities outside school and on weekends. Examples include Cubs, Brownies, Girl Guides, Boy Scouts, gymnastics, tennis, swimming, football, tramping, rowing, and so on. Letting children participate in two or three out-of-school activities is a good idea. However, some of these activities can be time-consuming for parents who can end up feeling like taxi drivers, ferrying their children to one activity after another. Some parents try to involve children in too many activities on too many days of the week. Kids need time to relax at home, and as a child moves through school some activities may need to be curtailed so he can complete homework, study, and work on other school-related projects.

Sometimes the choice of activities can be a source of friction between parents. How much choice should children have? Once they start an activity, should they be made to continue if they don't like it? What should parents do if children want to play 'dangerous' sports like rugby?

Many a child has been forced to participate in a sport simply because a parent likes the game. This is often a mistake. The child's own interests and natural aptitude should be taken into account. However, once a child makes a commitment to play a particular sport or to join an activity, she should be encouraged to see it through at least for the season, particularly if the parents have had to pay for expensive uniforms or equipment. Some children need a bit of encouragement to continue in an activity. If they are simply allowed to drop out, they may do so with the next new activity they try and end up not participating in anything at all.

It is important to remember that organised activities for children are also social events where children can meet other kids and make new friendships.

Strategies for dealing with difficult behaviour

So far we have dealt with ways of encouraging appropriate behaviour and helping children learn new skills. However, there is more to producing well-adjusted children than rewarding desirable behaviour. An important part of socialising children involves helping them learn to control their own behaviour by regulating impulsive actions, curbing inappropriate behaviours, and managing anger and other negative emotions. In this section we turn to the issue of how to discipline and set limits for children's behaviour. Several alternative strategies for dealing with misbehaviour are described and listed in table 3. Each strategy has its uses under certain circumstances, as well as its advantages and disadvantages.

Table 3: Summary of strategies for discouraging undesirable behaviour

- establishing clear ground rules
- dealing with rule breaking through directed discussion
- using good behaviour charts
- giving clear calm instructions
- backing up requests with logical consequences
- quiet time
- time out
- planned ignoring
- planning activities to prevent behaviour problems

Establishing clear ground rules

Recommended age range: 4 to 12 years

Children cannot be expected to behave appropriately unless they know what to do. They need some limits to be set for them. Rules help children to learn what is expected of them. Families with no rules can live in chaos; those with too many can be like a concentration camp. There are five things to remember when establishing rules with children: they should be

- few
- fair
- easy to follow
- enforceable
- positively stated

Also, where possible, children themselves should contribute to decisions about family rules.

Have a small number of rules.

The more rules there are, the more opportunities children have for breaking them. This means more problems with enforcement. Each family has to decide on the rules appropriate for them, but here are some examples of important rules for all children to observe:

- children should always let their parents know where they are
- they should always return home by the agreed time
- they should respect and look after other people's property
- they should speak to other family members in a reasonable manner.

Rules should be fair.

Rules should apply to all children in the family. For example, rules relating to the granting of independence, such as when children are allowed to do certain things on their own, should be the same for all children in the family. If Andrea is allowed to catch the bus to the movies with friends at 13, the same rule should apply to James when he is 13. Parents need to use their own judgement in deciding what rules to insist on. Don't be manipulated by children who claim that 'everyone else in our class is allowed to'. If you don't believe it is a good idea, stand your ground. Children will respect you more if they see you as being fair and consistent.

Rules should be easy to follow.

Children are more likely to follow rules that are simply stated and that they understand. They should be able to state a rule themselves and show you exactly what they should do in a particular situation. Parents can check on children's understanding of the rule by asking them, 'What is the thing to do when you first get into the car?' They should be able to answer, 'Put on your safety belt.'

Rules should be enforceable.

There is no point in having rules if you are unprepared or unable to enforce them. Enforcement should involve praise when the child obeys the rule and consistent consequences if the rule is broken. The ways to provide consequences for breaking important family rules will be discussed in more detail later in this chapter. They include withdrawing privileges for a set period, grounding children, requiring extra duties or chores, or withdrawing pocket money. Both parents must enforce the rules consistently, otherwise children will not learn to follow them.

Rules should be positively stated.

Rather than having a huge list of 'don'ts', state the rules in terms of 'do's'. Here are some examples. 'Walk when you are by the pool,' rather than 'Don't run by the pool'; 'Always let Mum or Dad know where you are going if you are out of the house.' 'Pick up your clothes and towels after having a bath,' rather than 'Don't make a mess in the bathroom.'

'Do' rules are specific in the sense that they describe exactly what is expected of the child. Avoid vague phrases such as 'Be careful when you ...', or 'Show respect to your elders.' Apart from sounding preachy, they don't tell the child exactly what to do.

Rules for particular situations.

Sometimes it is very useful to lay down ground rules before going to particular places, such as on shopping trips, visiting relatives, excursions into large cities, air travel, or going on boat trips. These are rules that apply to specific situations, and they do not operate after the outing has finished.

First ask yourself whether the proposed rule is really necessary. If it is, proceed as follows.

1. Set the scene. Call a meeting of all family members. Turn off the television or any other distractions. Choose a time that does not interfere with favourite TV shows or other important activities.

2. State the reason for calling the meeting. Let the kids know why they are there. 'Kids, Mum and I want to talk to you about this camping trip on the weekend. There are a couple of rules we would like you to remember about camp safety, to avoid the problems we had last time we had a weekend away. Remember, Ben, you got lost in the bush, and Sandy, you nearly burnt yourself on the gas cooker

when you were cooking the toast. This will take about 5 minutes. OK?'

3. State each rule early. 'There are three things we would like you to remember at all times. The first thing is always wear something on your feet. There can be broken glass in the grass, not to mention the bull ants which bite.'

4. Seek your child's opinion on the rule. If kids have strong feelings about the fairness or otherwise of the rule, it is better to discuss this in advance and, if necessary, work out a compromise. Sometimes children have very good ideas about how to make the rule workable.

Ask 'What do you think about that? Is that fair enough? Does it make sense to you?' Sometimes difficult children will not participate sensibly in these discussions. If so, state the rule quite clearly and end the discussion. Debating and arguing serve no useful purpose.

5. Ask the child to repeat the rule. This helps the child remember what is required. 'So, what do you have to remember?'

6. Repeat steps 4 and 5 for each additional rule. 'The second thing to remember is, stay near to the camp site unless an adult is with you. We don't want anyone to get lost this time.'

7. Summarise the rules. Ask the child to state all the rules covered. 'Let's see if you can remember them all.'

8. If necessary, write the rules down. Some parents find it helpful to write basic house rules down on a piece of paper and then stick them to the fridge with a magnet so everyone can see them.

9. Decide on specific consequences for complying with and breaking the rule. Rules are more likely to be followed if they lead to consequences, particularly in the early stages. Children should be praised for remembering the rules and, if they have been particularly good, some appropriate reward, such as an activity they enjoy, can be used to recognise their effort. If they break the rule, there should also be appropriate consequences. We will deal with selecting suitable consequences for misbehaviour later in this chapter.

10. Wind up the discussion. Close the discussion by making a quick summary of the key issues covered and agreed upon.

Dealing with rule breaking through directed discussion

Recommended age range: 4 to 10 years

Directed discussion is a way of promoting alternative behaviour when a child has done something wrong. It is useful with house rules such as not coming indoors with muddy shoes or gumboots, leaving school bags or dirty clothing in the wrong place, and running through the house instead of walking. It is best used when the child's behaviour has been a slip up rather than a frequently occurring event.

Gain your child's attention.

Obtain the child's attention through a request for a chat or a direct instruction. 'Tim, come here please. I'd like to talk to you about what happened just then.'

State the problem briefly, simply, and calmly.

For example, if your child walks in the back door with muddy gumboots say, 'Do not come inside with your gumboots on.'

Explain why the behaviour is a problem.

'It makes a mess on the floor and then someone has to clean it up. That someone is usually me.'

Describe or get the child to suggest the correct alternative behaviour.

'What's the right thing to do? Where should your gumboots go?'

Rehearse the correct behaviour.

If there is a chance for the child to practise the correct way to behave, get him to do so immediately. 'Now you show me the right way to come indoors when you're dirty. Go right back to the back door and start again.'

End the discussion by praising the child for the correct behaviour.

When you use directed discussion, try to avoid becoming annoyed. Keep your cool and speak in a matter-of-fact way. Avoid statements such as 'you silly boy' or 'what a grub'. Simply thank the child for completing the correct behaviour.

Using good behaviour charts

Recommended age range: 2½ to 9 years

Another very effective way of encouraging better behaviour is the use of a behaviour chart, also called 'happy faces' or star chart. A happy faces chart can be made out of cardboard or paper and displayed in a prominent and convenient place such as the refrigerator. The chart consists of a number of squares, about 2cm, large enough to draw in or stick on smiley faces, stars, or stickers. The basic idea is that the child can earn smileys for good behaviour. This strategy is often useful for children between the ages of about 2½ and 9. With older children, say between the ages of 10 and 13, points or ticks can be used instead. A sample chart appears in figure 2 on page 70.

When to use a behaviour chart

A behaviour chart is probably best used when a specific problem has arisen. For example, Rupert's mother decided to use a star chart, giving him a star each time he got into his own bed without protesting. Rupert had a chart beside his bed with 14 squares, one for each day for two weeks. At bedtime, Rupert's mother would ask him to get into bed. If he did so without a fuss, she praised him and put a gold star on his chart. When Rupert had earned three stars in a row he received a special treat the next day. Rupert decided his reward would be to choose his favourite dessert.

These charts are particularly useful for helping children learn daily routines in the home, such as completing set chores like drying dishes, keeping the bedroom tidy, completing homework, and so on. They take the heat out of a situation where the parent otherwise has to nag to get a child to cooperate. The charts work best when the stars or faces can be exchanged for a backup reward that the child likes. Some of the best (and cheapest) backup rewards involve activities rather than things, for example being able to stay up a bit later to watch a favourite TV show, going on a family picnic, being read to in bed even though the child can read for herself, being able to invite a friend over to play or to stay the night, or playing a board game with dad after dinner.

Concerns about using rewards with children

Some parents are concerned that using rewards for good behaviour

Figure 2: A sample happy faces chart

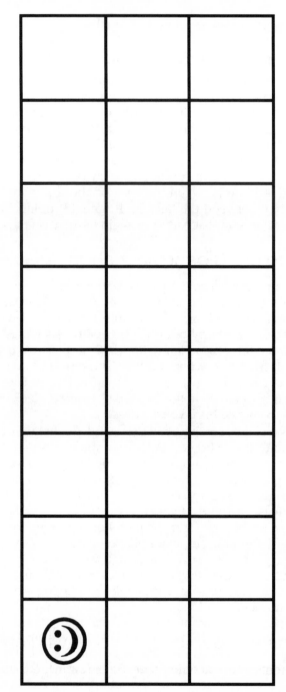

Each time the desired behaviour occurs, place a smiley face, star, or a sticker in a square.

might cause problems. Some of these concerns are quite real, but problems can be largely avoided if the plan is set up properly.

'Is it bribery?'

A bribe is usually thought of as an inducement to do something wrong, illegal or immoral. Parents sometimes feel that rewards are bribes, and that their children should comply simply because they are supposed to. Unfortunately, this is not the case for many children. Think of the reward as an encouragement or incentive for the child to try a bit harder at correcting a problem. Children who develop problems often need their parents' support and recognition in tangible ways.

'Won't he become dependent on rewards?'

Will the child learn to rely on getting rewards and so do nothing unless there is a payoff? This is a reasonable concern, but the danger can largely be avoided if the parent follows a few simple rules. First, always pair the material reward with some other form of attention such as praise so that the reward can be phased out. Second, use activity rewards rather than things you have to buy. Third, give the reward when the child has earned it rather than when she asks for it. Fourth, use the behaviour chart sparingly, for brief periods of time, and for specific behaviours. Most parents find behaviour charts most useful during the first two or three weeks, when the child is learning a new behaviour. Once the new behaviour is established, the child can be weaned off the chart gradually. Positive attention is often enough to keep the improved behaviour going.

'Won't it discourage self-motivation?'

Strategies like smiley faces charts, giving children stamps in their school books for good work, merit awards, and praising children for desirable behaviour are all based on the idea that good behaviour deserves to be recognised and rewarded. Nevertheless, some psychologists and parents believe that giving external rewards to children for improved behaviour is bad for them. They believe that it is disrespectful to the child, weakens his self-motivation and natural interest in the activity he is rewarded for, and, because the adult controls the reward, takes away the child's responsibility for his own behaviour.

I strongly disagree with most of the criticisms, for the following reasons. First, the children who benefit most from programmes that involve rewarding good behaviour are frequently not motivated to change and do not enjoy the tasks they need to perform. Such children may never have experienced the satisfaction of completing a task. Rewards can help them start to experience success. Second, there is nothing disrespectful about wanting to show appreciation to or encourage a child who has behaved well. Rewards can be used to strengthen rather than weaken self-discipline. Third, rewards can be used to enhance rather than restrict responsibility. Children can be rewarded for responsible behaviour, such as taking care of a younger sibling when crossing the road. Finally, rewarding desirable behaviour is one of the most effective methods of motivating children. Sensible parents learn how to use such strategies to their child's and their own advantage.

'How will other children in the family react to one child getting special treatment?'

The concern here is that if one child is on a special programme that involves rewards, other children in the family will resent it and may even misbehave themselves. This occasionally happens, but in my experience it is relatively rare. Other children often respond to a simple explanation as to why the child concerned needs special help. Usually there are advantages for all family members if a difficult youngster's behaviour improves. Of course, it is still important not to neglect the other children if one is put on a behaviour chart. Where several children have the same kind of problem, a separate behaviour chart can be used for each.

How to set up a behaviour chart.

1. Get ready. Get everything ready, such as the chart, gold stars, stickers, or felt pens if you intend drawing happy faces or small pictures.

2. Hold a discussion with your child. Tell your child what is going to happen. Get her attention either through a simple request for a chat or by a direct instruction. 'Jane, come here please. I'd like to talk to you about something.'

3. Prepare your child by describing the problem simply, briefly and calmly. 'Over the past week we have had a lot of hassles over keeping the bathroom tidy. I have had to remind you each night to hang up the towels, and to put your dirty clothes in the washing basket.'

4. Say why the behaviour concerns you. 'When you leave your mess on the floor someone else has to pick it up and that's usually me. This makes me annoyed and I don't like getting annoyed. I think you're old enough to do this on your own.'

5. Describe how the behaviour chart works. 'We're going to play a little game to help you remember. See this chart? It has seven squares on it. One for each day of the week. You can earn a special sticker like this, which we will put on here if you leave the bathroom tidy each night. When you earn seven of these stars you can have a little treat for your good work. OK?'

6. Describe how often the child can earn the stars, happy faces, or stickers. This will vary depending on the behaviour, for example each time the behaviour occurs, every half hour, one hour, two hours, once a day. At first, behaviours that occur only once or twice a day, for example making a bed, can earn stars each time. If the behaviour, for example whining, occurs very frequently, say at least twice an hour, it is better to use a system where the child earns a reward for each half hour that he speaks properly without whining. You have to make this decision about timing yourself. In other words, you reward the absence of the problem behaviour. In general it is better to reward a new behaviour frequently when you start. Once the desired behaviour is learned, rewards can become less frequent. For instance, in the whining example, you can start with short time periods then increase to one, two or three hour time blocks.

7. Describe what back-up rewards can be earned for a specified number of stars. Make sure a back-up reward, such as inviting a friend over, is available within the first two days so the child does not have to wait too long. Then, if all goes well, the reward can occur less often, maybe only at the end of the week.

8. Ask the child to state the rules for earning stars and back-up rewards. Praise the child for stating the rules correctly. If she does not appear to understand or gets the rules wrong, state the correct ones and simply proceed. Children learn what it all means by experiencing the plan in operation.

9. Decide on a procedure to follow if the child breaks the rules. Few children manage to correct their behaviour without the occasional slip up, so decide on how you will deal with breakdowns. There are several possibilities here. One is simply to withhold the reward. If the child forgets, he doesn't receive the star. Sometimes this is enough. For other children something more powerful is required. We will discuss some strategies in detail later in this chapter.

10. Explain to your child the consequence of breaking the rules. Ask the child to tell you what will happen if he breaks the rules.

11. Where possible have a practice run. Pretend first of all that the child has done the correct thing and place a star on the chart. Then pretend the child has forgotten the rule and take her through exactly what you plan for dealing with disobedience.

Managing the programme

Watch your child's behaviour closely.

There's no point in starting a behaviour chart unless you know whether the child has obeyed the rules, completed the required task or whatever.

Catch your child being good.

When you notice the desired behaviour occurring, give enthusiastic praise. Let your child know you are pleased with his efforts.

Describe the problem behaviour and the consequences to the child.

When the problem behaviour occurs, state firmly but calmly what has been done and then put the consequences into action. 'Jimmy, Sandra, you've been fighting over the TV. Now the TV will be turned off for 10 minutes.'

Fill in the chart at the required time.

If no problems have occurred, then at the end of the selected time gain your child's attention and let her know you are pleased with her efforts. Suggest that she might like to put a sticker on the chart. If she doesn't want to, simply put it on yourself. Use a kitchen timer set to the required time period to remind yourself when the time is up.

If an undesired behaviour occurred, describe that behaviour and ask your child to suggest what he should have done instead. Of course, no stars go on the chart. Do not use black marks on the chart or unhappy faces to indicate bad performance. This kind of negative feedback doesn't help.

Give the back-up reward.

When your child has earned the number of stars agreed on, provide the back-up reward for his efforts.

Giving clear, calm instructions

Recommended age range: 2 to 8 years

In chapter 2 we discussed how the kind of request we make of children influences whether they cooperate or not. Here are some ideas about how to give children instructions that work. If you really want a child to do something, then always be prepared to back up the instruction. If you're not, then don't follow this procedure. If you give the child a choice, be prepared for him to say no.

Get close.

Move to within arms' reach of the child so that she is sure to hear and will find it difficult to ignore what you say. Being close also makes it easier to follow through if the child disobeys.

Gain the child's attention.

Call the child's name. 'Paul, listen.' Don't require the child to look at you, just be sure he can hear.

Use good body language.

Turn your body towards the child, get down to her eye level, stop whatever else you are doing, and look at her.

State what you would like the child to do.

Describe exactly what you want the child to do. 'Paul, it's bathtime now. I would like you to pack up the game and hop into the bath, straight away, please.' 'Amanda, turn off the computer and come for dinner, please.' Do not always insist on instant obedience. Allow the child to finish what she is doing. Finding out where the child is up to in a game or activity can help because a natural break will occur at the end of a turn, set, or game.

Give the child time to comply.

After the instruction, pause for 5 seconds and say nothing. Children need time to get started.

Give positive feedback if your child complies.

Praise your child for complying with an instruction. 'Good girl, Linda, for doing as I asked straight away.' 'Thank you for doing as you're asked straight away.'

Repeat the instruction if the child does not obey.

State the request again in a firm, calm, matter-of-fact way. 'Paul, I asked you to do something. Pack up and hop into the bath.'

Wait another 5 seconds if necessary.

Once again, give the child time to comply. Remain close at hand and say nothing else. No debating, arguing the point, or losing your cool. Just pause.

Praise your child for complying.

If your child complies with the second request, offer praise.

If the child still doesn't comply, back up your request with an appropriate consequence.

If the child continues to be defiant use an immediate, decisive consequence such as quiet time or time out (see page 78).

After the time out period, return your child to the place where the problem started and repeat the instruction.

Repeat steps as many times as required until the child does what he is told.

This method relies on the parent being sure that the child is asked to do something she can accomplish. The aim is to break the cycle of yelling, hassling, and repeated nagging. It requires you to be firm and consistent and to keep your cool. It is a way of getting out of the escalation trap described in chapter 2 on page 26.

Backing up requests with logical consequences

Recommended age range: 4 to 12 years

Janice put Damian's bike away in the shed for two days because he rode without his crash hat, and on the wrong side of the road. Daniel removed a troublesome toy after Henry grabbed it from Lucy while she was playing with it. Nora refused to buy any iceblocks the next time she went shopping because the kids continually took them from the freezer at home without asking. Bill was grounded for four days for arriving home late from football training without any explanation. These are all examples of logical consequences for misbehaviour. Each parent has chosen a punishment that fits the crime, in an effort to discourage further problems. Here are some ideas for using logical consequences. It is a very useful strategy for behaviour that is mild and doesn't occur too often, and is most useful with basically well-adjusted kids who have a few specific problem behaviours that cause family conflict.

Describe the problem behaviour.

When you observe the undesirable behaviour, gain the child's attention and clearly state the nature of the problem. 'Johnny, you know you must not grab toys from your sister while it's her turn.' Try not to get angry or wound up.

Withdraw the activity.

If possible, remove the activity, such as a troublesome toy, bike, or ball, or take the child from the activity, for example turn off the television, or send the child to another room.

Give an explanation.

Tell the child why you are doing this and how long the consequence will last. 'Since you won't play nicely with your sister, these games will be put away for 10 minutes. Then you can try again to play without grabbing.'

Keep to the conditions.

Allow the child access to the activity once the time is up.

Be reasonable in the length of time the activity is withdrawn.

Banning a child from playing with something such as a bike for three weeks is excessive when two hours might have worked just as well. In general, long periods of deprivation are no more effective than shorter ones.

Avoid arguments.

Don't debate or argue the point with your child.

Be decisive.

When the problem occurs, act immediately and decisively. If you discover the problem after the fact, act as soon as possible when the opportunity arises.

Using quiet time to handle disruptions

Recommended age range: 1½ to 9 years

Quiet time is a mild but effective procedure for helping children learn more acceptable behaviour. It involves removing a child who is misbehaving or being disruptive from an activity and making her sit quietly on the edge of the activity or in a quiet time chair. This chair can be in the same room where the disruption took place. Quiet time is particularly useful for mild disruptions that involve a child disturbing the games or activities of other children. For example, Sheila decided to used quiet time to help David learn to take turns on the family trampoline when other children were visiting. When she saw David push in or refuse to get off after his time was up, she walked up to him and told him he must remember to let the other kids have a turn. She then led him to the edge of the activity and told him to sit quietly for 2 minutes. He was allowed to watch but could not join in. When Sheila first heard about quiet time she was convinced it would not work. However, David quickly learnt to sit quietly if he wanted to return to the activity, and it only took three quiet times before he was taking turns like everyone else.

Before you begin, explain how quiet time works.

Tell your child what behaviours will earn quiet time. Explain calmly why you will be using it. Show your child exactly what will happen the next time the disturbing behaviour occurs, in other words rehearse the procedure. Children under 4 often have to experience the procedure a few times before they understand what's involved.

When the problem occurs, give a terminating instruction.

When you notice the behaviour occurring, gain the child's attention and calmly but firmly give him a terminating instruction. 'Peter, stop pushing your sister right now.' Act quickly whenever you see the behaviour occurring.

Praise your child for compliance.

If the behaviour stops, thank the child for doing as he's told and suggest another activity.

Back up your instruction with quiet time.

If the behaviour continues or occurs again within the next hour, tell the child what he's done wrong ('I have asked you to stop pushing your sister.') and the consequence of disobeying ('Now go to quiet time').

Do not lecture, nag, or threaten quiet time.

Act, don't threaten to act. Make sure the child is taken to the quiet time place. Protests should be ignored. If the child protests or refuses, firmly but calmly guide her to the quiet time area.

Before you leave, let your child know the rules.

'After you have sat here quietly for 3 minutes, you can come out.'

Withdraw all attention while your child is in quiet time.

Once the child is in quiet time, do not speak to him, and ensure that he receives no attention from anyone else.

After quiet time, engage your child in an activity.

When quiet time is over, do not mention the incident. Encourage the child to find something to do, such as rejoining the activity, then look for an opportunity to catch him being good.

Questions parents ask about quiet time

'How old should a child be?' Quiet time can be used with children from about the age of 18 months to 9 years. Younger children will learn what it is about by experiencing what happens when they are disruptive. A toddler's cot or playpen can be used as a quiet time area.

'Shouldn't I also be encouraging good behaviour rather than just punishing her when she's naughty?' Yes indeed. Quiet time, like all discipline techniques, works more effectively if you praise your child when she does the right thing.

'What should I do if my child won't sit in quiet time?' Unless your child is particularly difficult he will soon get the idea that by sitting quietly for a short time he can rejoin the activity more quickly. If the activity is something the child likes to do, this often happens after three to five quiet times, sometimes more quickly. If your child simply refuses to stay in quiet time then you can back it up with time out, which is explained below.

'What should I do if my child sits but is not quiet?' Some children will sit in a quiet time chair but will cry, sob, or call out. Quiet time starts when the child is quiet. It stops when the child has been quiet for 2 to 3 minutes. Some parents make the mistake of letting the child out of quiet time while she is still upset. If this happens, the child will not learn to be quiet in quiet time. If she becomes quite disruptive and throws a temper tantrum, it is better to use time out.

Using time out to deal with disruptions

Recommended age range: 2 to 10 years

In time out the child is temporarily removed from the situation where a problem has occurred. It usually lasts for 2 to 3 minutes, and is used immediately after a problem behaviour. It can be a back-up to quiet time or the consequence of very disruptive behaviour such as aggression, temper outbursts, or disobedience. It works in much the same way as quiet time, except the child is typically put in another room such as a laundry, bathroom, or hallway. Time out is an alternative to shouting, threatening, and smacking a child who has misbehaved. When it is used correctly it can be an extremely effective way of helping children learn more acceptable behaviour. Its main advantage is that it requires the adult to remain calm. Becoming angry when a child is upset often leads to more anger on the child's part, causing the spiralling escalation referred to in chapter 2.

Sending a child to her bedroom is a variation of time out. The main problem in using the child's bedroom as a time out area is that it often contains toys and other things to be played with during the time out period. The best time out areas are rooms that are fairly dull and uninteresting, but well-ventilated, safe, with good lighting, and able to be closed off if necessary.

Parents who have tried a version of time out may have found that it hasn't worked for one of the following reasons. First, the child has been allowed to decide when to come out. For example, the parent may say, 'Amanda, don't speak like that in this house. Go to your room and come out when you're ready to behave yourself.' The child may simply walk into the room and come straight out again. Second, it has been used inconsistently. Time out works best when it is used every time a problem behaviour occurs. Third, the child comes out of time out while he is still upset. This is a major problem because he learns that if he yells long and loud enough he will eventually get out. Getting out of time out should depend on the child actually being quiet for 2 to 3 minutes rather than promising to be good, or simply being there for the set time. Time out starts when the disruption stops.

Many parents I have worked with choose the laundry area for time out, having first safety-proofed it by placing harmful products out of reach.

The guidelines for using time out are similar to those for quiet time.

Explain the time out routine to your child.

Before you begin using time out, explain the procedure. Tell your child what behaviours will earn time out and rehearse the entire routine with him. The rehearsal is a practice run of what will happen the next time your child, for example, throws a temper tantrum.

When the problem behaviour occurs, gain your child's attention and describe the problem behaviour.

Deliver a firm verbal reprimand such as, 'Jane, stop that fighting immediately.' Respond quickly, as soon as you see the behaviour occurring. Be sure to respond each and every time the behaviour occurs.

Praise your child for complying.

If the instruction works, praise the child for doing what he was told. If the behaviour continues, tell him what he's done wrong ('I've asked you to stop that fighting.') and the consequence for disobeying ('You haven't stopped. Now go to time out for 3 minutes').

Back up with time out.

Make sure the child actually goes to time out, but do not lecture, nag, argue the point, or threaten. If the child refuses or struggles, firmly but calmly guide her to the time out area and leave her there. Use the minimum force necessary to get the child to move towards the area. Reduce this physical assistance as soon as the child begins to walk.

Remind your child of the rules.

Once you have taken the child to the time out area, tell him he can come out after a few minutes providing he is quiet. Short time outs are just as effective as longer ones. With toddlers, a 30-second quiet period can be sufficient. With 3 to 5 year olds, 1 to 2 minutes can be used. With children from 5 to 10 years, 3 to 8 minutes can be used. Time out periods longer than these do not add to the effectiveness of the strategy. Leave the door open, but close it immediately if the child tries to leave the room.

Ignore disruptions in time out.

If the child become disruptive in time out (screaming, kicking the door or walls, or calling out), ignore it. She is trying to get your attention, and being successful will defeat the purpose of the exercise. If the child attempts to escape by opening the door again or by climbing out the window, be prepared to return her to the time out area immediately. If necessary, stand by the door until the time out period is over. Once the child is in time out do not speak to her, enter the time out area, or give her any attention at all until the time out period is over. You must be prepared to put up with the storm. Some children will try to escalate their behaviour, particularly if they have learnt to do this to get their own way.

After time out, try to catch your child being good.

When time out is over, don't mention the incident, encourage the child to play or amuse herself and then look for a chance to praise her for behaving correctly. However, if the child received time out for disobeying an instruction (such as 'come to the dinner table'), take her to the spot where the original instruction was given, then repeat it. If she complies, offer praise. If she continues to defy you, return her to time out for a further 2 to 3 minutes.

If the problem occurs again, reintroduce time out.

If there is a repeat of disruptive behaviour that has earned time out in the previous hour, reprimand the child and immediately put him back into time out.

When to use time out

Time out can be used for a wide range of behaviour problems, including refusing to comply with requests, teasing, fighting, temper tantrums, swearing, and destructive behaviour such as throwing or breaking objects or possessions. It can be used with children up to the age of 9 or 10. It can also be used as a back-up to other forms of discipline such as logical consequences and quiet time, both of which are discussed earlier in this chapter. Once a child becomes too strong to put into time out, other strategies should be considered.

Using planned ignoring to deal with problem behaviour

Recommended age range: 1 to 7 years

Not all difficult behaviour needs to be specifically corrected. Sometimes it is sufficient simply to ignore it. Planned ignoring involves withholding attention from the child while the behaviour is in progress. It is most effective for minor misdemeanours such as complaining after being refused something, accidents such as breaking glassware, or making a mess while playing. It works best when all attention is withheld from the child, including reactions from siblings, peers, and people like grandparents. Sometimes parents say they have tried ignoring a behaviour and it hasn't worked. One parent I worked with said that she ignored her son Bradley when he was cheeky to her. What she actually meant was that she had stopped hitting him. She still looked at him, stopped what she was doing, and often told him off. It is not surprising that 'ignoring' failed to work. The child still received quite a lot of attention for being cheeky.

When you observe the undesirable behaviour, decide whether you should ignore it.

If you decide to ignore a behaviour, make sure you ignore it every time.

Withdraw all attention.

Turn away from the child and, if necessary, walk away. Make no response at all. Avoid eye contact.

Continue to ignore the child if the behaviour worsens.

Be prepared for the behaviour to become worse before it improves. Children don't like being ignored and may become noisy and demanding before they finally realise that you mean business.

Attend to your child when the behaviour ceases.

When the undesirable behaviour stops, wait a few seconds and then attend to the child. Praise her for behaving correctly once again. 'Good, you finally stopped whining. What was it you wanted to ask me?'

If the problem starts again, once again remove all attention while it continues.

You must consistently ignore the child each time the behaviour occurs.

As soon as the child is busy and engaged in play, offer praise.

Catch your child doing the right thing.

Planning activities to prevent behaviour problems

Recommended age range: 1 to 10 years

Many behaviour problems can be avoided completely if adults take steps to ensure that children have interesting and engaging activities available. Bored children are often disruptive. Helen and Mark understand this principle. Whenever they go visiting with Daniel, their 2-year-old, they always take toys and games that Daniel can play with. Mary and Cameron also know what can happen when they take their three boys aged 7, 9 and 10 for picnics in the country if they don't take something for the kids to do en route. This family decided to set aside some special activities that are only allowed to be used in the car. They included two hand-held computer games and a variety of cassettes that the children chose themselves. Most of the time car trips are no hassle because the kids have something to do other than look out of the window.

Pinpoint high risk situations.

Think of situations where children have been disruptive or naughty in the past because there was very little for them to do.

Identify suitable activities for each situation.

In each situation, ask yourself how you might keep your child amused for at least some of the time. For example, on shopping trips children can be involved in locating the cheapest washing powder, locating goods of different colours or shapes, helping find Dad's favourite shaving cream or aftershave, and so on. In a bank, children can be given a deposit slip and can practise filling out their own while the parent waits to be served.

Discuss the ground rules in advance.

Discuss new ground rules in advance, and encourage your children to select something they would like to take that will keep them amused, for example colouring books, picture books, Rubik's cube, and so on.

Generate an activity list.

Involve children in thinking of activities during school holidays. Some parents have found that boredom during holiday periods or bad weather can be reduced by an activity list. This involves asking your child to try to think of all the activities he would like to do during the holidays. Encourage him to generate a list of about 20 to 30 items, including many things he can do on his own and that don't cost anything. This list can be stuck to the refrigerator. Whenever the child complains of having nothing to do, simply refer him to the activity list and ask him to choose something he would like to do.

Help your child get started if necessary.

Sometimes you will need to help your child get started. For example, if she wants to play with play dough, you may need to place news-paper on the table and get the necessary materials ready. If she won't get started, give her a gentle prompt. 'How about rolling the dough out until it's really smooth and I will come back to see how you're getting on.'

Attend to your child periodically.

Give your child attention for brief moments periodically while he is busy. The child is more likely to continue if you do this. Don't wait for him to finish the activity before providing attention. Offer snacks and drinks while he is busy rather than waiting till he is bored and whingeing for food.

General guidelines for coping with children's behaviour

There is a wide range of options for dealing with children's behaviour. Here are some general principles on dealing with misbehaviour in children. If you follow these general ideas, many headaches over children's behaviour can be avoided.

- Do set limits to your child's behaviour.
- Do praise your child for behaving appropriately.
- Do respond to misbehaviour immediately, consistently, and decisively.
- Do respond to misbehaviour by describing what the child has done wrong.
- Do respond to misbehaviour by telling the child what would have been more acceptable.
- Do back up your instructions or reasonable requests by using natural or logical consequences, quiet time, or time out.
- Do remain calm when speaking to a child who is upset or who has misbehaved.
- Do speak calmly but firmly to your child when she misbehaves.
- Do act quickly. Don't threaten to act.
- Do deal with the problem yourself rather than threatening someone else's action.
- Do try to prevent problems by ensuring that your child has plenty of interesting and engaging things to do.
- Do discuss rules with your child and give him a chance to be involved in deciding on family rules.

- Do expect reasonable behaviour from your child but don't expect perfection.

Many problems with children can be avoided completely if parents remember four other basic ideas.

- Give children positive feedback when they do the right thing.
- Encourage children to share their experiences with you.
- Create lots of opportunities for children to be involved with engaging and interesting activities.
- Show a genuine interest in what they are doing.

Seeking professional advice

Many parents will be interested not only in ways of preventing problems arising but also in practical ideas for handling specific problems. You will need to decide whether to tackle your child's behaviour problem on your own following the suggestions in this book, or to seek the help of a professional counsellor or therapist. Child psychologists can often be very helpful to families who have several different problems and are uncertain about where to begin. In chapter 7 on page 272, there is a list of the behavioural and emotional problems that probably require professional advice before you begin a behaviour change programme. While some of the material in this book may assist children with serious adjustment problems, you may need professional guidance in deciding which parts apply to your child. Your family doctor should be able to refer you to professionals in your area who specialise in working with children.

Be an informed consumer. Before entering therapy, ask some specific questions. What kind of approach does the person take in dealing with problems such as your child's? In particular, select a therapist who actively involves parents in the therapy process and who offers concrete, specific advice on ways you can assist your child. Ask how many sessions are typically involved and the cost per session. What qualifications and training does the professional have in dealing with children with problems? Are after-hours appointments possible so that working parents can attend? Are drugs used as part of the treatment? If your therapist refuses to answer these sorts of questions, or fobs you off with 'the doctor knows best' routine, or with psychological, medical, or psychiatric jargon, then seek an alternative referral. You can reasonably expect to be fully informed, that both you and your child will be treated with dignity and respect, and that you will receive treatment tailored to meet your needs.

Part II

Specific Parenting Guides

CHAPTER 4

Infants
and Toddlers

The first three years of a child's life are of special importance because it is during this time that the foundations for all subsequent development are laid. Children's physical, cognitive, language, social, and emotional development can all be dramatically affected by their early experiences. In the first year of life, infants should develop a basic sense of trust in their caregivers and in their environment. This means that the child should experience a positive, warm, and predictable world where pain and discomfort are minimised. Four main aspects of child care contribute to this developing sense of security during the first year of life: whether the child's basic requirements for food and nourishment are met; whether the child receives sufficient physical contact and nurturing; whether the child forms a close emotional bond with the primary caregiver; and whether the child's environment provides an adequate level of stimulation.

Infants who are fed when they are hungry and have their other physical needs attended to, who receive plenty of positive, warm physical contact through cuddling, holding, rocking, and being talked to, and who form an emotional bond with a caregiver, usually the mother, experience a positive and non-threatening world. Children's development progresses much more smoothly during the first few years in such a climate.

Children's development proceeds through a series of fairly predictable phases from birth to adolescence. New behaviours, skills, and capabilities, such as learning to crawl, walk and talk, emerge in a fairly orderly and predictable pattern for most children during the first two years of life. Newborns begin life equipped with a number of basic reflexes. For example, if a baby is stroked on the cheek, it will automatically turn its face in that direction. This reflex has survival value because it helps the baby locate the nipple for feeding. Despite such reflexes, the human infant depends on the care and supervision of adults for survival. During the first 8 to 10 months of life, much of a baby's time is spent sleeping, feeding, mastering basic motor skills such as kicking, and exploring the environment.

In the second half of the first year, the child becomes a true social being. It is an exciting period for parents because their children become far more responsive to people and things around them. They recognise their parents' faces and voices, and begin to smile, babble, and communicate. They make many exciting discoveries, including learning to crawl and explore, and they develop a curiosity about the world around them. This world consists of people, sounds, lights, smells, and objects which differ in shape, size and texture. Babies gradually become less dependent on their parents and occupy themselves for longer periods, even though most of their day is still spent close to a parent.

The first two years are marked by relatively rapid changes in the child's capabilities. Simple reflexive behaviours, such as sucking, are gradually replaced by more complex goal-directed ones, such as crawling, walking, feeding oneself, and talking. Children learn a variety of social behaviours, for example smiling, cooing, and laughing, through their daily interactions with family members. It is also a time where the rudimentary foundations of human intelligence and problem solving are laid down, as children learn to explore objects in their environment through tracking (watching and following), mouthing, and touching objects.

This chapter is not intended to provide an in-depth coverage of normal development during infancy and toddlerhood, or to cover all possible problems that might arise in caring for children of this age. I have been selective here, dealing with those issues that most frequently create difficulties for parents.

Specific issues or problems of infancy

During infancy, the main difficulties parents encounter involve adjusting to the day-to-day demands and responsibilities of taking care of a dependent human being whose very survival depends on the parents' attentiveness and capacity to provide loving care. In addition, however, three specific problems can be a source of considerable anxiety to parents during the child's first year. These include problems of accidental injuries to the infant, crying and fussing, and fear reactions. Strategies for dealing with each difficulty are discussed below.

A safe play environment

As infants and toddlers spend most of their time at home, it is important that this environment be made as safe as possible, particularly after the child starts to crawl, probably around 8 to 10 months. This will allow exploration to occur with as little restriction as possible as soon as the child is ready. Having a safe environment also frees parents from worry about a child getting hurt or injured. Accidents in the home are a leading cause of injury and death in young children, so it is important to recognise some of the dangers in the home and to take appropriate action to ensure that the environment is as safe as possible for your young child.

Check for hazards in the kitchen and living areas.

Start by looking for accident hazards in the kitchen and living areas. Young children spend most of their waking hours here. Make sure that breakables, cleaning materials, and sharp utensils are removed to high or lockable cupboards. Anything that may cause harm, such as sharp objects, household cleaners, bleaches, chemicals, medicines, or glassware should be well out of reach of young children. Be particularly careful to ensure that potentially harmful objects are removed from low areas, especially those below 1 metre.

Electrical plugs and cords can be a particular problem for toddlers. When power points are not in use, make sure they are cov-

ered — plastic covers that fit into the socket are available from hardware stores. Ensure that all cords are well insulated and not in need of repair. Keep all appliance cords, especially that for the electric jug, well out of reach so a child cannot accidentally pull an appliance down on top of himself. Turn pot handles towards the rear of the stove. Use the front elements or burners for low-heat cooking and simmering and the rear ones for high heat cooking. Keep children away from unstable or fragile furniture until they are well enough coordinated that they do not need to grab for objects to hold themselves upright.

Make sure that TV or stereo knobs can't be removed and swallowed. Objects less than 3 or 4 cm wide can be inadvertently swallowed by curious infants.

Ensure that pot plants are not poisonous.

Bathrooms

A bathroom can be a hazardous place for babies and toddlers. Water fascinates children and from the age of about 8 months many try to pull themselves into the bath or, occasionally, up on to the sink to turn on taps, or even on to the bench to get to the medicine cupboard. These exploration attempts can result in serious accidents such as falling into the bath, getting scalded, drowning, or taking dangerous medicines. Never leave an infant or toddler unattended in the bath. Children can drown in just 5 cm of water. Always check to make sure the bath is the correct temperature before putting the child in, and turn off all taps tightly so that the child can't turn them on. Keep all cleaning agents, cosmetics and medicines out of reach. Some parents decide to make the bathroom out of bounds for babies and toddlers unless they are supervised.

Stairs

Children from 9 or 10 months on are fascinated by stairs and inevitably want to climb them. Falling down stairs can cause nasty injuries, including head injuries. Supervise your child's attempts to negotiate stairs. Rather than making them completely out of bounds, put a safety gate on the third or fourth stair until the child can climb up and back down safely. It is quite natural and normal for young children to want to climb stairs.

Outdoors

Swimming pools should be fenced and child-proof safety catches fitted. Swimming activities should always be supervised, and parents should insist that older children walk rather than run when near the pool. Young children should always wear flotation aids and be taught to swim as soon as possible. When several children are in the pool, diving should be banned altogether. Too many head injuries, even in good swimmers, are caused by children misjudging the dive and hitting the bottom. Pool chemicals and pool filtration equipment should be locked away.

Outdoor play equipment should be kept in good repair and checked regularly for sharp edges and splintered wood. Young children should always be supervised near swings and slides. Infants and toddlers can easily crawl or walk into the path of older children on swings.

Watch out for dangerous toys.

Some toys are unsafe for young children. Marbles, Lego, small cars, and toys with small, removable parts can be put into a toddler's mouth and cause choking. Indeed, any object smaller than 3 or 4 cm in diameter is potentially hazardous. Problems can arise when older children play with these kinds of toys and they attract the attention of younger ones. Older children should be encouraged to play with such toys in their bedrooms, outside the house, or only if the younger child is closely supervised by an adult, and should be warned of the potential danger of the toy to their younger sibling.

Barbecue areas

Barbecues are extremely dangerous places for young children. Children are fascinated by fire and will often try to touch an open flame. An open fire should never be left unattended, and young children should be kept well away from the cooking area. Gas barbecues should have knobs firmly tightened when not in use. Children should not be allowed to play with matches at any time.

Fear of strangers

At around 7 or 8 months of age, most infants show a fear reaction to strangers. This reaction can include fretting or crying, or clinging to and refusing to separate from the parent in the presence of an unfamiliar person. Stranger anxiety is quite normal and usually disappears by the time the child is 2, however the intensity and persistence of the reaction varies from child to child. Some appear very fearful while others show hardly any reaction at all. The reaction tends to be most intense in unfamiliar surroundings rather than in the child's own home.

Infants also differ in how they reunite with their parents after temporary separations. Some want to be picked up and held but are not distressed, others snub or avoid their parents, still others show angry, resistant behaviour even though they want to be held after separations.

The fear reaction can be triggered by a variety of events, including unfamiliar adults looking at, speaking to, or trying to hold or interact with the child. It also can occur when the parent moves out of the child's sight, when there are strange, loud noises, or if the parent attempts to leave the child with unfamiliar baby-sitters.

The way a child reacts to a strange situation is believed to be related to the quality of the mother–infant relationship and the degree of attachment or emotional bonding between them. Children who show minimal distress on separation, but who want to establish contact with their mothers on reunion, are more likely to have mutually satisfactory and enjoyable experiences with their mothers. They feel safe and secure and are used to good things happening in their lives. Their mothers are sensitive to their needs and can accurately interpret any signs of distress or upset. Feedings are more harmonious, there is longer and more pleasurable face-to-face contact between parent and child, crying is responded to quickly and effectively, and the child is likely to have experienced tender and affectionate holding.

Fear of strangers gradually diminishes during the second year and many children come to enjoy the attention and company of friends and relatives. Parents have an important role to play in helping their infant cope and adjust to new experiences.

Here are some guidelines for dealing with stranger anxiety.

Spend quality time with your infant.

A child will cope best with new challenges if she has many warm, caring, and enjoyable experiences with her parents at other times. Look at, talk to, smile at, affectionately hold, and be responsive to your child's attempts to communicate with you, particularly her vocalisations and babbling sounds. Be prepared to interrupt what you are doing to respond to your child's signals.

Give your child time to become familiar with new surroundings.

When your child meets someone new, keep close to him until he indicates that he is ready to explore, move around the room, or be held by someone else. Bring some familiar things into strange surroundings, for example a toy, teddy, doll, cuddly blanket, or music box, to help your child feel secure.

Be prepared to intervene if your child is being upset by extra attention.

Be prepared to come to your child's aid if she becomes distressed. For example, if she starts to cry while being held or spoken to by another adult, hold her yourself for a while until she is calm.

Soothe and reassure your upset child.

Often simply picking the child up and cuddling and speaking calmly and warmly to him will settle a distressed infant.

Do not force an infant to be nursed by someone he is afraid of.

This can make the situation worse by heightening the child's fear reaction and uncertainty.

Keep calm when your child shows fear.

When a child is upset, avoid becoming uptight and anxious yourself. Your infant needs calm, confident, relaxed parenting when she is afraid. Hold her and demonstrate through your own relaxed actions that there is nothing to fear.

Do not chastise your child for being shy.

Even though you might desperately like your child to be held by a good friend or relative, you should never berate or criticise him for not wanting to go to another adult.

Respond warmly when your child smiles or reacts positively to new people.

When your child becomes responsive to the attention of others, pay warm, caring attention to her when she is returned to you.

Let friends and other trusted adults interact with your infant.

Try not to become overprotective when stranger anxiety surfaces. The more opportunities your child has to meet and interact with others on familiar ground, the more quickly his fear will be overcome. Experience will teach him that you are still there and accessible, even if he is temporarily with someone else.

Crying

Crying has a survival function for babies. It is a signal to parents that the child needs care. Infants cry when they are hungry, wet and uncomfortable, cold, in distress, or want attention. Children soon learn that they can use crying to control what happens to them. Because their child's crying is almost universally distressing for parents, most will frantically seek ways of pacifying the distressed baby, including picking up, rocking, patting, stroking, singing to, walking around with, or taking the child on midnight trips in the car. During the first year of a child's life and during toddlerhood, crying tends to decrease, much to the parents' relief.

From birth to 9 months, crying often peaks in the late afternoon and evening. After the first 3 months, both the amount and pattern of crying begins to change. There is a gradual decline in evening crying, and over the course of the first year the nature of the crying gradually changes. It becomes less a response to hunger or discomfort, and is more readily influenced by learning experiences. For example, some crying is to gain attention.

In the first 3 months of a child's life, parents differ a great deal in how frequently and quickly they respond to crying. Most parents take between two and nine minutes to attend to the baby. Parents who frequently ignore a young baby's distress tend to have children who cry more often and more persistently in the 9- to 12-month age group. The key, therefore, in dealing with infants' crying is promptness of response. If the parent is attentive to distress signals, the infant will be more secure, and less demanding or impatient.

When your child is awake, alert and not crying or fussing, give her plenty of attention and things to look at.

Infants cry less often if they receive plenty of loving attention, physical contact, and visual stimulation when they are awake and not fussing.

Respond promptly to crying.

When your child cries in situations such as after waking from a nap or when hungry, do not ignore him for a long period. It is better to attend to the child within the first minute, before he becomes really distressed. This means interrupting what you are doing.

Try to assess your child's needs as best you can.

Try to work out what, if anything, is causing the distress or discomfort. While this can be very difficult at times, many parents become quite skilled at assessing the situation and taking prompt action that settles the child. Most parents get to know their own child's cry very well. Is she hungry, wet, cold, too hot, or in pain due to nappy rash or wind? Is she grimacing? Does she appear to have a temperature or difficulty breathing? Has she vomited up milk or other food? Does she need a change of environment, stimulation, or attention from you? Has she got into an awkward position in a cot? Does she have something to look at, touch, explore, or listen to?

Attend to the child's needs.

Working out why an infant is crying is sometimes a process of elimination. Start by checking the basics relating to his physical comfort. While you do this, for example change a wet nappy, or feed the infant, make sure you interact with your baby. Look into his eyes, talk, smile warmly, hold him, or put something into his hands to hold. If the problem persists, try to distract him by rocking him, singing to

him, putting him in a bouncinette, moving him into a different room, or giving him a toy or object that makes a sound to hold or look at.

Make sure partners do not avoid their responsibilities.

Where crying is a persistent problem, particularly at night, it is an excellent idea for both parents to become skilled at settling the distressed, crying baby. Encourage your partner to share in this care. Some couples work out an arrangement whereby the father and mother alternate the task of attending to the baby at night. If the child needs to be breastfed, the father can still get out of bed to fetch the child when the crying starts, if the mother prefers to feed in bed.

Avoid becoming impatient, irritable, or angry.

Crying is distressing for both parents and children, particularly when it persists, and parents can feel very tired, vulnerable, and exposed. However, it is crucial that you don't take your negative feelings out on your baby. If you get to the point where you feel you could be in danger of harming your child in any way, have a plan for dealing with these times. Count to 10, take several deep breaths, and remind yourself that your child is not crying 'deliberately' to upset you; ring or visit a friend or someone else you trust; talk to your partner; take your child for a walk, or a ride in the car. If you must let off steam, go into another room, give yourself time out on the toilet, or weed the garden. If none of this works, ring a hotline number. Many cities have trained telephone counsellors for helping parents at risk of abusing their infants.

Listed below are 24-hour Help Hotlines in capital cities around Australia:
- Brisbane — Crisis Care, phone (07) 227 5999
- Sydney — Child Protection & Family Crisis Service, phone (02) 360 7200
- Canberra — Domestic Violence Crisis Service, phone (06) 248 7800
- Melbourne — Crisis Line, phone (03) 329 0300
- Hobart — Office of the Status of Women, phone (002) 34 2166 (9 a.m.–5 p.m.)
- Adelaide — Crisis Case Unit, phone (08) 232 3300
- Perth — Crisis Care Unit, phone (09) 325 1111
- Darwin — Crisis Line, phone (089) 81 9227

Areas outside the capital cities in many states also have a 24-hour free-call number:

- Queensland — phone 008 177 135
- New South Wales — phone 008 425 288
- Victoria — phone 008 015 188
- Tasmania — phone 008 001 377 (9a.m. – 5p.m.)
- South Australia — phone 008 188 118
- Western Australia — phone 008 199 008
- Northern Territory — phone 008 019 116

Specific issues or problems of toddlers

At around 8 to 10 months, most children will start to crawl and will also begin to test the limits that their parents set to their behaviour. At the same time, parents must provide an emotional climate where their children feel secure and loved. Toddlers can be great company; they can also be demanding and quite exhausting. Many of the difficulties that emerge now are part of normal growing up, and parents experiencing them for the first time should not feel that their child is abnormal, but they must be dealt with quickly to prevent more serious problems arising later. Toddlers need to get into good routines relating to sleeping, eating, and play, and they need to learn the meaning of the word 'no'.

Promoting independent feeding

During toddlerhood, children move towards an increasingly varied diet and learn to eat what the rest of the family eats, a diet containing all the necessary nutrients — proteins, carbohydrates, fats, vitamins, minerals, and water. They should become increasingly independent in their feeding habits. Many parents experience difficulties in helping their child make the transition from being a milk-fed infant to a youngster capable of consuming a mixed diet independently. One- and 2-year-olds are not known for their wonderful eating habits, and mess in the kitchen is an inevitable part of helping toddlers learn gradually to feed themselves. Many a parent has felt mildly nauseated on discovering a toddler with an upturned bowl and food all over her hands, hair, high chair and the floor. Other parents become irritated when the toddler drops his spoon from the high chair for the fifth time and then screams until it is picked up. However, it is during this period that children become independent in the act of eating. As a child's coordination and physical control improves, she becomes more skilled at handling eating and drinking utensils. Parents require a great deal of patience to prevent mealtimes turning into a battleground.

Changes in toddlers' feeding competencies

When toddlers are given as many opportunities to feed themselves as possible, there is a gradual but steady improvement in their feeding capabilities. By the age of 12 months, most toddlers can hold a cup with a lid and can drink liquids pretty well. However, spills are common, especially when drinking from cups without lids, as the toddler has trouble accurately coordinating the tilt of the cup to the mouth. Between the ages of 18 and 24 months, you can expect your child to control cups and small glasses quite well and to be less likely to drop or throw cups over the edge of the chair.

Spoon control develops slowly, partly because toddlers like to use their fingers. In the six months following their first birthday, most toddlers have difficulty scooping food and getting it to their mouths. By 18 months, scooping is improving but the load is still dropped frequently, sometimes just as it is about to go in. By the child's second birthday, wrist, elbow, and shoulder movements are well enough coordinated to get the spoon to the mouth with only a few spills.

Toddlers gradually become more adept at chewing, and with the arrival of a set of molars at around 12 months they start to grind some foods. By 2½, a child's chewing motions are well enough developed to handle most adult foods. From the age of 24 months, the child is skilled enough to concentrate less on the task of getting food into her mouth, and it is then that many parents find the toddler is easily distracted during meals and has difficulty sitting still.

A good diet

Good nutrition is a basic requirement for healthy development. Children should learn to eat a variety of foods that provide all the necessary nutrients. Appendix 1 provides a list of sample menus that meet daily dietary requirements for children of different ages.

During the child's second six months, most parents will have introduced their child to solid foods. This process often starts with the introduction of baby rice cereal, progressing to strained vegetables, strained fruits, dairy products, other cereals, then other protein foods. At one year of age, most toddlers still prefer mashed, puréed, strained, or moistened food because it is easier to chew. Cut harder food into small, bite-sized portions. Be particularly wary about food your child might choke on such as cherry tomatoes, nuts, hard sweets, and popcorn.

Toddlers can enjoy and digest most foods eaten by other family members, but they can also be quite fussy and refuse to eat particular foods or eat at certain meals. Your child may develop a particular fondness for a favourite sandwich and insist on it at every meal. This only becomes a problem if the child refuses to eat anything else and it continues for a long time. The primary goal during this time is to help your toddler learn to enjoy a wide variety of foods and to become as independent as possible in feeding.

Get everything ready.

Have everything ready in advance to avoid the problem of having a hungry child fussing and protesting while waiting to be served. Use a high chair until the child is ready to sit at a table along with the rest of the family, and provide unbreakable plates and cups.

Have predictable mealtimes.

Get your child into a set routine regarding mealtimes. Don't let him eat throughout the day. Meals should be served at particular times which coincide as closely as possible to the times other family members eat. Five small meals or three larger meals are sufficient.

Encourage self-feeding through finger foods.

Begin by encouraging your child to finger feed. Infants signal when they are ready to do this by trying to grab your spoon or plate. Try putting finger foods such as apple slices, sliced peaches, celery sticks, carrot sticks, or cheese segments, on a plate or directly onto the high chair tray, then simply let your child at them. Many children accept meals more readily when they can participate themselves. Toddlers will often gnaw on finger food and allow you to feed them at the same time.

Offer your child a spoon.

While you are feeding your child, offer her a spoon. Whenever she manages to get food on the spoon and into her mouth, praise and encourage her. As spoon control develops, you may need to gently guide your toddler through the motions of scooping and locating the mouth. Some spills are inevitable. As soon as your child loses interest in self feeding, continue to feed her yourself.

Gradually phase out your help.

As your child becomes more and more skilled at using a spoon, gradually phase out the help you provide. This means the child taking more and more control over the meal — as well as more mess to clean up initially.

Introduce new foods one at a time.

Take note of the time of day when your child seems to be hungriest. Introduce new foods one at a time at these meals. Introduce small portions of the new food along with familiar and accepted ones. Remember to praise the child and name the new food he has just eaten.

Provide opportunities for your child to learn through watching.

Toddlers learn a great deal about eating and mealtime behaviour through watching older siblings and parents, so, from 12 to 18 months, occasionally let your child eat in her high chair at the family dinner table.

Reward good mealtime behaviour.

Encourage competent and appropriate mealtime behaviour by providing plenty of praise and attention when your child is eating appropriately. Talk to, smile at, and touch her when she tries a new food, uses a spoon for the first time without spills, sits without wriggling in her high chair, or swallows a mouthful of food after having chewed it properly.

Avoid rewarding poor mealtime behaviour.

Do not provide positive attention for inappropriate mealtime behaviour. Avoid laughing at your child when he spits out or throws food, or throws or drops utensils, bowls, or cups. The best initial strategy is to withdraw your attention. Turn your head away and simply wait 10 to 15 seconds until the undesired behaviour has stopped. When it has stopped, re-establish eye contact, offer food again, and then give positive attention as soon as he eats correctly.

Don't expect toddlers to clean their plate.

It is better to serve small portions and allow the child to ask for more if she is still hungry rather than to have a battle over the last spoonful or two. Do not expect to provide the child's daily nutritional requirements in a single meal.

Excessive crying in toddlers

While most children cry less and less as their first year progresses, some cry a lot more than others. Sometimes labelled as sooks or cry babies, these temperamentally difficult children can wail after very minor upsets, bumps, or falls. They may cry loudly when put to bed, when they don't get their own way, and after mildly upsetting experiences such as a loud noise. Crying is often accompanied by attempts to get the parent's attention, which may involve being picked up and held, cuddled, reassured, or offered a drink. This kind of reaction from a parent is quite appropriate if a child is genuinely hurt or unwell. However, children also learn that upset behaviour leads to a great deal of positive attention. Some anxious parents feel that they are neglecting their children if they don't respond to all crying or distress. This kind of overprotectiveness is a mistake. Children have to learn to deal with a few minor knocks, discomforts, or frustrations without always bursting into tears.

When children cry frequently for little or no apparent reason, it is better either to ignore the crying altogether or to respond very matter of factly to it. 'Up you get. Give it a rub,' not, 'Oh you poor dear. Did you hurt your little bottom? Come over here and have a cuddle. Mummy fix it up.'

If you think your toddler cries excessively, try the suggestions but first ask yourself these questions. Does the child receive sufficient time and attention from you when she has been good? Are there any signs of emotional disturbance or evidence that the child has had an emotionally traumatising experience? For example, has he gone off his food, have there been any recent changes in his sleeping pattern, particularly more disturbed sleep, does he seem fearful or fretful? If the child is generally in good health and the answer to these questions is no, then it is usually safe to proceed as follows.

Quickly check on your child's state.

When your child starts crying, quickly check to make sure no major disaster has occurred. Try to do this without your child seeing you. Sometimes simply listening to the nature of the cry will give you the best clue. Children who are genuinely injured and in pain will often have a deep bellowing cry followed by a pause as they gasp for air. Other types of cries, particularly attention-seeking cries, are often less intense, are not interrupted by gasping for air, and are not as loud.

Ignore the crying

Withdraw all attention while the crying continues. Say nothing, turn your head away, and continue with what you are doing.

Listen for pauses in the crying.

Wait for a pause of a few seconds in the crying and then attend to the child immediately. When the crying has stopped, try to distract your child with another activity.

Do not pick up or cuddle the child while she is still fussing.

If the child seeks your attention such as by asking to be picked up while still crying or whimpering, use a neutral tone to prompt her to tell or show you what the matter is. Do not pick her up. Be neither overly sympathetic nor cold and harsh. A matter-of-fact expression is the best. For example, simply ask 'What's the matter?'

Praise your child for being brave.

If the child points to or tells you about the problem and at the same time stops crying, praise him. 'Aren't you a brave boy?'

Set the child up in a new activity.

Try to distract the child with another activity. If the crying continues or turns into whining, use the strategy for dealing with whining which comes later in this chapter.

Promoting children's language

One of the most important changes that takes place during toddlerhood is in the area of language. Children move from understanding an average of around 10 words at 12 months, to having a vocabulary of 800 to 900 words by the time they are three, when they understand most of the adults' sentences they hear. This tremendous growth in language use is closely related to intellectual development and the child's general understanding of her world. How quickly children learn to speak and the size of their vocabulary is influenced by their interactions with their parents and other family members. Children differ markedly in how quickly they learn to speak. Some children are speaking in complex sentences by the age of 3, while others are hardly speaking at all. If your child's language appears to be considerably delayed compared with other children of the same age, then it is worth seeking professional assistance to have the problem assessed thoroughly. Speech therapists and some child psychologists are expert in assessing language problems and can provide concrete advice on dealing with the problem. Here are some ideas about how to promote language development.

Be accessible.

Being accessible does not simply mean spending time with your child. It means being available when he attempts to communicate through language, and being prepared to listen to what he is saying.

Talk to your child.

A child's interest in speaking is increased when her parents speak to her frequently. This does not mean that you must spend all day chatting to your 1-year-old, but you should point out and name things your child looks at. Notice the objects she is interested in and give those objects names.

Respond positively to children's language initiations.

Learn to respond positively when your child attempts to use language. This involves listening to what he is saying, repeating it yourself, and perhaps providing more information about the topic or thing that has captured his attention. This is the key to the incidental teaching we discussed in chapter 3. If a child brings an object to you (a rattle) and makes a sound ('tattle'), this is an excellent time to teach your child language. His interest is focused on an object and he has approached you to show you how it works. A good response here would be to stop what your doing, look at the child, smile and say, 'What's that you've got?' Instead of simply saying, 'That's a rattle,' you have invited the child to tell you more about it. If this initial attempt does not produce any more language use, simply say, 'That's a rattle. Can you say rattle?' If he can, praise him. If not, don't worry, there will be plenty of other opportunities. Toddlers benefit greatly from these kinds of interactions, particularly when they are brief and occur often.

Provide a good language model.

Try to avoid babytalking to toddlers. Provide a good language model by using complete sentences and correct pronunciation. Children learn more quickly to speak in grammatically correct sentences when adults use language that is somewhat more difficult than they can yet produce. As children get older, they will often ask the meaning of unfamiliar words and thereby extend their own vocabularies. Of course, you should not use overly complex sentences that have too many unfamiliar words.

Describe what you are doing.

Children often enjoy watching their parents' various tasks, for example cleaning the car, vacuuming. They enjoy it even more if they can participate in some way, or can hold a conversation while they do so. Language can be encouraged if you take the time to describe what you are doing. These descriptions of simple everyday events, like weeding the garden, cooking, sewing, taking care of a baby, or building something, will often stimulate your child's curiosity, prompting her to ask further questions.

Share your feelings, ideas, and joys.

Another aspect of describing what you are doing involves sharing your feelings and experiences: telling your child about your day, the things that amused you, what you saw on the way home from work, the people you spoke to. Disclosing information about oneself is a skill that some adults never master. Those that do have often had these skills modelled for them by their parents. In the meantime, of course, it also helps to stimulate a child's interest in the world of words.

Act as an information resource.

By definition, parents know more about the world than their toddlers do. They can and should be information resource centres for their young children. Encourage your child to ask questions by answering her in understandable language. This takes patience and a willingness to be interrupted frequently. The parent who tells her 3-year-old not to ask so many stupid questions misunderstands the importance of this skill for a child's development. Children who don't ask their parents questions are also likely to have a very poor relationship with them.

Comment on your child's play.

Some parents are able to participate in their child's play without dominating or directing it. The key to doing this is observation. Watch what your child is doing and then make a comment that extends his interest in the activity without interfering with it. One of the best ways to do this is to ask a question about the game or activity. 'Where does baby Sarah sleep?' 'Where do all the blue ones go?'

Read to your child.

Toddlers love to have stories read to them and to look through picture books with an interested adult, particularly at bedtime. Infants and toddlers should be read to from a very early age. The world of words comes alive in books. Parents should obtain a good supply of books and read to their children regularly, at least once every day. Both parents should be involved. However, don't force children to listen to a story if they are interested in something else.

Whining

As children learn to communicate with their parents through words, whining can become a problem. All children whine from time to time as a way of gaining an adult's attention. Children whine for a variety of reasons: they may be tired, hungry, bored, have a wet nappy, be unwell, or want attention. Some children whine a lot more than others. Whining is a problem when it occurs frequently and becomes the child's usual way of gaining attention or making requests. If whining is successful because it produces attention or whatever the child wants, there is little incentive to learn to make requests appropriately. For instance, if a child simply points and grunts or whimpers to get an object which is out of reach, and then gets it, she does not need to learn the name of the object or to say please. Children whine less when they have the language to make their needs known. This involves learning specific words related to making requests, such as 'thank you', 'please', 'may I have', along with a pleasant expression and tone of voice.

Your main aim is to teach your child the proper way to make requests. Parents should not allow themselves to be bullied by a demanding toddler, so do not give the child what he wants until the request is more acceptable. The strategy also involves waiting until the form of the request is reasonable before considering the request itself. The idea is to model the correct way of asking and to reward the child when the desired behaviour is performed. Children under 2 who have yet to learn to speak can point, smile, or lead you by the hand to the wanted object. As long as the child is not whining and makes a language response that you can understand, comply with the request but prompt him to label the object requested. Each time he wants help he has an opportunity to learn a new word.

Here is a way of developing these skills in young children.

Stop what you are doing.

When your child approaches and makes a request in an unpleasant voice, stop what you are doing and gain his attention.

Calmly describe the incorrect behaviour.

'Sandy, you don't need to whine for a drink.'

Describe the correct way of asking.

Calmly ask your child to ask nicely. 'Say, Mummy, drink please,' or, 'Truck please, Mummy.' Use simple words the child can say. Initially, say all the words you want your child to use. Once he knows what to say, phase out your prompts. For example, you might say 'Pardon?', 'What's the magic word?', or even just look at the child expectantly with raised eyebrows.

Praise your child for speaking nicely.

Praise your child for speaking in a more pleasant manner. For example, 'That was a lovely way of asking.' Make sure you praise any time the child asks properly without first having to be reminded.

Decide whether the child's request is reasonable.

If the child asks for food, you might decide that dinner is being served in 5 minutes and you want the child to wait. The key here is not to say yes or no until the request is in an appropriate form. If the request is expressed appropriately and it is reasonable, then comply with it.

If whining continues, give one further prompt.

If the request is still unreasonable, prompt your child to speak properly once more. 'William, say, please Mummy, the truck'.

If the child protests, provide a logical consequence for the behaviour.

Describe the behaviour calmly but firmly. The most appropriate consequence is that the child does not get what he or she asked for. 'OK. If you can't ask nicely, the biscuits go away for ten minutes. Try again then.'

If the child becomes aggressive or throws a temper tantrum, immediately back up with quiet time for 2 minutes.

Remember to describe to the child what she has done wrong.

If the problem continues or the child won't sit in quiet time, put him into time out for 2 minutes.

Make sure the child is quiet before being allowed out of time out.

Children, like adults, eventually have to learn that despite being tired or run down it is not OK to be obnoxious to others. Be persistent and consistent and your child will more easily learn what is required.

Avoid losing your temper and yelling, telling the child to stop whining but giving her what she wants *before* she asks properly, or completing ignoring her. There are times when a bit more leniency is warranted, including when the child is physically unwell or has had an upsetting or frightening experience.

Whining often occurs in children who throw temper tantrums. Some parents worry that insisting on speaking reasonably might provoke a temper tantrum. However, don't let the threat of a temper outburst prevent you from dealing with whining as a specific problem. Tantrums can be dealt with as the need arises.

Minor fussing

Sometimes children whine for no apparent reason, they just seem in a grumpy mood. This sort of whining and whimpering can also occur when a parent refuses them something they want, such as food before mealtimes. It differs from the previous sort of whining because it is not immediately directed at the parent. Nor is it the result of the child having been hurt, or being wet or ill. Some children just seem to wander around aimlessly grizzling and whimpering. They often receive attention at some point from their parent or a concerned grandparent, who says, 'What's the matter with you then?' The child may or may not settle when he receives such attention. The best strategy for dealing with such behaviour is to ignore it completely.

Here are some guidelines.

Quickly check that your child is not hurt.

When you observe your child whining, quickly check to make sure he has not fallen over, been hurt, or got wet pants. If the child is OK then proceed as follows.

Completely ignore the behaviour.

Remove all attention from the child while the whimpering continues.

Attend to the child when the behaviour has stopped.

When the grizzling stops, wait a few seconds and then attend to the child. That is, the child receives attention for having stopped grizzling. For example, you might say, 'Would you like to come and help me hang up the washing?' It is important to wait for a pause in the whining before trying to distract your child.

Offer praise when your child is busy.

As soon as the child is engaged in play, look for an opportunity to praise her. Catch your child not whining.

Disobedience

During the toddler period, most parents first experience the problem of disobedience. As toddlers become more mobile and independent they will touch things they are not supposed to. From the age of 14 to 24 months, toddlers start to resist the will of parents. They become more assertive. They may climb on to furniture that is fragile, run out on the road, try to put objects into power points, pull hair, strike their parents or other children, or pour drinks on the carpet. Toddlers must learn the meaning of 'no'. Some children will deliberately repeat a forbidden behaviour to get a reaction from the parent. When the parent says no, it's like a dare. The child does exactly the same thing again, maybe even with a big smile or a grin. Toddlers are renowned for testing their parents.

Neil, a 2-year-old, was told not to touch the TV knobs, and then stood right next to the set, looked defiantly at his mother, and pretended to touch the knobs again. His mother rose to the bait every time this happened, saying, 'Neeeiil!' Occasionally she would be so amused by the child's antics that she would grin and say, 'You are a naughty boy.' Neil, of course, got a very confusing message and it took a long time before he finally lost interest in the TV knobs. Neil would have learned to leave the TV alone much more quickly if his mother had dealt with the behaviour more firmly and decisively.

Discipline after disobedience should teach your toddler at least two things. First, 'no' means stop what you're doing immediately. Second, the child should learn the appropriate behaviour.

Deal with disobedience firmly and decisively when your child is a toddler rather than leaving the problem unchecked. Children need firm adult direction and guidance at this age. Parents who have taught their toddlers to respond to directions find raising preschoolers and school-aged children much less of a drama.

Here are some guidelines for dealing with disobedience.

Safety-proof your home so there are fewer 'no touch' areas.

By reducing the number of times you have to say no, you will make each rule carry more weight.

Get close

If a toddler does something that needs correction, move closer.

Say 'no' in a firm, controlled voice.

Grasp the child's hands firmly and speak in a firm, controlled voice. 'No, don't touch.' This will not hurt the child and is an alternative to smacking. When you say no, frown and shake your head from side to side.

Suggest an alternative activity.

If the child stops, suggest something else for her to do. For example, if the toddler pulls the cat's tail, say 'no', then show her how to stroke the cat gently instead. 'No, don't be rough with pussy. Stroke her like this.' Praise the child as soon as she complies or is engaged in an appropriate activity.

Ignore whimpering or protesting.

Sometimes children will whimper or cry after being corrected in this way. Simply ignore these protests.

Use quiet time as a back-up.

If the child repeats the behaviour within the next hour, use quiet time in a playpen, chair or beanbag for 1 minute.

Biting and pulling hair

Toddlers can inflict nasty injuries on other children through biting. Apart from hurting, a bite that breaks the skin can easily become infected. It is unacceptable behaviour and should be dealt with firmly. Some children bite when they don't get their own way, others bite when they are frustrated or annoyed, and still others do it just to see what will happen. Toddlers also occasionally pull hair and hit other children. Parents are sometimes the prime target for this type of behaviour.

Some parents try to deal with biting and hitting by hitting or biting back. The idea is that if the child knows how it feels he will be discouraged from trying it again. Unfortunately, this tactic involves modelling the very behaviour you want the child to control.

The key to overcoming biting is to provide close supervision in the early stages. You must watch your child closely for a few days while she is playing with other kids so that you can respond promptly.

Give positive attention for not biting.

When you notice your child playing appropriately, that is without biting or disrupting others, give him attention or comment on the child's play. 'Aren't you playing nicely this morning?' or 'What are you doing with that truck? It can tow that car easily, can't it?.'

Give a terminating instruction.

When your child is about to bite or actually bites another child, intervene immediately. Give a firm terminating instruction, such as 'No, don't bite.'

Put your child into quiet time or time out.

Provide an immediate back-up consequence, such as quiet time or time out for 3 minutes. Follow this step and the previous one as often as you need to until the behaviour ceases.

Allow the child to return to the activity.

After the time out period, return the child to the activity so he can practise playing without biting.

Provide a back-up reward if no further disruption occurs.

If the child manages to last out the activity without biting, provide a small back-up treat such as raisins, a favourite drink, or a story. Explain why his behaviour has pleased you.

A variation of this strategy can be used for pulling hair including your own. However, before you give quiet time or time out get the child to spend a few seconds touching and stroking your or the other child's hair without pulling. If she struggles or resists, simply guide her through the motions and ignore protests.

Sleeping and bedtime problems

'Mummy, I not tired', 'Stay wiff me', 'Your bed, Mummy', 'Mummy, more drink'. These are familiar cries at bedtime. The most common bedtime problems include refusing to and protesting about going to bed, crying once being put to bed, waking up in the middle of the night, refusing to sleep in the child's own bed, and getting out of bed after being put to bed.

Most parents need time to themselves at the end of a day. They are often tired and thus vulnerable to a child's night-time antics. It is important, therefore, for toddlers to get into a good night-time routine: they will have sufficient energy for the next day's activities and their parents will have some child-free time to spend with each other as partners and companions.

Children should have a definite and predictable bedtime, should be expected to sleep in their own beds, and to remain there until morning unless something exceptional happens, such as the child being physically unwell.

Some sleeping problems are temporary and follow an illness or other disruption to the child's normal routine, such as having to sleep in a strange bed. These problems often correct themselves once normal routine is re-established.

The most common difficulty parents experience is crying. The parent puts the child to bed, reads a story, says goodnight, and then it starts. As soon as the parent attempts to leave, the child starts to scream. This screaming can be quite distressing for many parents. However, if a child learns screaming will bring his parents back into the room, or better still have them take him out of bed and into their own bed, there is little incentive for him to stay quiet. The crying pays off. What is more attractive than being able to snuggle in between Mum and Dad in a nice warm bed? Unfortunately, if this habit is established, you can expect the problem to continue, sometimes for many years.

Parents who give up trying to get their children to sleep in their own beds often have to put up with disturbed sleep themselves. Toddlers often wriggle, knee you in the back, and disrupt parents' normal sex life. Here are some ideas for helping to get children into a good night-time routine.

Establish a predictable, regular bedtime.

Decide on a reasonable time (between 6.30 and 8.00 p.m.) and stick to it.

Discuss the ground rules.

Explain to your child that from now on you would like him to go to bed at a specific time, to stay in bed, and not to call out.

Make sure the child's room is well ventilated.

The room should be neither too hot nor too cold. Purchase a night light for the power point if the child is afraid of the dark.

Give a warning.

Thirty minutes prior to bedtime, warn your child that he will have to get into bed in half an hour. During this time, get your child involved in a quiet activity. Make sure he does not run around, or get too excited with boisterous play. Suitable activities include looking at a book, watching television, or listening to a story on a cassette tape.

Wind up pre-bedtime activities.

Five minutes before bedtime, ask the child to finish what she is doing and get ready for bed. Tell her if she comes straight away without a fuss you will read a story in bed.

Help your child get ready for bed.

Help the child as necessary with teeth, toilet, and getting ready for bed.

Put your child to bed and review your list.

Put the child to bed and read the story, give him a kiss and a cuddle, then go through a list of all possible excuses the child may have for getting out of bed.

> 'Have you cleaned your teeth, David?'
> 'Yes.'
> 'Have you said goodnight to Daddy and Booma [the cat]?'
> 'Yes.'
> 'Have you been to the toilet?'
> 'Yes.'

Remind your child of the rules before leaving.

Explain what will happen if he stays in bed or gets out of bed. 'If you stay in bed and don't call out, there will be a surprise treat under your pillow in the morning. If you call out, I won't answer you even if you yell. If you get out of bed, you will have to go to time out in the bathroom. OK? Goodnight.' If the child wants the door left open or a hall light left on, that's fine.

Ignore calling out.

If the child calls out, completely ignore her. Say nothing at all and don't go back in. Be prepared for her to cry for quite some time on the first night, particularly if you have returned to her room when she has screamed in the past. If the child wriggles and squirms in bed, or lies there awake, ignore it.

If your child gets out of bed, return him to his own bed immediately.

If the child gets out of bed, take him back to his room immediately. 'Steven, you are not to get out of bed. Now get back to bed.' Ignore protests and return the child to bed.

Return your child to her bed if she wanders during the night.

If your child wakes during the night and wanders into your bedroom, immediately return her to her bed. Give very little attention at this time. Spend no more than 30 seconds trying to settle the child down, for example by patting her back, say goodnight and leave. Ignore protests.

Give a back-up reward in the morning.

If the child remained in bed throughout the night, place a small gift or treat under his pillow and, if you're using a behaviour chart, put a smiley on his chart. Remember to praise your child for being a good sleeper if he has been successful. If he screamed or got out of bed, do not give a back-up reward.

If you follow this routine consistently, many problem sleepers will be sleeping in their own beds and going off to bed without protesting within a few days. However, many will cry for anywhere from a few minutes to several hours the first few nights. You must be prepared to let them cry themselves to sleep. If you go in after the child has screamed for a long time you will probably make it worse. The child will simply learn to scream louder and longer. Remind yourself that no harm will come to him and that in the long run it is for his own good.

Some parents become quite upset during this time and are very tempted to attend to the child. Don't, see it through. By the end of the first week, children will often have given up crying when they are put to bed or will whimper for only a few minutes. The first few days are the hardest.

It is very important that both parents follow this routine consistently. Remember that an adequate amount of sleep is a vital energy-restoring process. We cannot make a child go to sleep, but we can organise conditions where sleep becomes more likely. If there is no progress after a two-week trial, double check to ensure that you are following the routine consistently.

Temper tantrums

Almost every parent has heard about the 'terrible twos', when their previously placid, cooperative baby becomes a demanding, stubborn, and uncooperative monster. Some toddlers will throw massive temper tantrums when they are not allowed to do something, or even for no obvious reason. The trigger can be quite minor, such as not being able to fit a block into a hole in a puzzle board, or being unable to open a packet of raisins. The first time a child throws a true tantrum, the parents may be stunned into embarrassed silence, particularly if the supermarket floor is the venue.

Some temper tantrums are short-lived encounters, lasting only 10 to 30 seconds; other children work themselves up into such a state that they can continue screaming for hours. They may throw themselves on the floor, throw objects, stamp their feet, even hold their breath until they are unconscious for a few seconds. It can be quite frightening to see your child change colour through lack of oxygen, but all breathholders eventually take a gasp of air. Temper tantrums can also be a sign of more severe behavioural disturbance, particularly if they occur frequently and persist over a long time. It is best to deal with them promptly as they arise. Here are some guidelines.

Gain the child's attention as best you can.

Stop what you are doing and move close to your child, within arms' reach.

Give the child a terminating instruction.

Tell your child that the screaming must stop or he will have to go to time out until it does. 'Bevan, stop that screaming right now or you'll have to go to time out.'

If the tantrum continues, describe the problem and the consequence.

'You have not done as I asked. Now go to time out. Right now.'

If the tantrum continues, take the child to time out.

Explain what is wrong and the rules for time out. Give the explanation even though the child might be quite distraught.

Follow the time out rules consistently.

Follow the guidelines for using time out in chapter 3 on page 80, and do not let the child out until the screaming has stopped and the toddler has been quiet for at least a minute.

When the child throws a tantrum, do not try to cuddle, reassure, or in any other way give positive attention. Do not give in to the child's demands or he'll learn to use temper outbursts to get his own way. Some parents try to ignore the tantrum as an alternative to using time out. This will only work if the child is completely ignored, and that may be difficult if other children are around or you have visitors. It's better to remove the child from the action. He will learn an important message: 'When you have got yourself under control, you are welcome to rejoin us'.

Be prepared to put up with quite a storm in the time out room. You may feel quite agitated to hear your child in such distress, and your natural instinct will be to try to calm and comfort him. This is a mistake and can actually make the tantrum worse. Children who throw tantrums, often five or six times a day, may need to be put into time out six to ten times on the first day. By the end of the first week, tantrums are usually occurring much less frequently and for a shorter time.

If there has been no progress after a few days of following this routine, check to make sure that you are following the guidelines for using time out correctly. If you are, and the problem continues, seek professional advice.

Wandering

Toddlers are notorious for getting lost. Parents are understandably concerned about their children wandering because they can run on to the road, get hit by passing cars, or be picked up by strangers. These dangers are not apparent to 2-year-olds who do disappearing acts. Wandering can occur on shopping trips, walking down the road, or just playing in the backyard.

Some toddlers seem to take off whenever there is an opportunity. Parents have told me that it can take just a split second. The parent may turn away for a moment and the child disappears. Children like these may refuse to hold the parent's hand when walking.

It might sound very obvious, but the key behaviour to encourage in a wanderer is **staying close to the parent.** Remaining close has to become more rewarding to the child than the excitement of exploring on his own, at least initially.

Set aside some time to teach your child to stay close.

This can involve going on a series of planned short trips, about five to seven of them, around the neighbourhood with your toddler. Don't take your child out less because she is a wanderer, give her even more opportunities to learn the correct behaviour. Start with a very short trip of, say, 2 minutes, perhaps down to the corner of the street. Each subsequent trip should be slightly longer, building up to about a 10-minute walk.

Get yourself ready.

Before setting out on each trip, get yourself ready, arming yourself with a packet of raisins or soft sweets that can be used to reward the toddler for staying within reach.

Explain the ground rules.

Explain where you are going and what the ground rules will be. 'We're going for a walk down to the shop for some bread. Would you like to come with Mummy?' Depending on the child's language, ask him to state the rules for going walking with Mummy. Praise him for correctly stating the rules.

Praise your child for staying close.

Initially, praise the child every 30 seconds or so for staying close, before he has had a chance to take off. Each time you praise him, offer him part of a snack. As you walk, engage him in conversation. Point out flowers, birds, trees, or any item of interest that catches your eye.

Deal with wandering by prompting the correct behaviour.

If your child starts to stray, immediately describe the incorrect behaviour. 'Paul, you are too far away.' If he returns, praise him for doing what he's told. 'Good boy for coming to Mummy.'

Provide a back-up consequence.

If the child takes off again, grab him immediately and give a firm terminating instruction. 'No, you must stay close to Mummy.' Stop walking and give him quiet time for 1 minute. Quiet time can involve sitting him on the pavement. If necessary, physically restrain him by wrapping your arms around him and holding him firmly so he can't move.

Continue the journey while remembering to praise your child for staying close.

Once quiet time is over, continue the trip and look for an opportunity to catch him staying close.

After the trip, give positive feedback.

At the end of the trip, make sure you make a big fuss over the fact that your child remembered to stay close today. Tell your partner and grandparents or family friends who can also give positive feedback.

Let your child practise staying close with other adults.

After your child has accomplished staying close on short trips, make sure he has a chance to practise staying close with both parents or even with grandparents.

Phase out rewards and positive attention.

Gradually phase out the rewards so that your child is required to last the whole trip before receiving the treat. If the improved behaviour continues, then phase out the back-up treats altogether. Just give occasional praise for remembering to stay close.

The key to overcoming wandering is a quick decisive response on your part. The child should be supervised very closely during outings where wandering occurs and immediately punished with quiet time if he attempts to stray. Some parents use restraining harnesses with young children who wander. This can be a useful strategy but it does not actually teach the child the correct behaviour. It simply prevents her from running off. Parents often find that the problem resurfaces as soon as the restraint is not used. Take the time and make the effort to train your child properly in the correct behaviour.

Toilet training

Learning to use the toilet or potty is a complex task. The child must learn to recognise internal signals such as a full bladder, to delay going in his pants, to tell his parent he needs to go to the toilet, or to walk to the bathroom, then to remove his pants, sit on the potty, pass water or defecate, wipe his bottom, pull up his pants, wash his hands, and return to play. It is a wonder that more children do not have problems.

It is best to begin toilet training at age of 20 to 24 months when the child has better control over the sphincter and abdominal muscles and enough language to understand what is required of him. Toilet training is accomplished quite quickly with some children; others take several months.

Here are some general ideas on how to toilet train your toddler.

Allow your child to watch.

The best preparation for many toddlers is to watch what their parents do when they go to the toilet. Let your child follow you into the bathroom.

Get everything you need ready.

Buy a child-sized potty that is easy for the child to sit on without falling in and a doll that will release water when squeezed.

Choose a day to begin.

Set aside a half day so you can concentrate on the task of toilet training.

Organise a practice session.

Have a practice session with the doll to show the child what to do when she wants to go to the toilet. Set this session up as a game where the child can help dolly learn to go to the toilet. 'Let's look at what dolly does when she wants to go wee wees.' Show the child how dolly first comes and tells Mummy. Praise the dolly for letting Mummy know. Then quickly take the dolly to the potty, take off her panties and sit her on the potty. Ask the child to tell dolly how good she is for sitting on the potty. Then squeeze the doll so that water goes in the potty. Offer enthusiastic praise for going to the toilet. Next let your child play Mummy and you be the dolly. Approach the child with the doll and say, 'Mummy, I want to go wee wees.' If the child spontaneously praises you (the doll) and takes you to the potty, praise the child for helping dolly go wee wees.

Next, let your child pretend to be dolly. Start off by asking what you should do when you want to go to the toilet. If the child tells you, offer enthusiastic praise. Take the child over to the potty and say, 'What comes next?' If the child says, 'take off my pants,' or takes off his pants, offer praise and sit him on the potty for a few seconds. If the child actually goes, offer praise. Take the child to the bathroom to wash his hands and once again offer praise.

Give plenty of fluids.

After this practice session, give your child plenty of fluids to increase the chances he will want to go to the toilet. Put the child in loose-fitting pants with an elastic waist, and no nappy.

State the correct behaviour.

Remind your child what you want him to do if he needs to go to the toilet.

Offer praise for each correct step.

If your child lets you know she wants to go to the toilet, then praise her enthusiastically for each step she accomplishes on her own.

Ask your child if he would like to go.

If your child does not approach you or the potty, then every few minutes ask him if he would like to go, particularly if you see him holding on to his penis through his pants or pulling a face that indicates he is about to go.

Teach your child to wash her hands.

After every successful use of the toilet, make sure your child washes her hands. Offer a back-up treat, such as a small packet of raisins or soft sweets.

Deal with accidents by describing the incorrect then the correct behaviour.

If the child has an accident, and almost all children will, describe what he has done wrong ('No. You don't do wees in your pants') and tell him what he should do instead ('You must do wees on the potty'). Make sure the child practises the correct behaviour. Take him by the hand into the bathroom, take down his pants, and sit him on the potty. Use a firm and matter-of-fact voice. Ignore protests. Do not get angry or abuse the child.

Phase out rewards and praise gradually.

Once your child is telling you regularly when she wants to go, and successfully completing the task, gradually phase out the amount of praise and back-up rewards. This can be done by waiting until the child has completed several of the steps, then all of the steps, before being praised.

It is often quicker to teach toddlers to urinate in the toilet than to teach them to pass a bowel movement in the toilet. Many children who are dry during the day will wait until their diaper is on during naps before they pass a motion. This is quite normal and should not cause any concern. However, if the child tries to pass a bowel motion while sitting on the potty, offer enthusiastic encouragement. If you notice your child straining to pass a motion, then quickly ask if she would like to go to the toilet and take her promptly to the bathroom.

Many children will continue to wet themselves at night until the age of 6 or 7. Bedwetting is dealt with in chapter 6.

Encouraging independent play

Toddlers are generally better able to amuse themselves than infants. Indeed, toddlerhood is a period of great discovery and excitement as children become capable of more complex play and games. However, they are not generally capable of truly cooperative play with other children. Their play tends to be parallel, where two children may be playing side by side but with no rules in common and each absorbed in her or his own activity. Children's play is extremely important. Through play they learn about their world. They discover objects have different shapes, sizes, colours, textures, names, and uses, and they make different noises.

Children's play also serves other important purposes. It is through play that children meet and learn to relate to other children. Children's play can be tremendously rewarding for parents as well, and they can participate from time to time without dominating the play.

Problems can also arise with children's play. If a child simply won't play on his own without an adult joining in, parents end up feeling harassed and as though they never get a break when the toddler is awake. If every time the parent stops watching the child play the child cries or follows the parent around, it is probably time to teach the child to play more independently. Many of these problems are quite normal and all children go through phases of being clingy. They may seem to want to follow you round all day, becoming upset whenever you are out of sight. The problem usually sorts itself out with time.

Here are some suggestions for encouraging independent play.

Make sure you have plenty of interesting and age-appropriate toys and other activities available.

Make sure the activities are easily accessible. Toys can be stored in low, open shelves within easy reach of the child. In general it is better for activities to be stored in areas where children spend most of their time. This is usually in family living areas. Having a beautifully equipped playroom can be next to useless if the child wants to spend her time near to you. Avoid storing toys in boxes that open from the top. This makes it harder for the child to select what she wants to play with. Set aside a low cupboard in the kitchen where there are things the child can play with.

Help the toddler get started.

Ask the child what he would like to play with. If he does not select anything, get out a few toys yourself and suggest something. Sometimes children will need to be shown how to play with particular toys.

Use incidental teaching strategies to encourage the child to continue with the activity.

Respond positively to children's initiations and questions.

Once the child has started, use 'strategic exiting'.

Suggest something the child might do ('See how tall you can make that tower') and follow with an offer to return shortly to see how the child has got on. Always tell the child where you are going. 'I'll just put on the kettle and then you can show me what you've done.' Initially, leave the child on his own for a very short period, say 20 seconds. If the child continues with the activity without stopping, come back and let him show you what he's accomplished. 'Isn't that a beautiful tower? You did it all by yourself.' The basic idea is to gradually increase the amount of time you are away before returning, so that the child gets used to you joining in then leaving his play without interruption. Your return should always be associated with positive comments or questions related to the child's activity, and the fact that he was playing all by himself.

Ignore further protests about leaving.

If the child protests or stops as soon as you attempt to leave, simply tell her to choose something else if she has finished with that game and then leave anyway. Ignore further protests.

Offer children snacks while they are busy.

Don't wait until children have become bored and have interrupted their play before you offer snacks. By offering them while a child is still busy, you will increase your child's attention and concentration span. It also serves as a reward for sustained play activity.

The combination of making activities accessible, the use of incidental teaching when children are at play, and the strategic exit, can be very effective in encouraging easily distracted youngsters to focus their attention on play activities. Don't be upset if the strategy doesn't work the first time; simply try again in a few days' time. Children who are very easily distracted can't concentrate on anything for more than a few seconds and those whose play seems aimless may be hyperactive or have a developmental disability, in which case you should seek professional assistance.

Dressing problems

Children begin toddlerhood needing a great deal of help with getting dressed. By the time they are 3 they should have acquired most of the skills involved in dressing themselves, but will need some help on occasions. During toddlerhood, parents should encourage more independence in dressing, but some children will resist these attempts and simply refuse to dress themselves unless the parent does everything. Teaching a child to dress is a long-term project and change will be gradual. Some dressing skills are much easier than others. For example, putting on a pair of shorts is easier than learning to tie shoelaces.

Dressing should be fun. It is not a time for harassing or nagging children. A toddler has at least two or three opportunities each day to learn about dressing and undressing. Try the following procedure.

Get everything ready.

Try to organise your morning routine so that everything the child needs is ready before you start. Have it all in the one place so that the child does not have to wait. Avoid distractions, like having the TV on, so the child can concentrate on what is happening.

Praise independent dressing.

Begin dressing your toddler, but any time he wants to do something let him do so. Praise him enthusiastically and frequently for any attempt to put on an item of clothing.

Describe what is happening.

Talk to him about what you are doing. 'First, we put on what?' 'Yes, that's right, your underpants.' Ask him questions about what he should do next. 'What goes in here?' as you point to the holes for his legs.

Only give assistance when it is required.

Only give your child as much assistance as she needs. For example, avoid pulling up her pants if she can do this. Over time, gradually reduce your assistance and withhold praising her until she has put on all but very difficult clothing items.

Give your child time to learn the skills.

Allow enough time for dressing so that you are not rushed and therefore tempted to simply dress the child yourself to avoid being late.

Prompt the naming of items of clothing.

Ask the child to identify each item of clothing. Praise the correct naming of items.

Provide consequences for non-cooperation.

If the child struggles, resists, tries to run off, or throws a temper tantrum during dressing, tell him to keep still. Back up this instruction with quiet time for 1 minute.

Sharing

Toddlers can become very possessive about their things. The word 'mine' surfaces early in the vocabulary of many children, and they get quite upset if visiting children dare to touch something of theirs. Appealing to the child's sense of reason simply doesn't work. The toddler may grab or push another child away from a favourite teddy, car, doll, or other toy. This kind of behaviour is common and nothing to be particularly concerned about. It often decreases once the child attends a playgroup or moves on to kindergarten or preschool.

In the meantime it can be a source of frustration and embarrassment, especially if your child is allowed to play with your friend's child's things when you visit. Here are some ideas to help toddlers get used to the idea of sharing.

Tell your child who will be visiting and what to expect.

When you know that other children around your child's age will be visiting, explain that you would like him to let the visitors play with some of his toys.

Involve your child in selecting toys for sharing.

Ask your child to select some toys she's prepared to let the visitors play with.

Give the visitor permission to play with selected toys.

When the visitors arrive, set out the toys and tell the visitors they are welcome to use them. Set the children up in an activity before you leave.

Praise your child for sharing.

Praise your own child periodically for letting the others play with his things.

Describe correct use of toys.

If the visitor plays with your child's toys dangerously or roughly, ask your child if she would like you to put the offending toy away. Tell the child concerned how the toy should be used and request that he do so.

Deal with snatching and disruptions by describing the incorrect and correct behaviour.

If your child tries to snatch, grab, or push the other child away from his toys, describe what he has done wrong, 'Steven, you mustn't grab when Andrew is using it', and prompt the correct alternative behaviour. 'Give it back and let him have a turn.'

Remove troublesome toys.

If the child disobeys, simply take the toy from her hands and give it to the other child.

Use quiet time as a back-up consequence.

If your child continues to protest or throws a tantrum, put him in quiet time for 2 minutes. After quiet time is over, return the child to the activity and tell him when it will be his turn.

Sometimes difficulties can arise when older or bigger children take over and do not let your own child have a turn. In these instances, be prepared to intervene to ensure that the children share the activity. Your child cannot be expected to let other children use her things if they don't take proper care of them or won't share. Don't wait for other parents to come to your child's rescue. In your house, and with your child's activities, be prepared to insist on fair play.

Arrival of a new baby

The arrival of a new baby means some fairly major changes for both the toddler and the parents. The toddler may have been quite excited about the prospect of having a baby brother or sister, but the reality can be a different story. The toddler must get used to not having his mother's undivided attention, and may resent all the interest shown in the new arrival, not only by parents but by others. If there have been problems with the delivery, the mother will be quite anxious about the new baby's every movement. The mother will often be exhausted and sore after the delivery, or may be quite depressed and need time to relax and recover when the baby is sleeping. This of course is the very time the toddler wants your attention, because he has you on his own.

Some toddlers can be very loving and caring towards a new baby, rushing to tell their mother any time the baby cries, and cheerfully watching and helping with nappy changes and feeds. Other children become quite jealous and aggressive towards the baby. They may hit the baby, pour things on her, or otherwise be too rough with her. Many of these problems can be minimised if the following steps are taken.

Prepare your child in advance.

Tell your child when the pregnancy is confirmed: talk about the birth, let the toddler feel the baby kicking, and let the toddler 'help' with the preparation of the nursery. There are several good books written for young children about the arrival of new babies into the family.

Involve the toddler in the care of the baby.

After the mother returns from hospital with the baby, involve the toddler in the care of the baby. It is important for the toddler not to feel excluded.

Make sure you spend some time with the toddler without the baby being around.

The toddler needs to come to terms gradually with not being the centre of attention all the time. This adjustment can be helped by making sure the toddler is not neglected.

Praise your child for assisting with the care of the baby or attending to his needs.

Let the toddler hold, cuddle, and nurse the baby. Praise him for amusing, entertaining, and being gentle with the baby.

Provide consequences if the toddler tries to hurt the baby.

If the toddler becomes aggressive by trying to pinch, hit, or hurt the baby deliberately, describe the incorrect behaviour. 'Jamie, no, don't pull Amy's hair.' Describe the correct behaviour. 'Stroke her like this if you want to touch her.' Deal with this behaviour firmly and calmly. Don't over-react by being too emotional. It is quite normal for toddlers to feel some resentment towards the new arrival. If the behaviour persists, put the toddler into quiet time for a minute with an explanation of what he's done wrong.

Despite your best efforts, your toddler may feel some resentment and jealousy towards the next baby. This resentment can become even worse once the infant herself starts to crawl and walk, and so becomes able to touch and interfere with the older child's possessions and games. Parents dealing with this situation should aim to teach the older child to distract the infant's attention on to objects or toys of his own. The parent should praise the older child for doing so. It is also important to avoid always chastising the older child for becoming upset about the infants 'disruptiveness' and never saying anything to the younger child. Many of these early adjustment difficulties resolve themselves with time. However, sibling rivalry and jealousy can be a persistent problem and indeed can continue right throughout adult life.

CHAPTER 5

Preschoolers

During the preschool period, from 3 until 5 or 6, many important developmental changes take place. These include further development in language use and vocabulary, improvements in both fine and gross motor coordination, and the beginnings of complex play and games that involve simple rules, sharing, and turn taking. At this age, children often spend time at some kind of organised preschool and have to learn to handle these separations from their parents. Some children go to play centres or play groups run by their parents. In either case, they become increasingly independent as many basic self-care skills are mastered, including being able to dress and undress themselves, learning to answer the telephone, developing table manners, and learning to pick up, put away, and take care of their possessions.

This is also the time when children need to be prepared for their entry into school. Preschoolers love books and should acquire many basic concepts about the printed word that are important for learning to read. These include skills such as tracking words from left to right, locating the top and bottom of a page, and the idea that words convey meaning. Some preschoolers learn to read before they start school.

During this time, children develop a stable notion of their own sex (gender identity) and begin to see themselves as being either a boy or a girl. They also start to display behaviour patterns that are characteristic of their gender.

This chapter deals with the more common developmental and behavioural problems that can arise in preschoolers. Some of the problems covered, such as disobedience and tantrums, are extensions of problems that begin in toddlerhood. Others relate to their greater involvement with the world outside the family, such as shopping trips, travelling in the car, visiting, separation problems, dawdling while getting ready to go out, and refusal to tidy away after themselves.

Specific issues or problems

Disobedience

Disobedience is the single most common problem of children referred to mental health specialists for behavioural and emotional problems. Serious problems of this kind can be avoided if parents have established good routines to deal with disobedience when the child is a toddler. It is important that preschoolers learn to respect adult direction and authority if they are going to be ready to enter formal schooling. At school, children are expected to comply with many basic rules. Those who are very defiant or disruptive at the end of the preschool period often have difficulty in settling into the routines of normal school life.

One way to tell whether your child is becoming very oppositional is to give her about ten instructions over a half-hour period. If she disobeys six to eight of the ten instructions, or more than 60 to 80 per cent, you may need to do something to increase her cooperativeness. Most children will disobey between 20 and 40 per cent of requests. When non-compliance occurs more often than this, the parent is likely to experience difficulties with many basic family routines such as getting into the bath, getting dressed, and shopping. Very disobedient children often receive lots of negative attention from their parents, who struggle to exercise control. These children are also often quite demanding. They may throw temper tantrums if they don't get their own way. Some are aggressive towards other children and their parents.

It is important to remember that blind obedience to all adult directions is also very undesirable. Insistence on blind obedience at all times is over-controlling and quite unreasonable. Children's creativity, initiative, and positive view of themselves can be threatened in such a highly authoritarian environment. However, if a parent has reasonable expectations and takes care to make fair and reasonable rules, then consistent enforcement of these rules will lead to more cooperative, better behaved, and happier children. It also leads to less stressed parents. The guidelines below are for children who *frequently* ignore parents' reasonable requests. Read the guidelines outlined in chapter 3 on page 75 for giving instructions to children, which cover most of the basic principles.

Set up a 'happy faces' chart.

Have about thirty 2 cm squares for each day and enough sheets for about 14 days. Have enough sheets for all the children in the family who have a compliance problem.

Choose a quiet day to begin.

Organise your time so that you begin this programme when you will be at home most or all of the day. Your child will find it easier to learn the basic routine if you avoid shopping trips or outings on the first few days.

Give a clear, calm instruction.

When you ask you child to do something, be careful to make sure that you get close and that the instruction is both clear and timed not to interrupt an important activity such as a favourite TV programme.

Praise compliance with the request.

When the child complies within 5 seconds of giving the instruction, praise him. 'Good boy for doing as I asked straight away.' Put a 'smiley' on his chart.

Back up your instruction.

If your child disobeys, repeat the instruction once, wait a further 5 seconds, then back up this instruction immediately with quiet time. Follow the quiet time guidelines in chapter 3 on page 78.

Repeat the instruction.

After quiet time, repeat the instruction. Do not put a smiley on the chart if a reminder is required.

Give back-up rewards as appropriate.

Initially let the child have a back-up reward from a lucky dip after earning four smileys. If the child is put into quiet time, start the count again. For example, if the child has earned three smileys then goes into quiet time, wait until four more instructions have been complied with before offering a lucky dip. After the first two days, give the child a lucky dip after six, then eight, then ten instructions. Increase the number gradually and simply go back one step, for example from eight to six, if the compliance drops off as you increase the demands.

Make back-up rewards more unpredictable.

After the first week, make the lucky dips more and more unpredictable. Sometimes after five, sometimes after 15, sometimes after eight. The idea here is that the child never knows when compliance is going to be rewarded. It becomes like a surprise.

Phase out the happy faces chart.

After the second week, phase out the happy faces chart. Don't put up a smiley after every instruction he complies with. Make the earning of smileys unpredictable, but continue to praise your child occasionally for complying with requests.

Follow this routine consistently every time you give an instruction and after three weeks your child should be complying with most requests. Often it only takes a day or two.

This programme requires parents to become very conscious of when they give instructions. It works best when both parents consistently follow the routine. Avoid giving your child a smiley or a lucky dip if she asks for one. Simply tell her that she can't get a smiley just by asking. This is to prevent the child from repeatedly asking the parent for a reward. Make sure you don't forget to provide the lucky dip if you have promised one and the child has reached the goal.

Temper tantrums

Temper outbursts are not confined to the 'terrible twos' and displays of temper can occur throughout childhood and indeed adulthood. Anger is a normal emotion. However, in the process of growing up, children need to learn to express their annoyance and disagreements constructively. Failure to do so can produce young adults who resort to violence whenever they don't get their own way. Temper tantrums are common problems in preschoolers. The most common triggers include being asked to stop an activity the child is involved in, such as being requested to turn off the TV and get ready for bed, a parent's refusal to agree to the child's request or demand, for example to buy an iceblock, and fights while playing with other children. Some very difficult preschoolers can throw 10 to 15 tantrums a day. These children are often very disobedient as well. Both the tantrums and the disobedience often need to be dealt with at the same time.

Some preschoolers only throw tantrums at home, never when they are at preschool or kindergarten. Preschool teachers can be quite surprised to learn how difficult a child is at home because the child is so well behaved at preschool. Others will throw tantrums anywhere.

Tantrums can be difficult to deal with, particularly when they occur in the middle of the night, in the supermarket, or if the parent lives in temporary accommodation such as a women's shelter, a caravan park, or with relatives. Neighbours may complain to the police and welfare agencies when they hear a child screaming repeatedly. Usually the fear is that the child is being abused.

Most of the guidelines for managing tantrums in toddlers apply equally well to preschoolers. However, tantrums with preschoolers can take a bit longer to bring under control and some parents may have to endure several fairly long screaming episodes before the child finally learns that tantrums no longer work.

Set up a behaviour chart.

Set up a behaviour chart similar to the happy faces chart described for dealing with disobedience on page 134, but this time make up a sheet with half hour time blocks corresponding to the child's waking day, for example from 7 o'clock in the morning until 7 at night, like the one in figure 3 on page 138.

Discuss the time out procedure with your child.

Prepare the child for what will happen next time he loses his temper, by rehearsing the time out procedure.

Set the timer.

Set your kitchen timer for 30 minutes. If the child lasts 30 minutes without throwing a tantrum, she earns a smiley face. Let her put the smiley on the chart if she wishes.

Back up instructions with time out.

If the child throws a tantrum, follow the procedure for managing tantrums in toddlers on page 118, that is give an instruction to stop, back up with time out in the laundry or bathroom, let the child out of time out when he has been quiet for 3 minutes, and ignore the child completely while in time out. Remember to make sure that the room used for time out is safe, and follow the guidelines very carefully.

Phase out the chart and back-up rewards.

After two weeks, providing the tantrums have reduced to about once or twice per week, phase the child off the happy faces chart and back-up rewards, but continue to praise her for being cooperative.

Many preschoolers quickly learn not to throw tantrums at home but may do so outside. If a tantrum occurs in the car, pull over and stop the car. Tell the child firmly to stop. If the tantrum continues, be prepared to put the child out of the car and on to the footpath for 2 minutes. If necessary, hold him still. Ignore other people's reactions as best you can. If struggling persists, give the child one firm smack on the bottom. When the tantrum has stopped, let him get back in the car, put on the seat belt, and continue on your way. If it is simply not possible to give time out, as in the supermarket, completely ignore the behaviour. Look away, turn away, and as soon as there is a pause in the screaming, comment on the fact that the child is quiet. Finish your shopping as quickly as possible and put your child into time out in the bathroom or laundry as soon as you get home. Remind him why he is going into time out.

Figure 3: A sample behaviour chart

Day:_____   Date:_____

Times	Faces	Times	Faces	Times	Faces

7.00
 	
    7.30
	☺	11.00
		
		    11.30
				3.30
				
				    4.00	

7.30
 	
    8.00
		11.30
		
		    12.00
				4.00
				
				    4.30	

8.00
 	
    8.30
		12.00
		
		    1.00
				4.30
				
				    5.00	

8.30
 	
    9.00
		1.00
		
		    1.30
				5.00
				
				    5.30	

9.00
 	
    9.30
		1.30
		
		    2.00
				5.30
				
				    6.00	

9.30
 	
    10.00
		2.00
		
		    2.30
				6.00
				
				    6.30	

10.00
 	
    10.30
		2.30
		
		    3.00
				6.30
				
				    7.00	

10.30
 	
    11.00
		3.00
		
		    3.30
				7.00
				
				    7.30	

Place a smiley face in the faces columns for the appropriate time period to indicate the absence of a behaviour you wish to reduce, or the occurrence of a desired behaviour.

Trouble shooting

If there has been no noticeable change in the tantrums after the first week, then check out the following list.

1. Make sure you and your partner are following the routine every time. Grandparents, baby-sitters, and child minders should also be aware of the time out routine and should follow the same guidelines.

2. Make sure you do not threaten time out. Don't say, 'If you don't stop, you will have to go to time out.' Act, don't threaten.

3. Are you letting your child out of time out before she is properly quiet? Some parents will let their child out while they are whimpering or calling out instead of requiring silence.

4. Make sure that the child is receiving sufficient positive attention when he is not in time out. Are there enough activities available for the child? Time out works best when 'time in' is positive and rewarding.

5. Don't get trapped by the child's attempts to treat time out as a game. He may say things like, 'I like time out anyway,' 'Can I go into time out?', 'Time out's fun.' Don't let these tricks put you off. Completely ignore such comments and follow through every time the problem behaviour occurs.

6. Make sure that the child cannot escape from time out before the time period is up. Some children may run out, open the door, or climb out the window to avoid time out. If necessary, put a lock on the door or window, or hold the handle so he can't get out.

7. Check to make absolutely sure your child is being completely ignored while in time out. Sometimes children will call out things like, 'I'm quiet now mummy. Can I come out?', or 'Mummy, I can't breathe,' or 'I want to go to the toilet.' These manoeuvres must be ignored otherwise your child will use them to gain attention when she is in time out.

8. Are you remembering to keep your cool? Some parents forget this and give time out only when they are really angry. They may shout and drag the child into time out, giving her a whack for good measure. None of these things make time out more effective.

9. Does your child know the rules? Sometimes parents will tell their child one thing but act as though different rules apply. For instance,

the parent tells the child he will go to time out for hitting, then puts the child into time out for not coming to the dinner table quickly enough. If you change the rules, make sure the child knows what they are beforehand.

10. Is the noise getting to you? Some parents abandon using time out because the child's screaming gets to them. If you give in while the child is screaming in time out, it is likely you will make the problem even worse. They will simply learn to scream louder and longer next time. Find something to do when your child is in time out, for example watch television, read a book, get a friend to hold your hand, go for a walk in the garden, get some ear muffs; remind yourself it's for his own good.

11. Is the time out room a dull, uninteresting place? Make sure you don't use the child's bedroom for time out.

12. If the child makes a mess during time out, for example by throwing clothes from a laundry basket around the room, make sure it's cleaned up before allowing the child out. If necessary, manually guide the child through the motions of tidying away.

If you are following all of these guidelines correctly and the child's behaviour is still not improving, then you should seek professional assistance. However, if these guidelines are followed accurately, time out will be effective with the vast majority of preschoolers who throw tantrums.

Getting ready to go out

The early morning rush of getting children ready for preschool or school can create chaos. It is a pressure time and one that often leads to behaviour problems. This is particularly likely if you were late waking up yourself and have to get yourself ready for work. Beds are left unmade, dishes are in the sink, the place is in a mess, and children leave without having everything they need for the day's activities.

Some children add to these difficulties by being persistently slow or demanding. Just when you need them to be cooperative they run away, hide, refuse to get dressed, or start to whine. When adults are under pressure they may yell and shout, and many a child has left for a morning's activities at preschool after getting a whacking at home. Other children just seem disorganised in the morning. They have to be reminded every step of the way, sometimes several times.

Have you done your teeth, been to the toilet, got your kindy bag, and so on?

The key to overcoming this kind of dawdling is organisation.

Get yourself organised.

For activities that occur often such as taking a child to day care or preschool, have an organised morning routine. If you need to leave by 8.15 a.m. at the latest, do not get out of bed yourself at 7.30 a.m. when you know it takes an hour to get ready. Some parents are habitually late in bringing their children to organised activities such as preschool, parties, or play at other children's homes. This shortens the time a child has to enjoy outings like these and creates unnecessary additional pressure on both parents and children.

Avoid last minute rushing.

Try to avoid last minute rushing, and perhaps arriving late, by getting some things ready the night before, by going to bed at a reasonable hour, and by waking up early in the morning.

Get yourself ready first.

Explain to your child where you will be going, then get yourself ready first. If you get ready early it will give you the time you need to deal with any disruptions with the children.

Discuss the day's activities with your child.

Answer any questions your child may have about the day's activities.

Use 'ask, say, do' in helping your child get ready.

Involve your child in the getting ready time by using 'ask, say, do' as a way of promoting independence and self-dressing as outlined in chapter 3 on page 60. If you use this procedure your child will not only learn what she has to do when she goes out but will be able to help.

Give positive attention for cooperative behaviour.

Speak up and praise your child for getting ready without making a fuss. Initially, any time your child gets ready without first having to be asked, praise this behaviour enthusiastically.

Provide appropriate consequences for disruptions.

If any disruptions occur, such as whining or temper outbursts, deal with them decisively, using the strategy suggested for the specific behaviour, for example quiet time. Sometimes you will have to endure an outburst while the child is in quiet time or time out. Don't let this put you off. Be late if necessary. Next time it will be easier.

Use the 'beat the clock' game as a way of dealing with dawdling.

Beat the clock involves setting the child a goal of being ready before the clock alarm sounds off at a set time. If the child wins, he earns a small treat or reward for his efforts, such as a favourite snack in his lunch box.

Explain what is involved

Explain to your child that you would like her to learn to get ready more quickly. Show her the timer on the stove or an egg timer and tell her that if she can get dressed and ready to leave before the alarm rings she will get a small treat. Set the timer for the amount of time that you consider reasonable. Avoid giving repeated instructions or nagging the child to hurry up.

Reward your child for beating the clock.

If the child is ready before the timer rings, offer praise and encouragement and give the back-up treat.

Phase your child off the programme.

Once the child is regularly beating the clock, phase out its use. This can be done simply. First stop the back-up treat, using only praise as the reward but keeping the clock going. Next, let the child set the clock and tell you when the time is up. Finally, leave it to the child to decide whether to have the timer set as a reminder. This can often be accomplished over a two-week period.

Some early morning problems are difficult to solve because the child expects everything to be done for him. Watching television first thing in the morning can be very disruptive. It is often better to get children dressed before they have breakfast. If you feel you must have TV on in the morning, then make watching TV dependent on being ready and beating the clock. If the child beats the clock, put something special in her lunch box that day. Parents themselves should also try to model being organised and on time. A child who observes his parents being consistently late for appointments or outings may develop this behaviour himself. While you don't want to become too time conscious, good organisation in the morning certainly helps. It also helps if children learn to help out with tidying up. Smooth organisation is much easier when all family members pull their weight.

Teaching children to tidy up after themselves

Preschool children should be encouraged to take care of their possessions. This includes learning to clear away toys and activities after they have finished with them. If children simply leave everything for someone else to clean up, they will quickly lose parts or pieces of their toys and games. Play equipment will be more likely to be damaged, the house will always look messy, and there will be much more work for parents.

Don't have unreasonable expectations. Having play things strewn all over the place is often part of children's play, and interrupting such play so that the house is neat and tidy can be quite disruptive to their spontaneous interest and involvement in what they are doing.

It is better to wait for natural breaks in children's activities before cleaning up. These breaks can occur when children move locations, from indoor to outdoor play, go from one activity to a clearly new activity, such as from dressing up to painting or colouring-in books, have a meal break, or when the family is getting ready to go out. Some parents decide that only one clean up a day is sufficient, say before bedtime. The disadvantage of this tactic is that the task will be much bigger and therefore harder for the child, who may need a lot of help. Two or three quick tidy aways are often sufficient to keep the house in order, and have the advantage of taking place immediately after the play activity.

Getting children to tidy away is another story. Some children refuse to cooperate and even insist that it's *your* job. It is better to focus initially on getting children to clean up shared family living areas rather than their own bedrooms. Huge messes in shared areas are an inconvenience to everyone, not just the child. Here are some ideas for helping children learn to pick up and put away.

Store children's toys so they are easily accessible.

Use low, open shelving where possible rather than boxes or containers which open from the top. Boxes make finding toys harder and often lead to everything being tipped out on the floor which means more work later.

Choose the right moment to ask the child to tidy away.

Look for natural breaks in the play activity.

Give your child a warning.

Tell your child she will have to finish the activity and tidy away in a few minutes.

Suggest a natural consequence for complying.

'When you've put the Lego away, you can come and have morning tea.'

Calmly ask your child to begin.

In a calm voice, tell your child you want him to begin putting away the game or toys. Be specific. Rather than 'Tidy up this mess please,' say, 'John, put the train back in the box please.'

Pause, then prompt your child to begin.

Wait 5 to 10 seconds to see if your child complies. If she does not, or cannot, go over and tell her what to do. 'First of all put all your train carriages in this slot here. Show me how you can do this.' If the child completes this, give praise 'Nicely done Jane, those carriages are very neatly put away.'

For each game, activity, or item that has been used during playtime, follow the previous two steps.

You will notice that this strategy initially relies on giving the child assistance in getting started by breaking down the task into smaller parts. This assistance can be reduced as the child learns what to do.

Deal with protest with a terminating instruction.

If the child begins to whine or complain, or becomes aggressive, give a terminating instruction using a calm but firm voice. 'John, stop complaining right now. I want you to gather the crayons together and put them in your pencil case.'

Use 'manual guidance' to help the child get started.

If the misbehaviour continues or increases, avoid becoming angry and harassed. Stay beside the child, ignore protests, and manually guide the child's hands through the motions until the activity or game is completely cleared away.

Provide a logical consequence.

Afterwards, if the child has misbehaved during the cleaning up time, tell her that the games were not put away in an acceptable way today and that there is a consequence: the games will be put away and out of reach for a period of time, maybe the rest of the day or until the next day.

Speak up and praise cooperative behaviour.

If the child cooperated during clean up time, praise him for being a good helper. 'Stephen, you picked up all your books and put them away beautifully today. Good boy.'

Gradually reduce the assistance you give.

During subsequent clean up times, gradually reduce the amount of assistance needed to get the child started. This can be done by giving her more responsibility for deciding what to do first, for example asking, 'What do you want to pick up first?' followed by praise, by getting the child to pick up several different items before praise is offered, and finally by getting the child to pick up all items before receiving praise.

Some parents only experience problems when they try to get their child to clean up by herself. In other words, even though the child can do the task on her own, she refuses to unless the parent helps. This kind of behaviour can be very irritating and is often a form of attention seeking. To overcome it you may need to be quite firm and deal with it as disobedience rather than a pick-up-and-put-away problem. Time out can be used as a back-up consequence for refusal to cooperate.

There will be times, however, when the child needs help or indeed where the parent decides to do the task, for example, if the child is very tired, unwell, or the mess is not of his making. Young children understandably object to having to clean up other children's mess on their own. They are learning to act and think independently and will resist tasks they see as being unfair. View the task of teaching your child to look after his possessions as a long-term process that takes time to perfect. There is an important balance between looking after possessions and being overly rigid, fussy, and conscious of tidiness. A bit of a mess often makes a home appear lived in, relaxed, and homely.

Difficulties during meal preparation

The period between 4.30 and 6.30 in the afternoon can be a difficult time for many parents of young children. Parents and children are often tired at the end of the day. Parents often have a lot to do at this time including preparing meals, helping older children with homework, and getting children bathed and dressed ready for bed. It is a time when parents often like their children to amuse themselves while household tasks are completed. The children may have other ideas. Common problems at this time include children complaining about being hungry, or whining and demanding attention. These problems are often worse if the family is late arriving home. The child is more likely to be hungry and the parent disorganised. Children are often better behaved if there is something they can do to help during meal preparation. Not all parents like this idea and prefer the child to be out of the way so they can organise the meal without interruptions and distraction. These parents may often tell their child to go away, get out of the kitchen, or go and play. However, if children are eventually to learn to assist in running a home, they need opportunities to learn what to do. This means occasionally putting up with a bit more kitchen mess than you might like. Both boys and girls should learn to help under supervision, otherwise they may grow up seeing their mother as the kitchen slave.

The best way to overcome this problem is not to compel pre-schoolers to 'help', but to give them the *opportunity* to if they wish, always with close supervision to avoid accidents. Here are some guidelines.

Involve your child in a weekly discussion involving the planning of the family's evening meals.

Seek your child's opinions about the foods she and other family members like. Make a note of these suggestions. Thank the child for her help.

Plan a weekly menu of balanced meals.

Include some of the child's favourite meals and avoid serving meals that the child does not particularly like on consecutive nights.

Prepare a shopping list.

Have a regular time for meals each day.

Organise your time so that you have your family meal prepared at the same time each night.

Plan meals for the following night.

Decide on the meal for the following night. The idea here is to be one day ahead of yourself.

Check that all necessary ingredients are on hand.

Where necessary, make a note for the following day to take items from the freezer or to shop for specific ingredients.

One hour before each mealtime, ask your child if he would like to help.

Let your child know you are about to prepare dinner. Suggest something simple that the child can do safely while you watch, for example setting the table, helping prepare vegetables, and getting items from the refrigerator. Sometimes children suggest things that are too hard or dangerous such as chopping vegetables. If they do, explain why they can't help in this way and suggest something else. If the child prefers to continue playing, then that is fine.

Interrupt what you are doing every so often, speak up, and praise your child for appropriate behaviour.

This is particularly important for children who have been disruptive and demanding during meal preparation.

If the child interrupts, demands, or whines during meal preparation, describe the problem behaviour.

Calmly but firmly tell your child that you don't want to be interrupted while you are preparing dinner. Offer a choice of either playing quietly or helping with the meal.

If disobedience or grizzling continues, follow the steps suggested for dealing with these behaviours on pages 133–136.

Try to pinpoint what might be contributing to the behaviour.

Give your child warning before serving the meal.

Tell your child 10 minutes prior to the meal being served to clear away any game or activity and to go to the bathroom to wash his hands.

Invite your child to assist you in serving the meal.

Serve child-size portions and eat the meal.

If your child is frequently disruptive during meals, is a fussy eater, or has any specific feeding problem with swallowing or vomiting up food, refer to the guidelines relating to severe feeding problems with preschoolers on page 152 and the suggestions for handling mealtime disruptions below. Have a second look at the diet you are offering your child.

These suggestions about meal preparation are designed to give children a chance to participate if they wish. There will be times, however, when this is not possible because you are running late and simply prefer to get the job done as quickly as possible without children underfoot. It may be a special dinner occasion. At these times let your child know and, if necessary, suggest an alternative activity.

Handling mealtime disruptions

When family mealtimes run smoothly, they can be an enjoyable part of the day. The family is all together in one place; they can share the highlights of their day, plan family activities, and enjoy each other's

company. However, for some families the experience is quite different. The meal may be eaten while everyone is glued to the television, children may complain about the food served, try to leave the table, refuse to eat at all, or not use utensils properly. Some parents dread mealtimes because they seem to spend the whole time dealing with disruptions ('Don't be a pig.' 'Eat properly.' 'Leave your brother alone.' 'Come back here.' 'Sit down and be quiet.' 'Eat up your carrot, it's good for you.'). In other families, one partner arrives home late from work and effectively there are two mealtimes. Other parents have quite unreasonable expectations, such as 'No talking at the dinner table'.

If your family mealtimes are like this, then you might find the suggestions below helpful. Before you decide to try out any of these ideas it is important to make sure that your child is not underweight, not showing signs of malnourishment, has no physical disorder such as gastric reflux, or specific problem with swallowing. These sorts of problems may need specialist assistance and you should consult your family doctor to get the problem thoroughly assessed.

If a child is physically healthy and active, most mealtime problems are behavioural problems, not medical problems, and respond well to a simple change in the mealtime routine.

Eliminate between-meal snacking.

Explain to your child that from now on she will not be allowed any food other than at mealtimes. This is to ensure that she is hungry when the meal is served. Tell her she must not go to the fridge or cupboards to help herself. Explain that if she breaks these rules she will have to go to time out for 3 minutes.

Discuss the new ground rules.

Involve your child in a discussion of the rules that will apply during mealtimes: remaining seated at the table until you are excused; using utensils appropriately; not speaking with your mouth full; swallowing one mouthful before attempting another; no whining or complaining.

Reduce fluid intake immediately before meals.

Do not give your child any milk or juice for one hour before the mealtime. If he is thirsty, give him water.

Describe the positive consequences for good mealtime behaviour.

Explain to your child that if he keeps to the rules then some small treat will be given, for example a story or family game of his choice.

Get everything ready before calling the child to the table.

This reduces the necessity for waiting at the table while food is still being prepared.

Praise your child for eating nicely.

Comment on specific good behaviour such as remaining seated, chewing properly before swallowing, using the fork correctly, and so on. 'That's a good sized mouthful.' 'Good boy for staying in your chair.'

Allow conversation at the table.

If the child is making good progress, ask her questions about her day and encourage pleasant conversation between mouthfuls. Be careful here, however. Some children will quite happily chat away and eat nothing, or will eat very slowly.

If the child refuses to eat, ask him once only to continue eating.

Avoid threats such as 'If you don't stop playing with your food you'll get a smack.' Do not insist that the child eat everything on his plate but encourage him to try everything.

If the child refuses to eat, have her remain at the table until everyone else has finished.

If the child still refuses, calmly tell her that she must sit quietly and wait until the rest of the family has finished and that there will be nothing else to eat after she leaves the table.

Ignore complaints.

If the child protests or complains, completely ignore him and continue your meal.

Use time out for disruptive behaviour.

If the child leaves the table, won't sit still, or throws a tantrum, put her into time out until the crying stops for 3 minutes, then return the child to the table until the family finishes.

Give positive feedback for good mealtime behaviour.

Speak up and praise any behaviour you liked during the meal. 'Kate, you had beautiful manners at the table tonight. Well done.'

Provide a back-up reward.

Offer the child an extra back-up privilege such as some individual time with you, or additional playtime before bed.

Offer no other food.

If the child did not behave well during the meal, do not make any reference to it. However, make sure that no snacks or other food are given either between meals or before bedtime.

Some parents are very reluctant to be firm over between-meal snacks because they are afraid that their child will starve or that it is unfair to send a child to bed without something to eat. However, if a child can eat whenever he likes, there is no incentive for him to learn to eat normally, and problems with food can continue over many years. It also makes it more difficult to take the child anywhere because he turns on such a performance. It is important to establish good eating habits and a nutritionally adequate diet as early as possible.

More persistent feeding problems

An appropriately balanced diet is vital for a child's normal growth and development. However, some children are a handful to feed. It has been estimated that about 5 per cent of children have an eating problem which is severe enough to require specialist professional assistance. Children with feeding problems can exhibit a wide variety of behaviours. They may spit up their food, vomit during or after meals, only eat a narrow range of selected foods such as a bottle of milk or a sandwich, simply refuse to eat, try to get down from their high chair or table, play with the food, or refuse to feed themselves or to use utensils. Other children have problems chewing and swallowing and may gag when they attempt to eat solids. You may know of children who only eat potato crisps and icecream, or who have biscuits and drinks as snacks but who never eat at the table. Every mealtime turns into a battle. Some children's feeding problems become so serious that they fail to gain weight or begin to lose weight. However, the most common problem parents report is that the child simply 'won't eat'. Most feeding difficulties with children are transient and decrease as the child moves through toddlerhood and the preschool years. However, other feeding problems are more persistent and require both medical and psychological evaluation before the problem is resolved.

Parents of children with feeding problems are often deeply concerned that all is not well, but they are assured by family and friends that 'it is just a stage', or 'they'll grow out of it'. The situation only seems to get worse.

During toddlerhood, a child makes the important transition from being a largely milk-fed infant to a child who independently consumes a mixed diet. Feeding problems can result from physical causes, specific food intolerances, or behavioural problems relating to the parents' feeding practices.

Physical causes of feeding problems

Physical causes that need to be investigated include central nervous system disorders such as cerebral palsy and epilepsy, or degenerative diseases that occasionally present as feeding problems. Swallowing problems can be due to a cleft palate, pharyngeal incoordination, or gastroesophageal reflux. True food intolerances are a much less common cause of feeding problems than is often thought. However, occasionally children have a lactose (milk) intolerance. In many but not all instances these problems would have been diagnosed earlier.

Feeding practices

Some feeding problems result from the way the parents organise family mealtimes. **Unpredictable mealtimes** can be a problem. If a child's evening meal is at 5 o'clock one day then 8 o'clock the next, it is difficult to achieve a set routine.

Between-meal snacking can reduce a child's appetite, particularly if it occurs within one hour of the scheduled mealtime. Some parents give up trying to get the child to eat at set times and simply let her eat whenever she wants. This usually makes the problem worse. While the parent may be relieved because 'at least she's eating something', the child may not be receiving a balanced diet of proteins, carbohydrates, fats, vitamins and minerals.

Juiceaholics and milkaholics are children who consume large amounts of fluids but rarely eat solid foods. Children can sit at the table like other children but spend most of their time sipping drinks and refusing to eat anything.

Parent-child interaction at mealtimes

Some mealtime problems are directly related to the kinds of interactions between parent and child that occur at the dinner table. Refusal to eat is sometimes a very effective way of gaining attention. By refusing, going slow, or complaining about the meal, children often get a reaction from their parents. Often this is in the form of an instruction. ('Tania, eat your dinner.' 'Don't play with your food.') At other times the parent may end up bargaining and negotiating with the child over the amount of food to be eaten ('Why not try just a little spoonful of your carrots?'). This is not necessarily a problem except when the child repeatedly manipulates the parent into allowing him to eat the most meagre of portions. Often these responses result in the child becoming the centre of attention at dinner times. This can be a hidden payoff for refusing food.

The child's feeding problem may also result from the parent providing inconsistent consequences following food refusal. On some occasions the child is allowed to get away with eating next to nothing, at other times the same behaviour leads to the child being sent to bed, threats of no TV, no dessert, or other dire consequences.

If these consequences are too unpredictable the child will not know whether refusal will be successful.

Avoiding a painful experience

Children who have suffered from gastric reflux problems as infants may associate the ingestion of food with pain and discomfort. Even though the child may have been treated quite successfully using drugs or surgery, she may still be a reluctant eater long after the original physical cause has been removed. An almost universal response to pain is to try to avoid the thing that causes it. In this case, the result is that the child won't eat.

Fear and anxiety

Some older children develop an intensely fearful reaction to eating. Prior to meals they become tense and upset, they may cry or even shake. These children may be genuinely 'food phobic'. A phobia is an intense irrational fear of some object, event, or situation. For these children, eating is truly a major ordeal. The fear can occur in a child who is otherwise well-adjusted. Young children cannot express why they are afraid. However, food phobia is sometimes related to a fear of choking or gagging.

Family chaos at mealtimes

All families with young children sometimes experience disorganisation at mealtimes. Parents can be rushed, exhausted, home late from work, late in picking up their child from child minders or day care. Unforeseen circumstances can lead to a temporary disruption to meal preparation and service. Such events don't cause major problems unless they occur frequently. A disorganised household at mealtimes, particularly when it occurs often, can be a formula for producing feeding and other behavioural problems.

Unrealistic expectations

Sometimes parents can have unusual ideas and expectations relating to their children's meals. For example, parents who insist that every single morsel on the child's plate be eaten at every meal will often create unnecessary battles. Children, like adults, have food preferences. They like some dishes more than others. Parents who insist that children eat a specific vegetable when the child will quite happily eat something else just as nutritious make life unnecessarily difficult for themselves.

Consequences of feeding problems

Some quite serious problems, both physical and psychological, can result from persistent feeding difficulties. These include nutrient deficiencies leading to failure to gain weight. Common dietary problems include iron deficiency and protein deficiency caused by reliance on milk and fluids and late introduction of solids, caloric deficiency, and vitamin B_{12} deficiency caused by a strictly vegan diet (i.e. exclusion of meat, dairy, and other animal products). Other problems, such as dental caries due to prolonged bottle feeding, and diarrhoea due to excessive juice or cordial intake, can occur. Severe malnourishment can of course lead to death, bone malformations, intellectual deficiencies, and behavioural and other emotional problems.

Handling more persistent feeding problems

The goal of this programme is to help children with persistent feeding difficulties learn to eat independently and appropriately. It works best for children between the ages of 3 and 7.

If necessary, consult your doctor first.

If you are concerned about your child's weight or growth, consult your family doctor. He or she may suggest seeing a specialist before tackling the feeding problem on your own.

Get your smileys and chart ready before the meal.

See chapter 3 if you have not used a good behaviour chart before.

Set up a quiet time and time out area.

If your child behaves unacceptably at mealtime, follow the guidelines for using quiet time and time out in chapter 3 on pages 78–83.

Seat your child at the table.

It is important to warn your child that it will soon be time to eat so that he can finish what he is doing or stop his game at a convenient time. Most people eat sitting at a table. Children with eating problems have often developed the habit of eating anywhere *but* at the table. By seating your child at the table, he will learn that this is a prompt to eat and that when he is sitting at the table he will be expected to eat.

Give your child a balanced diet.

Prepare meals that provide a mixed, nutritious diet. The actual food you prepare will depend somewhat on the child's age. Appendix 1 gives some sample menus for children of different ages. If a child is eating solid foods but is simply very fussy about what she will try, then prepare the same meal as for other family members. Your child may initially eat only *some* of the same foods but by the end of the programme she will probably be eating *most* of the same foods.

Set a goal for the amount of food to be eaten.

Tell your child how much he has to eat 'James, I would like you to eat all of the vegetables and half of the stew.' Set a goal that the child has a reasonable chance of achieving. Don't try to make him eat everything on the plate. It is more important to sample the variety of foods presented. It is better, too, to serve small portions and let the child ask for more if he is hungry.

Establish a clear time limit for the meal.

Sometimes it is necessary to set a time limit for eating. This should be clearly understood by the child. The time should be long enough to allow the child to eat the meal with time to spare, and short enough so that it doesn't interrupt normal family routines. Twenty to 30 minutes should be plenty.

Expect appropriate table manners.

Some children with eating problems develop ways of eating that are different from those of other family members. They may gnaw at a sandwich, slurp juice, or only eat with their fingers even though they are capable of using a fork or spoon. Sometimes parents are so pleased to see their children eating anything that they don't insist on the appropriate table manners, but this is a mistake. As soon as a toddler is old enough to hold a spoon or fork, she should be encouraged to do so. Before you start the meal, tell your child what manners you expect.

Explain quiet time and time out to your child.

Before you use quiet time, tell your child what behaviours will earn quiet time and calmly explain why you will be using it. Behaviours which should earn quiet time at mealtimes include throwing a plate across the room, screaming and shrieking, and kicking or biting.

Help your child get started.

After serving the meal, wait for 10 seconds to see if your child will begin by himself. If not, help him get started by giving an instruction.

'Nicholas, eat your lunch please.' If the child still does not start, give him a specific instruction relating to a food item. 'Steven, pick up your spoon and put some yoghurt on it.' Limit your prompts to one per mouthful.

Praise and encourage your child for good eating.

Eating becomes an unpleasant business for children with feeding problems. Mealtimes should be pleasurable occasions. This can be achieved by letting your child know you are pleased with what she is doing. 'You're chewing well, Carla.' 'Terrific. That's three mouthfuls you've eaten, Bea.' Be clear, specific, and immediate when you praise good eating.

Give smileys to start with.

Initially, each time your child swallows a mouthful offer praise and put a smiley or whatever your child prefers on the chart. You might set a goal of five mouthfuls, perhaps two more than the child managed the night before, then draw up five squares on a piece of paper. The meal might go like this:

'What would you like in the squares tonight, Simon?'

'Clown faces.'

'OK. Have your first mouthful, and when you've swallowed it we'll draw your first clown face.'

Simon puts a spoonful of mashed potato in his mouth. While he chews he keeps his eyes on his father who is watching him, smiling.

'That's good chewing, son'.

Simon takes a big breath and swallows. This is a major achievement for Simon because the previous week he vomited up each mouthful when he attempted to swallow. He is pleased with himself.

'That's great. You've swallowed your first mouthful.'

His father starts to draw the first clown face. As Simon swallows each mouthful, his father draws a clown face in each square and tells Simon how well he's doing. After the fifth mouthful he says, 'That's five Simon, you've eaten well. That's all you have to eat tonight.' Simon grins because he knows that he'll get his back-up reward.

When your child reaches the set goal, increase it by one or two mouthfuls for the next meal. How quickly you progress will depend on your child.

Use a drink as a reward.

Children with eating problems often drink a lot, particularly at mealtimes. You can use their preference for drinks to encourage them to eat. Let your child have a sip of her drink only after she has had a certain number of mouthfuls of food. In the beginning it might be only one or two mouthfuls, but after a while you should expect her to earn several smileys before she has a drink. This strategy will be even more effective if the child is not allowed fluids for about one hour before the meal.

Use terminating instructions to deal with avoidance tactics.

Some children will try to avoid eating by playing with their food. If, for example, your child starts to stack slices of sausage on his plate, say, 'Stop playing with your food.' When he looks at you, say, 'You put a fork in your sausage to eat it.'

Some children will put a spoonful in their mouths then hold it there without chewing or swallowing it. Some will try to get out of their seat, move food around their plates without eating it, or take tiny nibbles of food and chew it endlessly. These behaviours can be dealt with by describing what the child is doing wrong, then asking him to behave properly.

Use quiet time for inappropriate behaviour.

Use quiet time for 1 minute as a back-up for refusal to comply with the terminating instruction. 'Tracey, I have asked you to stop pushing your food with your fingers. Now go to quiet time.'

Use time out for disruptive behaviour.

If the child refuses to go to quiet time, throws a tantrum, or continues to protest in quiet time, put him into time out for 2 minutes. After time out, return him to his meal and continue as previously until he has reached his goal for that meal.

Give a back-up reward.

When your child reaches her goal, have a back-up reward ready. This might be something like staying up 10 minutes later, or having a dip in a lucky dip box. (A lucky dip box for a 3-year-old girl might include cheap treats such as hair ribbons, little soaps, junk jewellery and fancy hair clips.)

Phasing out prompts.

During the first few meals, you may have to help your child get started by giving one prompt for each mouthful. Once your child is eating ten to 20 mouthfuls, you should start to eliminate these prompts. Start near the end of the meal when there are only three or four more smileys remaining to reach the goal. Explain that to earn smileys the child will now have to eat a mouthful without being asked first. Get the child to tell you when the mouthful is swallowed. Give a time limit for each mouthful, 1 minute for mashed food and 2 minutes if they need to chew it. Check that your child is taking small to medium mouthfuls that can be chewed and swallowed easily in the set time. If your child does not swallow the food within the set time, put him into quiet time for a minute.

When your child can eat several mouthfuls without prompting, withdraw prompts earlier and earlier until he is eating the whole meal without instructions.

Always make sure you stop prompting before you increase the number of mouthfuls needed to earn the back-up reward.

Increase food variety.

Once your child is eating 15 or so mouthfuls per meal, you can start to increase the *variety* of food she will eat. Add a very small amount of one new food to the meal. It might be a mandarin segment for lunch, or half a teaspoon of pumpkin for dinner. Reward your child with an extra smiley and lots of praise for trying the new food. Only give one extra smiley the *first* time she tries the new food. At the next meal try another new food, such as a 1 cm cube of cheese, or half a teaspoon of broccoli. Once your child has tried these new foods occasionally add them to the regular meals you serve. Gradually increase the amounts and keep adding new foods. If your child has a particularly negative reaction to one food, leave it for a couple of weeks and try again. Don't worry about it. Everyone dislikes some food. The aim is to have your child eating a range of food from the different food groups in the same way as the rest of the family.

Phase out the smileys.

When your child is able to eat 15 to 20 mouthfuls, increase the number of mouthfuls required to earn each smiley. Start by requiring two more mouthfuls for each smiley for a couple of days, then increase to three, and so on. At the same time as you increase the number of mouthfuls for each smiley, *decrease* the number of smileys needed to earn the back-up reward. Don't rush it. Take it slowly.

Some children will start to lose interest in the smileys fairly quickly once they have learned to eat independently. After all, the aim is for eating to be an enjoyable activity on its own.

Children who persistently refuse to eat properly need parents who are very consistent in how they handle mealtimes for the first few weeks. For some children eating has become so unpleasant that going into quiet time or time out may not seem to work. After all, by refusing, the child can be sent to a place where no eating is required for a short time. The key to overcoming this problem is to make being at the dinner table as positive and rewarding as possible. This goal is best accomplished by setting reasonable attainable goals and by providing positive attention for correct eating.

Once a child finally discovers that you mean business and will follow through consistently, mealtimes become much less of an ordeal. Some children with severe feeding problems even start to suggest new foods they would like to try and, more importantly, start to enjoy their food.

When visitors arrive

Have you ever had the experience of inviting friends or family over for a meal, perhaps a barbeque, a party, or just so the children can play, and then found that your own children were an absolute embarrassment? You are not alone. Many parents find this a trying time. Preschool children often get quite excited about having friends over, particularly children their own age. However, the reality of having someone else on the child's home patch can lead to problems such as silly, noisy, and showing off behaviour. Your child might be quite defiant, refuse to share, refuse to play with the visitor, or constantly demand your attention.

Several aspects contribute to these problems. The first is having visitors stay too long. Children may be fine for a few hours but then become tired and grumpy if their normal nap times or mealtimes are disrupted. Second, children are sometimes left to their own devices and unsupervised a bit too long. If children only get attention when there is a problem, for example when one child starts crying, and are ignored the rest of the time with no organised activity, problems can arise.

Having visitors provides many opportunities for young children to practise social skills, like learning how to greet visitors, how to be a good host, how to think about activities other children might be interested in, how to make polite conversation with other grownups, and how to entertain friends. These are complex skills that many adults never learn properly. Here are some ideas to help your child learn to behave appropriately when visitors arrive.

Plan visits that do not disrupt the child's mealtimes and sleep routines.

This is particularly important for children who are difficult at these times.

Let your child know in advance about the visit.

Explain who is coming and the reason for the visit: 'Sheila and Brad are coming over for lunch today.'

Discuss the ground rules.

Explain the rules for the visitors' arrival. 'What do you have to remember when visitors come?' If your child cannot tell you, let her know what you expect. 'When Sheila and Brad are here I want you to ...' Ask your child to repeat the rules. 'OK, so what do you have to remember?'

Plan some appropriate activities.

Invite your child to choose some things that she would like to play with during the visit. The idea is to encourage her to find something she might do so she won't be bored. It may also be useful to think of activities yourself that might be suitable to entertain the children.

Let your child practise greeting visitors.

When the visitor arrives and greets your child, praise your child for answering appropriately. If he doesn't answer, prompt him but don't force him to answer. A battle at the beginning of a visit starts the whole thing off on the wrong foot.

Before starting your own adult conversation, set the children up in an activity.

Before getting too engrossed in adult conversation, take a moment to suggest something that the children can do. If your child takes the initiative, you may not need to say anything. If necessary, help them get started.

Interrupt your own conversation periodically to give attention to your child.

Be prepared to interrupt your own conversation every so often *before* a problem arises to speak to and praise the children for playing nicely. Ask a few questions about their activity, and before leaving say you will return shortly to see how they are getting on. Don't wait for problems to arise before you speak to your child when you have visitors.

If possible, offer a snack or drink while the children are busy rather than waiting for whining to occur.

This will help you avoid the trap of rewarding bored, disruptive children with food.

Deal with rude interruptions by describing the correct behaviour.

If your child rudely interrupts while you are talking, or whines for attention, prompt her to say 'excuse me' and to wait until the adults have finished speaking. Do not expect your child to wait for long if she has interrupted politely.

If the interruption or demanding occurs again, give a terminating instruction and back it up with quiet time if necessary.

It is important for your child to realise that you mean what you say. There is no point in having rules unless you are prepared to enforce them.

Give your child positive feedback.

Praise your child enthusiastically if he behaved appropriately during the visit. Spend some time with him after the visitors have left.

Complex skills take time to perfect. You should not expect your child to be a perfect angel when you have visitors unless you have put in the time to teach her how to behave appropriately. Many parents ignore obnoxious behaviour when they have guests so as to avoid a scene. This is a mistake as children quickly learn that having visitors is a time when their parents are vulnerable. Many problems can be avoided with a little planning as to how to keep your children amused. Once a child has learned that you are not constantly on call when you are entertaining, things often go much more smoothly.

Interrupting

Preschoolers have to learn to occupy themselves when their parents are busy, for example when they are speaking on the telephone, engaged in conversation with visitors, speaking to the doctor, or speaking to their partner. Some preschoolers seem to resent their parents directing their attention to anyone else.

There are three important things to remember about teaching children to wait and not to interrupt. First, we have to be reasonable. It is quite reasonable to expect a 4-year-old not to interrupt while you have a 5-minute telephone conversation. It is quite unreasonable to expect the child not to interrupt if the conversation lasts an hour, or if it's the tenth conversation that morning. Second, while children need to learn how to wait, they should be given something to do while they are waiting. Third, children need to learn how to enter adult conversation appropriately. It is polite to say 'Excuse me, Mummy' and wait for her to finish what she is saying. It is rude to barge into a conversation by demanding instant adult attention.

Several problems get in the way of teaching these kinds of social graces. Sometimes parents of preschoolers are desperate for adult contact. After spending perhaps days on end without speaking to anyone over the age of 5, parents need social outlets where adult conversation can take place. Unfortunately, some parents in this situation can expect too much. For example, they might visit a friend and simply stay too long. The children may have been able to amuse themselves for a couple of hours but not four or five. Other parents completely ignore their children when visiting, happily chatting until there is a crisis. Children learn to amuse themselves best when they receive some attention from adults while they are busy. Don't wait till your child interrupts before giving attention.

If your child frequently interrupts or is naughty while you are on the telephone, follow these guidelines to overcome this problem.

Explain that you would like your child not to interrupt when you are on the phone.

Explain the ground rules to be followed when the phone rings. These could include answering the phone unless Mummy wants to answer it (see guidelines for teaching the child to answer the phone, page 165); finding something to do quietly while Mummy is on the phone; not interrupting while Mummy is on the phone.

Ask your child to state the rules.

'What do you have to remember when the phone rings?' Praise the child for stating the rules correctly.

Set aside a morning to help your child learn the correct thing to do.

You need to decide here whether to teach your child the necessary behaviour in a concentrated session or to spread it out over several weeks. The former is quicker but requires you to be organised and to set aside the time.

Get out some quiet toys or activities that the child can play with while you are on the phone.

Examples of quiet activities include colouring books, picture books, soft toys, puzzles, and blocks. It is also a good idea to purchase a toy phone the child can use while you are on the phone.

Remind your child of the rules.

On the day you start, quickly restate the ground rules.

Dial a number.

Dial your own telephone number. Speak briefly on the phone as you normally would. If the child continues to play with the toys, speak for a few seconds more and praise the child enthusiastically for letting you speak on the phone without interrupting. 'Good girl, Danielle, for waiting while I was on the phone.'

If your child interrupts, prompt the correct behaviour.

If the child stops what he is doing and tries to interrupt, prompt him to find something to do: 'Remember the rules. When Mummy's on the phone, find something to do.'

Praise compliance with the rules.

If the child complies, praise her for finding something to do.

Use quiet time as a back-up consequence.

If the child does not comply, say 'excuse me' to your pretend caller and immediately put the child into quiet time.

Increase the length of the pretend calls.

Practise this basic routine with pretend callers about ten times, gradually increasing the length of the conversation up to about 2 minutes until the child is performing the correct behaviour. Spread these calls out over an entire morning.

Arrange for a spouse, friend, or neighbour to call you at a specific time.

Keep the conversation brief, about 2 to 3 minutes. If the child copes with this real call, praise her enthusiastically and offer a snack or treat as a back-up reward. Over the next few days give the child several further practice runs.

Phase out reminders.

Gradually phase out reminders of the rules before beginning to speak on the phone. Every time the child complies without having to be reminded, offer praise enthusiastically.

Keep calls brief.

When your child is around, try to keep calls brief. If you wish to have a long conversation, wait until your child is having a nap, is in bed at night, or is at preschool. Any time your child interrupts, be prepared to back up your instructions with quiet time as soon as the problem arises. Don't wait until the child is screaming before you act.

Teaching a child to answer the telephone

It is also important for children to learn how to answer the phone politely and, eventually, to learn how to make their own calls under supervision. They need to know what to do if the phone rings when the parent is outside, on the toilet, in the shower, or otherwise temporarily unavailable. Some children never learn these skills properly. Many problems can be avoided if parents teach their preschoolers correct telephone etiquette. It is interesting that even some adults find making telephone calls a difficult experience, and become anxious whenever they have to ring someone other than close friends or family. Some simply avoid using the phone unless they absolutely have to.

When preschoolers answer the phone they can make several blunders. They may pick up the phone then not speak; use a silly, rude, cheeky, or impolite voice when answering; or answer then not tell the person for whom the call was intended, and so on. One way to teach a preschooler to answer the telephone is to buy a toy phone to practise on. Using the telephone correctly is quite a complex skill and preschoolers should always be supervised when they answer the phone.

Choose a time when you have about 30 minutes to spend.

Ask your child to get her toy phone.

Explain the rules of the telephone game.

The rules for answering could be: when you hear the phone ringing, first ask Mum or Dad whether you can answer it. If the answer is yes, then lift the receiver and say 'hello' and your name: 'Hello, Julian Palmer speaking.' Speak in a nice voice. If the caller wants to speak to Mum or Dad, say 'Just a minute please', put the phone down and get your parents quickly.

Ask the child to state the rules.

'What do you do when the phone goes ring, ring?' If the child can state the correct sequence, praise her. If only some parts are correct then praise the correct parts and tell her what she missed out. If after three attempts the child is still confused, move to the next step.

Model the first step in the sequence.

This might involve an interaction such as the following.

> 'Watch what I do. Let's pretend the phone rings. "Ring, ring." What should I do first?'
> 'Mummy, can I answer it?'
> 'Good girl. Yes, you ask Mummy or Daddy first.'
> "Mummy, the phone's ringing. Can I get it?"

Let the child practise the first step.

'OK. You try it. Ring, ring.' If the child correctly performs the first step, offer praise and encouragement and move on to teaching the next step in the same way.

> 'Now let's do the first two steps. Watch what I do.'

Let the child pretend he is you. Pretend the phone rings, ask the child for permission to answer, then pick up the receiver, say hello, and give your name.

> Now let your child practise the first two steps.
> 'OK. It's your turn now. Ring, ring'
> 'Mummy, can I get it?'
> 'Yes.'
> 'Hello, Rebecca Smith speaking'.
> 'That was excellent. You remembered to ask and then said your name very nicely.'

Practise all other steps.

Continue in the above manner until the child masters all steps in the sequence.

Arrange for a friend to call you.

If the child remembers the first step, praise her immediately. If she needs help, offer it. It may take several weeks before she can answer the phone confidently. Each time the correct sequence is remembered, offer praise.

Deal with silly behaviour on the phone by immediately taking the phone from the child.

Tell him what he's done wrong.

Back up your action with quiet time.

If the child protests or becomes disruptive, back up with quiet time or time out.

Problems on shopping trips

Shopping with children can be an exhausting experience, particularly when they are tired or hungry, or when they misbehave. In one study we conducted, 99 per cent of the parents who were interviewed as they were leaving a major supermarket said that shopping with children was difficult for most parents, and 66 per cent had actually experienced problems with their children on that trip. Common problems include children demanding that parents buy them things, touching merchandise without permission, running up and down aisles, getting lost, whining, and occasional temper tantrums.

Most preschoolers tire quickly and become bored easily. This is especially so if the parent has a lot of shopping to do or becomes so preoccupied that the children are ignored until they become disruptive. Many parents prefer to shop without children but others simply have no choice. Single parents are often in this position. If they work full time they may have to shop at times when the stores are very busy, and usually there are other time pressures, too. Parents on tight budgets can also find shopping a nightmare because they constantly have to spend a lot of time searching for bargains and specials to make ends meet.

The main reason children become difficult on shopping trips is that there is nothing for them to do. Bored kids often become disruptive. This is particularly likely if the parent does not involve the child in the shopping trip and simply ignores him unless he is naughty. This is a formula for bad behaviour.

The following suggestions form a step-by-step guide that teaches children to become good shoppers and to behave appropriately when they are on shopping trips with parents. Rather than seeing shopping as a headache, try to view each shopping trip as an opportunity for your child to learn something about becoming a skilled shopper. Focus on what the child should be doing rather than on how to stop bad behaviour.

Plan a series of brief shopping trips over a period of a week. Your first trips should be quite short, about 5 minutes, gradually increasing up to a 30-minute excursion to the supermarket.

Discuss with your child what you expect from good shoppers.

Gain the child's attention through either a simple request for a chat or a direct instruction: 'Tim, come here will you? I'd like to talk to you about what we're doing this morning.'

Prepare the child for the outing by describing what is going to happen.

'We're going to the supermarket this morning.' Tell the child how long the trip will take.

State briefly, simply, and calmly what the problem was the last time you went shopping.

Describe the four rules for being a good shopper.

- Good shoppers stay within an arm's reach of their mother or father.
- Good shoppers do not touch anything on the shelves or displays without their parents' permission.
- Good shoppers do not run down aisles, fight, yell, scream, or have tantrums.
- Good shoppers do not ask for things until the shopping trip is over.

Tell the child why you would like him to obey these rules: 'I don't like it when you demand things when we go shopping'.

Ask your child to state the rules for being a good shopper.

Praise your child for stating the rules correctly. Help out if she can't remember them all.

Discuss rewards for being a good shopper.

Explain to your child that good shoppers can earn special privileges for keeping to the rules. Every two minutes that the child obeys the rules he will be able to earn coloured buttons which can be exchanged for money at the end of the trip (see below).

Ask the child if he has any questions. Praise him for being involved in this planning ahead of time.

Get everything you need ready.

Check to make sure you have everything you need: a watch, a child's purse or wallet, and about 20 coloured buttons.

Plan the trip to avoid disrupting your child's normal routine.

Plan the shopping trip so that it does not disrupt your child's usual mealtimes. Avoid shopping trips just before lunch. Plan your day so that the shopping trip occurs after rather than before a nap. This reduces the chance that your child will be tired.

Just before leaving, remind the child of the rules for being a good shopper.

Praise your child for being a good shopper.

If at any time during the trip the child does something you like or tries hard to keep to the four rules, look directly at her and say what she has done: 'Good girl, Peta. You are staying nice and close to Mummy today'.

Break the trip up into 2-minute time periods. At the end of each 2 minutes, if the child has kept to the rules, take out a coloured button and place it in her purse or pocket. Say that she has kept to the rules and how much you like it and how helpful it is: 'Jeannie, that's lovely, you have remembered the four rules. Here's your next button for being so helpful'.

Keep your child busy.

Find something for your child to do during the trip. Some examples include asking the child where certain items are; asking the child to pass things to you; asking the child the price of an item; asking the child what he would like to eat; giving the child information about certain products; having the child help you place items in the trolley; letting him help unload items from the trolley at the checkout; having the child help you plan a shopping list.

Deal with disruptions by making your child wait.

If your child misbehaves by breaking any of the four rules, stop what you are doing, gain your child's attention, and say that she can't earn any more buttons for 2 minutes. 'Sarah, you touched something without asking. Now you will now have to wait another 2 minutes before you get a button.'

Allow your child to do some shopping.

Once you have completed your shopping, count the number of buttons the child has earned, exchange them for money, and let the child shop by himself for some small item. Each button could be worth between 2 and 5 cents and therefore a 20-minute trip could be worth 50 cents. One way of working out how much each button should be worth is to simply calculate how much you usually spend on your child on shopping trips then divide that amount by the number of 2-minute time blocks on the planned trip.

Review the trip.

Praise your child's accomplishments. Briefly and calmly describe any rules the child forgot to follow.

This programme tries to overcome the problem of disruptiveness on shopping trips by preparing the child in advance, having clear set rules, by giving the child something to do to help, by catching her being good, and by giving the child a chance to practise being a shopper. The money children earn becomes their budget. They need to find something they can afford. They have to learn to handle money by paying the correct amount and by receiving change if there is any. If we expect children to learn to make wise choices in their purchasing when they have pocket money or work for wages, start preparing them as early as possible.

This programme works best for children who are reasonable at following directions. If your child is also difficult at home, use the plan for increasing compliance with requests before you tackle this programme. When practising a new skill such as becoming a good shopper it is better for parents to give their child more opportunities to master the skill. This is why several short trips over a period of a few days is better than taking your child shopping only once a week.

Leave difficult shopping trips, such as shopping for clothing or a long supermarket trip, until your child can cope with shorter ones without difficulty. In the first few weeks, avoid situations that require the child to wait for long periods.

Travelling in the car

'Jaasson! Daddy, Jason's on my side!' Family outings can become disasters when children play up in the car. Kids often seem to choose the car to try out some of their most irritating behaviour, whether it be whining, complaining, screaming, refusing to stay in their seat belts, fighting, teasing, or generally being a pest. These behaviours can actually be quite dangerous; they can distract the parent from concentrating on driving and thus cause accidents and even fatalities. Misbehaviour in the car is a traffic hazard.

All passengers, including children, should wear safety restraints at all times while travelling in the car. Children must also be taught to behave themselves in the car so that the driver can concentrate. Parents are often vulnerable while they are driving. Kids in the back are not within easy reach and the adult has to try to concentrate on two things at once, the road and the children's behaviour. It is a time when many parents are quite inconsistent and don't enforce ground rules.

From the child's point of view, car travel can be boring. It can seem to them that the ride takes forever, particularly if they have nothing to do. Some children are fine on short trips around town but become quite difficult on longer journeys. Others are difficult every time they get into the car. Here are some ideas to help your child learn more acceptable behaviour in the car.

Avoid disrupting your child's normal routines.

Plan your trip if possible for shortly but not immediately after a meal so children don't get hungry or tired too soon.

Discuss your travel plans.

Tell your child the destination and how long the trip will take. Answer any questions about the trip.

Have some special activities available.

Select some special activities or games for the children to amuse themselves with on the journey.

Discuss the ground rules.

Explain what you expect in the car by describing the desired behaviour: 'Elizabeth, when we travel in the car, I want you to remember to stay in your car seat and sit quietly. Don't squeal or ask me to buy you anything. Can you remember that? I will be trying to drive us all safely to the shops and home again'.

Ask your child to repeat the rules.

'So what do you have to remember?'

Speak up and praise your child for cooperative behaviour.

'That's right. You remembered what you have to do when we're in the car. Good boy.'

Explain consequences for good and bad behaviour.

Let your child know what will happen if she behaves well on the trip, for example there might be a small treat when you arrive. Let her know, too, what will happen if the car rules are broken. You should decide ahead of time exactly how to deal with disruptiveness.

Keep your child busy.

Engage your child in an activity shortly after setting off. Speak to, ask questions, and praise the child every so often during the trip. If the trip is a longish one (over an hour), offer a snack when he is behaving appropriately. On long trips, schedule breaks every few hours so that he can get out, run around, go to the toilet, and so on.

Deal with disruptions by describing the problem behaviour and then the correct behaviour.

If a disruption occurs, gain the child's attention. Calmly but firmly describe what the child has done wrong: 'Tanya, don't push your brother' and then describe what she should do instead: 'Keep on your side of the car and get out your scratch and sniff book if you want something to do.'

Back it up with a terminating instruction and a warning.

If the problem continues, give a terminating instruction, and a warning that further disruption will lead to the stopping of the car: 'Peter, sit up properly and leave Daniel alone. If it happens again I'll stop the car'.

If the problem occurs again, be prepared to stop the car.

Tell the child that her behaviour is unacceptable and must stop immediately. If the problem continues or occurs again, stop the car and put the child out on the side of the road for a 1-minute quiet time. Ignore protests.

Review the trip.

If your child has behaved well on the trip, praise him, describing the correct behaviour.

Provide a back-up reward

Offer any back-up rewards that you agreed to before the trip.

Disruptions during business trips

Sometimes it is necessary to take children to places which involve standing in a queue or sitting in a waiting room, for example banks and doctors' surgeries. These kinds of situations can result in misbehaviour, particularly if children need to remain in one place for any prolonged period. They get bored, squirm, wriggle, and make a fuss. For important business trips that you know will take considerable time it is better to leave your child with someone. Sometimes, however, this is simply not possible. Here are some suggestions for dealing with children during such outings.

Tell your child where you will be going and what you expect of her.

Prior to leaving, explain where you will be going. Tell the child she will have to stand or sit quietly next to you and wait until it is your turn to be seen.

Find something the child can do.

Ask your child what he could do while he waits. Suggestions could include sitting quietly, playing with toys, looking at a book, or drawing on a piece of paper. If the appropriate materials are unlikely to be available, suggest what might be taken along. Ask the child to get these items ready.

Select a suitable back-up reward for good behaviour.

Ask the child what kind of small reward, activity, or treat she would like to earn for behaving appropriately on the business trip.

Praise your child for good behaviour in the car.

If the child behaved appropriately in the car, praise him.

Remind your child of the rules.

Once you have arrived, remind the child of the ground rules that apply when you both go inside.

Set your child up in an activity.

Set up the child in a chair or on the floor away from the main thoroughfare and provide an activity, for example give her a pencil and paper. Before turning away from the child to seek services ask her if she remembers what to do.

Attend to your child periodically while you wait for service.

If you have to stand in a queue, tell the child where you will be moving to and invite him to bring what he is doing to show you every so often. Use these instances as opportunities to praise his good behaviour and to make comments that will extend play: 'That's a great horse you've drawn there John. Now you could try to draw a fence around the horse'.

If you have to sit in a waiting room, follow the same procedure.

Give a terminating instruction to deal with misbehaviour and provide back-up consequences.

If the child misbehaves, go to her and give a terminating instruction.

Calmly but firmly describe what you want her to do. If the misbehaviour continues or increases, go to her, tell her you don't like it when she ... (describe the behaviour that bothers you). Ignore further protests and attempt to restrain the child either by picking her up or holding her firmly at your side until she has calmed down. Avoid cuddling the child or nagging about the misbehaviour. As soon as she is quiet, attempt to set her up in an activity while you wait.

Provide positive attention for good behaviour.

If the child has behaved well on the trip, praise him then offer the small treat or reward previously selected.

Describe any problem behaviours that arose.

If any misbehaviour occurred, calmly explain what it was and describe what you want the child to remember next time. Do not provide the back-up treat. Tell the child she can try again next time you go on a trip to the bank.

Leaving children with friends, relatives, or child minders

All children have to learn to cope with temporary separations from their parents. Parents need time to themselves occasionally. They get sick, need a break from constant child care, start work, have appointments, and so on. Children often benefit from the opportunity to spend time with someone else. However, some will not tolerate separation from their parents. They cling, scream, and protest quite furiously if the parent tries to leave and they appear terrified by the prospect.

Giving in and deciding not ever to go out on your own because of your child's reaction to temporary separations is a mistake. It will encourage more clinging behaviour and, rather than relieve the child's anxiety, can make it worse. You should also investigate as best you can that your child minder, whether friend, relative, or paid help, looks after your child properly. Some children are neglected in child care and can even be sexually abused.

If you have persistent problems when you attempt to leave your child with sitters, check to make sure that the problem has not been made worse because of the way the separation takes place. Prepare your child in advance and follow these guidelines.

Get everything ready.

Make sure you have all the materials that the child minder needs to take proper care of your child, for example favourite toys, games, equipment and medicine.

Explain what is going to happen.

Prepare the child for the separation by explaining where she will be going, where you are going, and when you will return to pick her up.

Ask your child what he should do.

Tell your child what he can expect and ask him to tell you how he is expected to behave while you are out. If he can't tell you, describe the expected behaviour yourself. Answer any questions he has.

Take something special.

Make sure your child takes any special toy or other item.

Introduce your child to the child minder and any other children present.

Many preschoolers need their parents to pave the way in new situations.

Set your child up in an activity.

Suggest something the child might like to do.

Prepare the child minder.

Explain any special needs to the child minder, and always give a contact number in case of emergencies.

Say farewell to your child.

Remind your child of where you are going and when you will return. Say farewell to the child without fussing. Ignore protests or complaints and leave.

Greet the child warmly as soon as you return.

Ask questions about what he did and about his day. Spend some time with him on his own. Be prepared for him to be a bit clingy; this is quite common after brief separations.

Praise your child for any accomplishments.

If the child minder tells you about something interesting the child has done or accomplished, show an interest and praise her efforts. Also remember to praise your child for not fussing when you left.

CHAPTER 6

School-age Children

When children start formal schooling, their parents' influence on their development begins to change. Parents, while remaining the most important figures in a child's life, have to confront the reality that their child is increasingly influenced by experiences and relationships outside the home. Children's experiences at school have a major impact on their development. Their academic success and relationships with teachers influence how competently they view themselves. Their friendships with other children affect how they behave and cope with social situations. By the time children reach 7 or 8 they become capable of more complex thinking and problem solving. They also become more independent and able to do many more tasks for themselves.

Children of this age can contribute much more to the smooth running of the household. They should be encouraged to help with making beds, dishes, house cleaning, and other chores. Many parents start giving children pocket money during this time and children often want to participate in outside social, musical, sporting, and recreational activities. Many children start to learn a musical instrument, and some become avid readers.

The period from the age of 6 or 7 until 12, when many girls and some boys start to mature physically, can also be a testing time for family relationships. If parents have been unable to establish basic adherence to family rules by the time the child reaches 10 or 11, they can have a very difficult time indeed. Children at this age are bigger, stronger, heavier, and more difficult to handle. Parents can experience a variety of new challenges relating to their development and behaviour. Several issues can arise that relate to school. These include difficulties in getting a child to attend school, problems with learning to read, maths, and other academic areas, problems with disruptive behaviour at school, and completing homework. At home, many of the externalising behaviour problems seen during the preschool period, such as disobedience, aggression, sibling rivalry, excessive demanding, and complaining, can continue. Other children develop more internalising problems during this period, including fear and anxiety, depression, shyness, and low self-esteem.

As children proceed through their primary schooling, parents' strategies for dealing with their behaviour also need to change gradually. Children become better able to think of solutions to their own problems, particularly after the age of 10. They start to have opinions about how they are treated and will express them. They will also express opinions about fairness and justice, and about how they or their friends are treated. They can become more secretive and skilled at breaking adult-imposed rules.

These changes mean that parents cannot simply be authoritarian ogres and hope to have harmonious relationships with their children. Some parents whose children have been generally cooperative up to the age of 8 or 9 may be unprepared for challenges to their authority as their children approach adolescence. Parents need to be able to compromise and seek out children's opinions. They also need to help children learn to express their opinions and disagreements in socially acceptable ways.

Specific issues or problems

Preparing children for school

In most Western countries, children start school at the age of 5 or 6. Most children will have had some kind of preschool experience involving separation from the parent for periods of time. However, starting regular primary school somehow seems different for both parents and children. For a parent, this may mean that for the first time they have time to pursue their own career or other interests. It is also a stark reminder to many parents that their darling little girl or boy is growing up. This is something many parents have mixed feelings about.

Some children cannot wait to start school and eagerly look forward to their first day. For other children the reality of starting school creates anxiety and worry. It is a time of transition for most children and several important adjustments have to be made. The excitement of getting new uniforms, clothes, books, and other materials for school is often counteracted by fears of leaving the familiar and predictable routines of home and preschool. Children cope better with these transitions when they are prepared for them and parents have an important role in assisting children settle into school and indeed throughout the whole of a child's education.

Here are some ideas for preparing children for school entry.

Choosing a school.

For some parents there will be little choice available. The child may be required by local education authorities to attend the closest school unless parents are prepared for the expense of sending the child to a private school. The advantage of attending a local primary school is that your child will get to know other children in the neighbourhood, there will be less travelling to and from school, and it will be easier for the parents to become meaningfully involved in the child's school activities. It is often extremely difficult for parents to gauge the quality of education a child is likely to receive at a particular school, whether public or private. It very much depends on the particular teacher and classroom your child is placed in in a given year. A school is only as good as its current complement of teachers. Schools develop reputations both good and indifferent for reasons other than the quality of education they provide. There are many excellent teachers in socio-economically deprived areas, and there can be incompetent teachers at schools with otherwise good reputations. A parent may not know who their child's teacher is going to be until just before the beginning of term. There is an element of luck involved, and in any case parents are forced to accept that teachers are professional people trying to do their best to cater for the needs not only of your child but of many other children as well.

Nevertheless, there is a lot parents can do to find out about schools. Speak to other parents whose children have recently attended local schools. Find out who will be taking your child's class and seek opinions from parents who have had children in that teacher's class. Don't speak to just one parent, talk to several. Speak to the teacher personally as well as to older children at the school who know the teacher. When you enrol the child at the school, be prepared to ask quite specific questions about its general philosophy and approach. Find out whether the school provides special pro-grammes for slow learners, remedial help, extension programmes for children with special abilities in maths, languages, reading, and so on. Find out about school rules and policy on discipline problems. Find out who the child's teacher will be and what the child needs to bring on the first day. All schools provide some information to parents on many of these issues. However, be prepared to seek clari-fication if you are unsure about particular points. Take particular note of how the school's headteacher and office staff deal with your questions and concerns. Do they answer your questions openly and honestly? Do they suggest ways in which you might help the school or become involved in school activities? Remember to take care and be tactful with your questioning.

Talk to your child about starting school.

Long before your child actually begins school, you can raise the topic. This is best done by answering her questions about school in the 6 months or so prior to starting school. It is generally better not to overload the child with information all at once. It will be confusing and probably upset her as she must gradually get used to the idea of starting school.

Read to your child about starting school.

There are a number of children's books concerned with starting school. Check out a local bookstore that specialises in children's literature. These books can be read often to children as a way of preparing them for what lies ahead.

Tell your child when he will be starting.

Tell your child the starting date about two months beforehand.

Take your child to visit the school.

Ask the head teacher if there is an 'open day' at the local school. Otherwise, one weekend, take your child down to the school to have a look around. It is helpful if you can take an older brother or sister who can explain where the junior classes are, what happens on the first day, and where the toilets are.

Let your child know that you will be there on the first day.

On the first day, most schools permit parents of new entrants to stay with their children until they are settled into the new environment. This is often reassuring to a youngster who may be feeling anxious. If you say you are going to stay, make sure that you do.

Involve your child in buying things she needs for starting school.

This will include stationery, schoolbags, lunch box, clothes or uniform, and other items required by the school.

On the first day at school stay with your child as long as you are required. Make yourself as unobtrusive as possible but gently prompt the child to become involved in the classroom's activities rather than clinging to you. Some children who have had separating problems at preschool will experience similar problems now. If your child usually gets upset when you leave but settles quickly once you are gone, then be prepared to explain you are going, say goodbye, and leave. It might take a few days for the child to get used to being in the new situation. However, most children quickly adapt to the excitement and challenge of starting school. Occasionally children can develop a marked fear of going to school (school phobia). Usually such children are not frightened of school per se, although some can be, but they are afraid of separating from their parents. If your child is extremely difficult to get to school, complains of aches and pains on school mornings, screams and in other ways protests about going to school, be prepared to seek professional advice on how best to handle the situation. Generally speaking, it is very important that such a child miss as little school as possible. Speak to your child's teacher, headteacher, or family doctor, who can tell you where appropriate professional assistance can be obtained.

Homework problems

As children progress through school they will be expected to spend at least some time doing homework and independent study. Schools and individual teachers vary in the amount of such work expected. Children from Grades 4 to 7 can expect anywhere from 10 to 60 minutes of homework a night. However it is important for all children to get into good study habits and to complete set work if they are to make satisfactory progress in their studies. Most homework is revision, and children will normally have done similar examples or exercises at school.

Many parents experience difficulty from time to time over homework, and children sometimes make it hard for parents by telling them the night before a project is due in that they need help

and, perhaps, a trip to the library to get resource material. Some children refuse to do homework at all, or their attempts are poorly done, with little care. Parents often blame the child's attitude for such problems, and can accuse her of being lazy, irresponsible, and the like. This often makes the problem worse. One father I know used to require his 10-year-old to do at least one hour of maths study each day. He would sit next to the boy with a ruler and quiz him on his times tables. Every time the boy got a sum wrong, the father would yell at him and whack him with the ruler. The child did not learn his tables correctly and became so uptight about school work that his grades became worse and worse.

Nevertheless, parents do have an important role in helping their children get into proper study habits and routines. This ranges from organising a well-lit space where children can work and where there are few distractions to taking an interest in their work and assisting them to find resources and other materials as well as establishing consistent rules relating to completion of homework.

It is important to remember that you are not the child's teacher. Even though you may be convinced that the way you were taught to solve maths problems is the right one, children will generally be expected to tackle problems in the way they have been shown at school. Children differ widely in their abilities and the time they need to grasp concepts and new ideas. Doing homework should not be a time of stress or pressure. It should be a pleasant interaction where parents can be resource people who can encourage and offer help if the child needs it. Here are some guidelines for dealing with homework problems.

Let your child relax after school.

Children need a bit of time to wind down after school, just as adults do after work. Let your child tell you about her day at school. Have afternoon tea prepared so that she associates coming home with a pleasant interaction before commencing homework. Do not let your child turn on the television as soon as she walks in from school.

Arrange a proper place to study.

Primary school children often want to do their homework in the family living area rather than in their bedroom. A space should be cleared at the kitchen table and all distractions eliminated. Children do not need absolute quiet to work; after all, the classroom is rarely peaceful. Nevertheless, it is a good idea to buy or build your child a desk with a desk lamp to do some project work. Once in high school children can be expected to work completely independently in their bedroom or study.

Select a specific time for doing homework.

Homework is probably best done immediately after children have had time to wind down after school but before they are allowed to go out and play or watch television. If other children come around to play, tell them to come back at a specific time when your child has finished his homework.

Ask your child about homework.

Most children will tell their parents honestly what they are required to do. It might involve learning spelling words, writing a sentence or two, working on a project, summarising a paragraph, doing a few maths problems, and so on. Find out when the work has to be completed.

Help your child get started.

Many children who have had difficulties with homework, either because they don't understand the work or because they would rather be doing something else, need some help in getting into a good routine. Helping your child get started does not mean doing the work for her. Be prepared to sit down at the table with the child. Ask her what needs to be done. Remind your child of the ground rules. Playing or watching TV comes *after* completing her homework.

Offer praise and encouragement while your child is working.

Comments such as 'You're working well on your homework tonight Dean,' which attend to the fact that the child is on task, or 'Great. That's five questions you've done already,' are particularly useful in the early stages of motivating a child to persist with homework.

Wait until your child asks for help before giving it.

Children should be given the chance to tackle the task on their own before parents come to their rescue.

Deal with requests for help by using incidental teaching.

Requests for help are a good time for parents to use the incidental teaching strategies discussed in chapter 3. The basic idea is not simply to give the answer but to prompt the child to solve the problem himself. Be careful not to overdo it. For example, if a child asks you how to spell the word 'factory' without having attempted to spell it first, you could say 'How do you think you spell it? Get out a piece of paper and try to spell it yourself first and I'll come and have a look'. Offer praise when the child attempts the word. If he gets the word right, offer further praise. If the word is wrong, rather than saying 'No, that's wrong,' point out the letters that are correct first. 'That's nearly right. The first four letters are right. Have a look at the ending. Is it "ery" or "ory". Yes "ory", that's right. Good boy.' If after one prompt he still cannot get the correct answer then tell him what it is. Children will sometimes get frustrated if every question they ask is met with responses such as 'Look it up in the dictionary first'. Parents will find that their children are more cooperative if help is given relatively freely initially, with perhaps one or two attempts at incidental teaching.

Avoid criticising the child's work.

When children are doing their homework, they need encouragement for correct work and for attempting the task rather than abuse for mistakes. You may be very tempted to criticise work that is messy or incorrect. Such criticism often backfires and only discourages the child, particularly if it occurs too often. It is often a good idea to encourage children to do rough copies of work first; a final neater copy can be done for handing in at school.

Check your child's work before finishing.

Children often want to show their parents the work they have completed. Some will ask whether it is correct or ask you to give your opinion on how good the work is. Do not feel you have to make sure your child's work is perfect before allowing her to hand it in. It can be a devastating experience for a child who has worked hard for 15 minutes writing a paragraph only to have the parent point out 20 spelling or punctuation mistakes. The ideas the child has expressed in the story may be very good. When checking work like this, correct, if you must, only two or three mistakes. Try to find something positive to say about the child's effort.

Offer a reward following the completion of homework.

This could involve praising the child for finishing his homework or allowing him to watch television or go and play before dinner. Some parents may feel that a more powerful incentive is needed if the child has been very difficult at homework time in the past. For example, Jonathan and Andrea, Peter's parents, set up a special homework chart on the refrigerator like the one in figure 4 on page 186.

Each day that Peter completed his homework without a fuss he

Figure 4: A sample homework chart

Week beginning: _____

Tasks	Points	Mon	Tue	Wed	Thurs	Fri	Totals
Brought h/w notebook home today	1	1	1				
Started h/w by 4.15 p.m. today without complaining	2	—	2				
Worked for 15 mins without interruption	5	5	5				
Total points earned	8 (max.)	6	8				

Fill in the points earned for each task and total them at the end of the week.

could earn points which were exchanged at the end of the week for a back-up reward. His parents wrote down three things he had to do each night. These were bringing home his homework notebook each day (1 point), starting his homework by 4.15 without complaining (2 points), and working on his homework without interruption for a minimum of 15 minutes (5 points). If he earned 36 points by the end of the week, he received his back-up reward which was $2 towards a new skateboard he wanted.

If your child continues to have problems with schoolwork, be prepared to discuss the problem with her teacher. She may need remedial assistance or help in one or more subject areas. Remember that children's learning and academic performance is strongly influenced by motivation as well as ability. One of the best ways to encourage better motivation is to focus on the child's successes, the things she does right rather than the things she does wrong. Giving a child lectures and pep talks, or scolding, nagging, or threatening because of her 'attitude' to schoolwork often achieves very little other than making the child feel even more incapable than she really is.

Parents may need to accept that their child is not brilliant and no amount of pressure to succeed will alter this. Nevertheless, all children can be encouraged to perform to the best of their abilities by helping them get into good work habits and routines and by providing encouragement, support, and help as needed.

Disruptive behaviour at school

One of the most worrying problems for parents relates to a child's conduct at school. Children can be labelled as disruptive for a variety of reasons. Common problems include inattentiveness, not following the teacher's directions, distracting other children through silly behaviours such as swinging on chairs, pulling faces, or making loud noises, getting into fights in the playground, failing to complete set work, calling out, and wandering in the classroom. Teachers generally expect a certain standard of conduct from pupils. Children who consistently break basic classroom rules will find themselves getting into trouble.

It can be very difficult for parents to know what to do in these circumstances, particularly if the school does not contact them about the child's behaviour. It is not uncommon for parents to become aware of a conduct problem only after a serious incident has arisen, for example the parent is contacted when the school is considering suspending the child.

Children can be disruptive for a variety of reasons. Some children's disruptiveness at school can be an extension of their disruptive behaviour at home. These children are generally uncooperative and defy adult authority. Other children can be disruptive because the work is too hard, or not challenging enough in the case of very bright children. Sometimes disruptiveness is due to teachers trying to enforce excessively rigid rules. Many of the same factors that can contribute to behaviour problems at home can be at work in the classroom, for example the teacher only attends to the child when she is disruptive and ignores good behaviour. A child may also have lower intellectual ability, or a specific learning difficulty in one or more subject areas such as reading or maths, which influences his behaviour at school.

There are several things a parent can do to try to resolve a school-related behaviour problem. Most of these strategies require the active cooperation of the child's teacher. A home–school behaviour contract is one such strategy.

Clarify the problem.

The first step is to obtain accurate information about the child's behaviour. Make an appointment to speak to your child's teacher at a convenient time. After school is often the best time as the teacher will have fewer distractions.

Ask the teacher to describe specifically what the child is doing that is causing concern. Try not to be defensive or to make excuses for the child. Be prepared to listen to the teacher's point of view and understand the problem she or he experiences.

Share information with the teacher.

Tell the teacher about any similar difficulties you may experience with the child and let her teacher know what steps, if any, you have taken in trying to resolve the problem, such as taking the child to see a psychologist. It is often helpful to teachers to know about the steps that you are taking or intend taking in dealing with home problems. This often helps the teacher gain a better appreciation of your child and her circumstances.

Ask the teacher what you can do to help resolve the problem.

Find out first how the teacher thinks the problem might be solved before suggesting a solution yourself. This will convey your interest in trying to help solve the problem and will also encourage the teacher to share his own ideas on handling the difficulty. If the teacher is considering referring the child to an educational psychologist, for example, or requesting that the child be suspended, you need to know about this. Some teachers will make quite specific suggestions about things you can do to help, such as supervising homework and making sure the child brings to school everything required for the day's activities.

Find out what specific rules the child needs to observe in the classroom.

This involves encouraging the teacher to be as concrete and specific as possible about what the child is expected to do. For example, a Grade 4 pupil might be expected to begin set work promptly, put up his hand if he wants to speak rather than calling out, work quietly on set work without disrupting other children, and to write down his homework for that day.

Suggest a home–school daily report card as a way of dealing with the problem.

Take along a sample booklet for the teacher to look at, similar to the one in figure 5 on page 190. The main idea is that a system of communication be established between home and school regarding the child's behaviour in the classroom. The agreed set of rules the child is to observe in class is written down in the column marked 'classroom goals'. The child brings to school and takes home from school each day this home–school contract booklet. If she observes the rules during different lessons in the day, the teacher signs the appropriate column and allocates an agreed number of points for each behaviour. These points are then exchanged at home for an appropriate back-up reward, but if the child fails to earn an agreed upon number of points the parent can provide back-up consequences.

The main advantage of having the teacher record the child's behaviour is that you as a parent are more likely to have accurate information about what is happening at school. If the teacher is willing to try the programme, offer to work out the details and to discuss the plan with your child. Some teachers may prefer to do this themselves. Suggest that the programme be tested for one week initially, and arrange another time to review progress.

Explain the programme to your child.

Tell your child you have spoken to his teacher and that you are concerned about his conduct in class. Let him know he will have to take

Figure 5: Home–school daily report card

Home goals before school	Possible points	Points	Signature	Comments:
Take homework to school	2	2		
Ready to leave for school by 8.20	3	—		

Classroom goals	Possible points	9.00–10.30	10.45–12.30	1.15–3.00
Begin set work promptly	2	2	—	2
Obey teachers' instructions	4	4	4	—

Teacher's signature:

Comments:

Points earned in class (12) + home (2) = 14

Fill in the points earned for each goal and sign in the appropriate place. Total the points earned for the day.

the signed card to school each day and give it to the teacher. The teacher will fill in the card three times each day, and will sign the card at the end of the day. The card must be brought home each day, and you and your child should add up the points together.

Select appropriate rewards for satisfactory performance.

If the child earns 80 per cent or more of the possible points on that day, provide an appropriate reward on the same day. If the child earns 80 per cent or more of the possible points over the whole week, then another back-up reward should be provided. Andrew and his parents worked out that for the daily reward he would be allowed to choose his favourite dessert, watch an extra 30 minutes television, or have a game of cards with his father. As a reward at the end of the week he chose being able to have a friend to sleep over on Saturday night and to watch a video-movie.

Select a suitable consequence for poor performance.

If the child earns below 80 per cent of the possible points on any day, provide an appropriate consequence. Andrew's parents decided that he would not be allowed to watch any television on that night and would be banned from using the family computer.

Test the programme for one week.

Tell your child that the programme will stop at the end of one week and his progress will be reviewed at that time. During the first week, make sure you praise your child for good behaviour at school, check the daily points, sign the card, and make sure the card goes to school each day. Provide rewards and consequences as agreed.

Review progress with the teacher.

Arrange to meet with the teacher to discuss progress. Make any necessary adjustments to the programme, such as providing clearer definitions of the goals. Make sure you thank the teacher for her efforts in helping your child overcome the problem, and arrange for the programme to continue for a further two weeks.

Phasing your child off the programme.

This can be done over a two-week period as follows. In the first week, only give rewards every second day. To earn the back-up reward, the child must earn 80 per cent or better on two consecutive days. When this goal is achieved, increase to three days, then require a whole week before the child receives any back-up rewards. As you phase out the rewards, make sure you keep praising the child for his good performance. Then phase out the use of the monitoring card. Do this by alternating the days when the child has to take the card. As you phase out the monitoring, arrange to ring the teacher at least twice in the week to ensure that the child's behaviour has continued to be satisfactory. The following week the child need not take the card at all. If the child's behaviour deteriorates during the process of phasing him off the programme, simply go back one step and try again.

Discussing problems with teachers

It is important that parents establish open channels of communication with their child's school, particularly if the child is experiencing difficulties.

Avoid running down your child to the teacher.

Most teachers react negatively to parents abusing their children, even if the child has been quite difficult to deal with at school.

Avoid criticising the school or the teacher's handling of your child, even if you feel your criticisms are justified.

This will prompt defensiveness and will often make the school less receptive to your ideas and suggestions about how to solve the problem.

Avoid trying to make excuses for your child's conduct.

If there is clear evidence that your child has done something wrong, accept this reality. Don't get into long-winded explanations of your child's behaviour.

Avoid becoming irate.

This strategy often backfires and can make others irritated and defensive.

Avoid claiming your child has special gifts or abilities, unless you know this for certain.

Some teachers become quite annoyed by parents who claim their child is very bright but who has never done very well at school. Parents can easily over-estimate their own child's ability. Teachers see your child's performance in relation to hundreds of other children of the same age.

Avoid giving teachers advice on how they should teach.

Teachers are professionals and often react negatively to well-meant advice from parents about how they should run their classroom.

Remedial reading with your child

Reading is perhaps the most important academic skill children are expected to learn at school. Despite its generally recognised value, a significant number of children experience difficulties in learning to read. The reasons are complex. However, it is becoming increasingly clear that parents can play an important role in helping children with reading problems in their own home.

'Pause, prompt, praise' is a way of training parents to become remedial tutors for their own children at home. The procedures were devised to help children who had fallen several years behind in their reading. The basic idea behind the programme is that parents regularly listen to children read material of an appropriate level of difficulty in a positive atmosphere. Parents also learn how to attend positively to correct reading performance, and how to correct their child's mistakes. Children's ability to read is strongly influenced by motivation. Children feel discouraged and don't enjoy reading when their efforts are unsuccessful or meet with disapproval. Children with reading difficulties are often afraid of being wrong and it takes patience and persistence to help them to regain their confidence, and to sit down and tackle the task again.

Arrange a suitable time and place for hearing your child's reading.

Set aside 10 minutes, three or four times per week. Choose a time that does not clash with your child's favourite TV programme or other important activity. Sometimes a few minutes just before bedtime is a good time. To avoid interruptions, ask someone else to answer the phone and make sure other children have something to do. It is important that distractions are minimised so make sure the TV is turned off. Sit beside your child, either on the couch or at the kitchen table. Make sure the session lasts no longer than 10 minutes.

Select suitable books for your child.

This is one of the most important steps in helping your child with a reading problem. Most schools use a series of learning to read books that are graded from simple to difficult. Different schools use different series. Teachers often send home books for the child to read which are at the same level or below the level the child is using in the class-room. Contact the child's teacher and ask him or her to send home a book that is at an appropriate level of difficulty for your child.

Check on the difficulty level of the book.

Count off 50 words of text and note this point in the book. On a piece of paper write the date and the name of the book. When your child begins reading, put a mark on the paper for each mistake made.

Mistakes can be of several different kinds including leaving words out, adding words, or reading different words from those in the text. Count only one mistake for each text word incorrectly read. If your child corrects a mistake don't count this. Count the number of mistakes made. Take this number away from 50 to give you the number of words read correctly. The book is too difficult if there are more than ten mistakes and too easy if there are fewer than four mistakes. If your child makes a number of mistakes between these two numbers, the book is at the right level of difficulty. Speak to the child's teacher if your child needs a book of a different level.

Use 'pause, prompt, praise' to help your child become an independent reader.

This involves helping children learn to solve problems for themselves. The problems referred to are the words that they get wrong. Figure 6 on page 196 shows the basic technique. In essence the procedure is divided into two main parts: the steps to follow when your child reads correctly and those to follow when he reads incorrectly. When a child reads correctly, he should be praised. When a child makes a mistake, first of all you should wait for a few seconds (the pause component) to give him a chance to correct the mistake. If the child does not accurately self-correct, then prompt, that is give the child a clue to solve the problem. When he gets the correct word or words, offer praise and encouragement. This basic strategy eliminates any need for the critical comments that are so discouraging to reluctant readers.

Check on your child's progress.

It is important to continue to assess whether the material your child is reading is at an appropriate level. To do this, simply repeat the procedure you used in assessing the difficulty level to select an appropriate book. Make sure during this check that you don't give your child any help if a mistake is made or praise for correct reading. If your child makes fewer than four mistakes it is time to move on to a more challenging book. Speak to the child's teacher to get one a little harder, or search out the appropriate level at the local public library using the expertise of the professional librarian.

If you are to become an effective remedial tutor for your child, it is important that the time you set aside to listen to your child read be a positive experience. If you are feeling irritable or impatient, it is not a good time to listen to reading. Your feelings will come through and

Figure 6: 'Pause, prompt, praise' home tutoring procedures

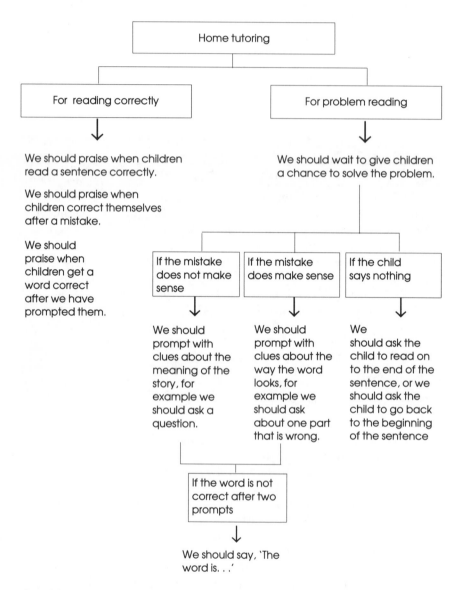

We should prompt with clues about the meaning of the story, for example we should ask a question.

We should prompt with clues about the way the word looks, for example we should ask about one part that is wrong.

We should ask the child to read on to the end of the sentence, or we should ask the child to go back to the beginning of the sentence

If the word is not correct after two prompts

We should say, 'The word is. . .'

From McNaughton, S.S., Glynn, T., and Robinson, V. (1987) *Pause, prompt, praise: Effective tutoring for remedial reading.* Birmingham, England: Positive Products. Reproduced with permission.

make the activity seem a chore. Success in helping your child improve his reading also involves getting into a consistent routine for regular practice, as this is what your child needs more than anything else.

Stealing

If you ask most adults whether they ever stole anything from their parents when they were children, the vast majority will say yes. Many families go through a phase when money seems to go missing from parents' purses or wallets. Most children stop when they are caught and firmly disciplined. However, some develop a serious problem with stealing. One 11-year-old I worked with found out his mother's personal identification number (PIN) and over a period of two weeks withdrew $400 from an automatic teller machine. This child had also been caught stealing money from a teacher's purse at school and had stolen things from other children's bags. Stealing is a potentially serious problem, particularly when it occurs outside the home, and it needs to be handled carefully.

Children are more likely to steal when parents are careless with their money, for example if they leave notes and coins around the house in easily accessible places. Some children start to steal because of bad peer influences. They may be involved with older children who have also stolen from their parents. Others continue to steal because they get away with it. Because stealing is sometimes hard to detect, there are likely to be many times when the child has stolen and is not caught. Stealing is often a problem in children who spend a lot of time unsupervised. Parents should always know where their child is, what he is doing, and who he is with. Parents of children who steal frequently cannot answer these questions.

Persistent stealing can also be a sign of serious family problems. Some children come from homes where one or both parents have a drinking or drug problem, have been in trouble with the law themselves, or where there has been violence within the home.

Children who steal persistently are at risk of becoming delinquents and criminals later on. The majority of adult criminals started their life of crime well before their teenage years. Children who steal repeatedly often have other problems as well, such as difficulties at school, aggressive behaviour, disobedience, poor peer relationships, and low self-image.

The best time to deal with stealing is when it first begins. If a child has been a successful thief for several years, he is likely to have become quite good at it. When children start stealing they are not very skilled and are often fairly easy to catch. For example, the child might arrive home from school with items that you know you have not paid for, claiming they were gifts from another child.

The key to overcoming stealing is to reduce the opportunity for stealing to take place, to supervise the child's activities more closely, and to use a no-stealing behaviour contract to prevent any further theft.

Keep track of your money.

Make sure you know exactly how much money is in the house. Count notes and change before your child goes to bed each evening. Do this laborious task every day for at least one month.

Keep your money in a safe place.

Do not leave it in the kitchen or family living areas where it may be a temptation.

Check your child's room.

Regularly check your child's room twice a week while he's out, and be on the lookout for any unexplained items, money, or other goods that you have not paid for and know your child has not been given the money to buy.

Make sure that you know where your child is at all times.

Minimise the amount of time your child spends unsupervised either at home or out of home. This is particularly important if your child has been stealing from local shops.

Start an allowance system.

Give your child a regular allowance that he has to earn by doing chores and odd jobs. This will make sure that some of the things he wants can be bought with money he has earned rather than stolen.

Establish a 'no stealing' contract with your child.

This should be a written contract which both parents and child sign. An example of such a contract appears in figure 7 on page 199. The contract is an agreement between parent and child which states in very specific terms what the child is expected to do, and the incentives and penalties that will follow if the child breaks the agreement.

This was a contract worked out between Phillip, aged 10, and his parents after Phillip was brought home by a policeman when he was caught shoplifting at a local newsagent. Phillip had also been

Figure 7: An example of a behaviour contract

Conditions

I _____
hereby agree to the following
conditions for a period of 4 weeks
commencing 3 June.

We_____
hereby agree to the following:

1   I will return home each day
    from school by 4.15 p.m.

1   That one of us should be at
    home each school day by 4
    p.m. to greet Phillip.

2   I will come directly home from
    school and not go near the
    shopping centre on school
    nights.

2   We will be available each
    school day to help Phillip with
    his homework should he want
    help.

3   I will not take anything that
    does not belong to me (steal)
    from my parents or anyone
    else. This includes money and
    any other items.

3   We will provide Phillip with the
    agreed incentives should he
    keep to the terms of this
    contract.

Incentives

For each day Phillip keeps to these conditions, he will
be able to earn $1.00 towards a new skateboard.

Penalties

If Phillip breaks conditions 1 or 2 of this agreement, he will be fined 50
cents for each condition broken. If he breaks condition 3, he will be fined
the entire amount saved up to that point plus be grounded for a period
of four days.

Signatures

Child's name:_____   Date:_____

Parent's name:_____   Date:_____
     (Mother's name)

_____
    (Father's name)   Date:_____

Commencement date:_____

Termination date:_____

taking small amounts of money from his mother's purse for about 6 months. The contract was used for 4 weeks. There was one episode of stealing in week 2, then not a single further episode that the parents know of for the next 2 years.

Involve your child in other interests, hobbies, and activities.

The turning point for some children who steal comes when they develop an interest or hobby that captures their imagination. Many kids who steal have very little to do in their spare time other than watch television. Give preference to activities that have adequate adult supervision. This might involve learning a new sport, learning to play an instrument, or joining a team.

Monitor who your child spends time with.

Be prepared to ban your child from playing with children who seem to be a bad influence. If your child is mixed up with children who are unsupervised for much of the time, or are involved in stealing, smoking, drinking, drug taking, or other antisocial behaviour, severely limit the contact your child has with them. This may be easier said than done, particularly if they attend the same school. One way of tackling this problem is to help your child get involved in organised activities that none of these children attend. If this is not possible, then encourage your child to bring children home to play so you can keep an eye on what happens and can provide supervision.

Establish firm rules relating to times for arrival home from school and times your child is allowed to spend away from home.

This is particularly important for children who have been getting into trouble after school hours. Wherever possible, make sure there is someone at home to greet the child after school. Primary school children should not be left unsupervised after school. If necessary, arrange after-school care. Don't leave the responsibility to older siblings, particularly if they do not get on well together.

If you find your child stealing again, act on your informed suspicions.

If you discover money or other items missing and you strongly suspect that your child is involved, be prepared to act on your suspicions rather than waiting for absolute evidence.

Confront the child with the facts.

'Two hours ago I had two twenty dollar notes in my purse and now there is only one. We are the only ones at home and I haven't been near my purse.'

Ask the child to return the money.

Many children will at this point hand over what was taken if it is still in their possession.

Do not require an admission of guilt.

Many children who steal also lie about it. Asking for a confession often simply gives the child an opportunity to lie and cover his tracks.

Impose the penalty as appropriate.

If the child admits taking the money and returns it, firmly and matter-of-factly impose the penalty agreed to in the contract. Do not lecture, nag, or shout: simply state the problem and the consequence. 'Brad, that is stealing. You are grounded for three days, have lost 40 points off your contract, and are banned from going to the movies with Henry this weekend.'

Ignore protests.

If the child protests, claiming her innocence, then ignore it and carry out the penalty. While this may seem a bit harsh, it is even more of a problem if the child is lying and is let off the hook. 'I am not saying you did it. I don't know this for a certainty. However, I strongly suspect that it was you and so you'll have to suffer the consequences. If I'm wrong I'm sorry, but what I've said goes.'

Test your child's honesty.

Once your child has stopped stealing, begin to test his honesty. This can be done quite simply by starting to leave amounts of money where you know your child will discover it. Do not let your child know that you plan to do this. If your child resists the temptation or returns the money to you, praise the child enthusiastically. If the money goes missing then deal with the problem immediately and decisively, and impose the penalty on the contract.

Create opportunities for your child to demonstrate that she is acting honestly and responsibly.

This can involve letting your child go down to the shops to purchase groceries on a shopping list. Give her more money than the goods will cost. If the child returns the correct change without having spent anything, thank her for being responsible with money.

Start a savings plan.

Help your child open a savings account and encourage him to deposit a portion of his pocket money each week. The idea here is to encourage the child to learn to save money he has earned rather than always spending impulsively when money is received. Make sure there is a portion available to spend or save as he sees fit.

Sometimes parents discover long after the event that something has been stolen. For example, on routine cleaning of a child's room, some unexplained item is uncovered. You don't know where it came from, how long it has been there, or how it was paid for. It is better to establish a basic rule that your child doesn't bring anything into the house that is not his, that is, no borrowing or looking after things for friends. The only things the child is allowed to bring into the house are articles of his own that have been paid for by you or that the child has bought from his allowance. You can then assume that a strange item has either been stolen or brought home without permission. The rule should not be relaxed until there have been no incidents for at least three months.

Lying

A lie is a deliberate distortion of the truth. Children lie for many reasons. They may lie to avoid getting caught when they have done something wrong. Lying is an understandable response when one remembers one of the side-effects of punishment. When children are under the threat of punishment, many will do things that enable them to avoid or escape the punishment. One of those things is to lie. Lying is more likely to continue if it is successful, that is if it allows the child to avoid punishment.

Other children lie as a way of gaining attention and approval from peers. Children can tell white lies about some strange things. They may tell other children or teachers lies about what they have done, seen, or own. These kinds of boastful white lies are often short-lived once a child starts school and has been caught out once or twice.

Lying becomes a problem when children start to be deceitful in an attempt to cover up activities such as getting into trouble at school, stealing, cheating, and behaving inappropriately in the community. For some very antisocial youngsters, lying becomes a way of life. These children are often engaged in activities they know their parents would disapprove of, and lying and deception allow them to continue these activities without getting caught. When lying has become

a well-established pattern of behaviour, it can be difficult for parents to deal with. Parents may feel unable to trust their children and become sceptical about many truthful things their children tell them. When children persistently lie, parents may need to make a number of important changes in their approach. This may include how much time and positive attention the child receives for good behaviour, the severity of discipline the parents typically use, a child's acquaintances, and the amount of supervision the child receives. Here are some guidelines.

Hold a discussion with your child.

Explain to your child that lying is unacceptable behaviour and that you would like this behaviour to cease immediately. 'Daniel, I would like to talk to you about what happened last night. You lied to me about where you had been after school and as this is the fourth time this has happened in the last two weeks, I think we have a problem. It is important that your father and I can trust what you say and I would like this lying to stop.'

Describe the problem from your perspective.

Briefly and matter-of-factly point out how lying affects you and why you consider it a problem. 'I feel angry and disappointed when this happens and it makes me want to question other things you tell me. You'll find that if the problem continues other people simply won't trust you.'

Seek the child's opinion on the nature of the problem.

When they are caught lying, many children don't have much to say about why they lied, but occasionally they will make excuses or even try to blame someone else for the problem. Avoid trying to get into a 'yes, but' type of argument with your child if this happens. Simply restate the problem as you see it and close the discussion with a statement of what you would like to happen from this point on.

Create opportunities for your child to practise accurate reporting.

This involves identifying occasions where your child is telling the truth about her activities and then responding favourably to these reports. To do this, you need to know that your child is telling the whole truth. The best way to do this initially is to ask your child questions about events and happenings around the home on which you are fully informed. 'Have you tidied your bedroom?' 'Done your homework?' 'Finished raking up the leaves in the yard?' 'Cleaned your teeth?' are examples where you can quickly check on the facts *before* asking the child. The reason for doing this is that the child can practise describing his experiences accurately and truthfully and you can detect deception immediately it occurs.

If the child reports accurately, give praise and positive attention

If the child accurately describes the event under question, then give positive attention and feedback, regardless of whether the child has or has not done whatever she was supposed to do. 'Good girl, Rachel, for telling me the truth.' The idea here is that the child is always praised for owning up and telling the truth whatever else has happened. Try not to create the impression that you are continuously suspicious.

If the child lies about what has happened then give corrective feedback.

Simply describe the problem. 'Kevin, you are not telling me the truth about that. You have not finished raking the yard.'

Back up corrective feedback with an appropriate consequence.

The consequence will depend on the circumstances. However, for failing to report accurately on chores, you might require the child to do extra work. Alternatively, time out could be used as an immediate consequence for a child up to age 9. The important point here is that the consequence is provided for lying, not for failure to complete the task or chore.

If your child lies to cover up some other inappropriate behaviour, for example stealing, smoking, or cheating at school then deal with the two problems separately.

Deal with the lying first, then the problem which prompted the lie. Provide appropriate consequences for both. If money is found in the child's room and he lies about where it came from, provide a consequence for the lying, such as withdrawing privileges. Then provide an additional consequence for the stealing itself, for example loss of points on a contract as described earlier.

Consider establishing a 'no lying' behaviour contract.

If the problem is persistent, establish a behaviour contract similar to the one described on pages 198–199 for managing stealing. An alternative is to incorporate lying as a behaviour into an existing contract for another problem.

Lying can be a difficult problem to solve when parents aren't sure whether the child is lying or not. Younger primary school children, however, can give the secret away because they smirk or smile while telling you a lie. Sometimes the child's story simply doesn't add up. For example, when asked to explain how they happened to have $10 in their room, they might tell an unlikely tale about finding it on the way home. Questions about when, where, who was with them, or the sequence of events, lead to a confession. Most children eventually confess when confronted directly, but others will maintain a lie in the face of the strongest interrogation. These children have become skilled liars and are often engaged in many other antisocial behaviours as well.

The best time to deal with lying is when it first begins. Children need to get the consistent message that regardless of what they have done they need to be honest with you. After all, parents cannot assist children who get into trouble, whether at school or in the community, unless they know what has happened. Many of the strategies discussed earlier in relation to fostering good communication with children can also help in overcoming lying.

Swearing

Children often learn to swear from their peer group between the ages of 7 and 11, although swearing can occur in preschoolers if they have older siblings or indeed have parents who swear a great deal. Swearing is considered by most adults to be an unacceptable behaviour, particularly at school. Swearing in the peer group may meet with the opposite reception. Some children swear as part of projecting a tough, aggressive image. It can be used to intimidate or threaten other children into submission, as an alternative to direct violence. Swearing in both adults and children is much more common in some groups than others. For many street kids and runaways, swearing is a part of life and a way of defying adult authority.

Swearing in the home can occur as part of an outburst of anger or rage. It can be a form of abuse directed at siblings or, less frequently, at parents themselves. There are hundreds of choice expressions that children can discover. Parents may find some expletives offensive while others are not a problem, and indeed they may use them themselves. You really need to decide for yourself which potentially offensive words, phrases, or expressions are acceptable and permissible in your home and which ones are not. The guidelines below are designed to help children learn more socially acceptable expressions.

Decide what words, phrases, or expressions are acceptable.

It is generally best to have a small number of completely banned words that are commonly used but which you find personally offensive than to have a large list of unacceptable words which will be difficult to enforce. Remember, you might be able to control the language your child uses at home but you can't control what happens in the playground at school, or on the street.

Make sure you do not model swearing.

You cannot expect your child not to swear if you use offensive words yourself.

Only use words, whether in general conversation or as expletives, that are on your list of acceptable words.

Every parent gets frustrated at times. We break things accidentally, hit our fingers with hammers, and bang our shins or elbows. These are the times that many parents will let out a swear word. It is very hard to control what we say when we are in pain, but if you must swear choose a non-offensive word if possible.

Explain the ground rules to your child.

Hold a discussion with your child relating to swearing at home. Describe the problem from your point of view: 'James, I don't like it when you use that word in this house. Don't use it again'. Describe acceptable alternatives. 'If you must use that sort of language, you may say ...[tell the child the acceptable words], but from now on these words are banned...[list the banned words]'.

Provide an incentive for complying with the ground rules.

Start a behaviour chart for monitoring swearing at home as shown in figure 8 on page 208. You will notice that it has one column for each day of the week. At the end of each day, your child can earn a merit award if she has gone through the whole day without swearing. At this time, you should thank and praise her for speaking properly at home during the day. When the child has earned seven awards in a row, give her a back-up reward. Keep this chart posted in the kitchen and have enough copies for 3 to 5 weeks.

Figure 8: A chart for monitoring swearing

Date:	20/6						
Day:	Sat						
Merit Award:							
Daily Total:	1						

Weekly Total

Fill in a merit award for each day that swearing does not occur, and total at the end of the week.

Deal with swearing by using a terminating instruction.

If you hear your child swearing at home, give her a firm terminating instruction. 'Jane, stop using that language immediately. That word is banned in this house.'

Describe the correct behaviour.

Tell your child what would have been a more acceptable way of dealing with the problem. 'If you want to borrow some paper from your sister, ask her pleasantly.'

Describe the back-up consequence.

Tell your child that he will not get his award today. Decide on an additional back-up consequence such as the withdrawal of a privilege, for example watching his favourite TV show, or time out for 3 minutes.

Ignore protests and follow through with back-up consequences as necessary.

After stating the consequences, simply remove yourself, ignoring protests. Make sure you follow through if it happens again.

One problem that can arise with this strategy is that other siblings may begin telling tales to get the offending child into trouble. Telling tales can be as much of a problem as swearing so you will need to be prepared to deal with this as well. One way of doing so is to act only on things you have heard yourself. It might mean that you have to keep a closer eye on your child's activities for a few days so that you detect swearing before other children feel they have to tell. If telling tales occurs frequently over other things as well, then read the guidelines on pages 64–67 for establishing clear ground rules.

Chores

How old should children be before they are required to regularly help out around the house with chores such as doing dishes, tidying their bedroom, clearing away the dinner table, cleaning the house, and working in the yard? The answer to this question will depend on at least three things: first, whether you view running the household as a shared responsibility or something that is the sole province of the parents (usually mother); second, whether you believe children should have regular assigned responsibilities as opposed to 'helping' now and again; and third, whether the child has the physical and mental capacity to carry out the necessary task.

Children need to learn the value of work from an early age. By having regular chores that are their own responsibility, children can learn to apply themselves to a task, can learn the skills involved in running a family household, and learn something about self-discipline. However, the key to helping children learn to undertake these responsibilities cheerfully and competently is to move slowly. The process starts right back during the preschool years when young children are taught how to take care of their belongings and to tidy up after themselves. By the time children reach the age of 8 or 9, they should be encouraged to have regular household chores. If you do this, you will find that your own work is more manageable, that you have more time to spend with the children on other activities, and of course more time for yourself and your spouse.

It is often better to introduce all children in the family to chores at the same time, even though they may differ in age and so have different capabilities. Children often accept new responsibilities if they don't feel they are being singled out. Here are some ideas for establishing a family roster for household duties. However, remember that premature introduction to unsuitable tasks will frequently turn the child away from such tasks in the future.

Call a family meeting.

Arrange a meeting with all family members at a convenient time. Eliminate distractions by making sure the TV is off. It is important that both parents have discussed the plan in advance and agree that there should be greater role sharing within the family. This can be a problem in very traditional marriages where one or both partners assume that it is the mother's responsibility to do the majority of the work around the home. Reluctant fathers might more readily accept that children should do more, than that they themselves might need to change.

State the issue from your perspective.

Explain to the children that from now on they will be expected to help out with chores around the home. Tell them that every family member will have certain assigned responsibilities each day. There will also be occasional jobs that need to be done less often.

Explain why children must be prepared to help out around the home.

Try to keep the explanation simple. 'Living in a family involves a lot of work. Our family will run more smoothly and there will be more time for things we can do together as a family if everyone pitches in and helps. It is not Mum or Dad's job to do everything to keep the place clean and tidy. You are now old enough to share in some of these jobs. One day you will have to know how to run your own house. Now is the time to start learning about these things.' Ignore protests or claims that none of their friends have to do any work. Simply restate the fact that from now on they all will have set jobs to do.

Generate a list of the daily, weekly, and monthly chores that need to be done.

Get out a piece of paper or use a blackboard to make a list of jobs that need to be done around the house. Involve your children in this process by asking for their opinions. Write each item down. Try to select items that children can do with a minimum of adult supervision and that are not too time consuming, such as placing their dirty clothes in a clothes basket in the bathroom, and taking their plates from the table after dinner and placing them in the dishwasher. The list should show the chores in order, from the beginning of the day till bedtime. At this stage do not assign jobs to children, simply pinpoint what needs to be done.

Put Mum or Dad's name beside any chores on the list that you feel you should do.

You might decide for a variety of reasons that there are specific things, such as loading the washing machine and preparing meals, that you should continue to do, either because the children are too young or because you feel these should be adult responsibilities.

Ask the children for their opinion on any chores they would like to do.

Children should be given an opportunity to express their opinion on jobs they would like to take on. Be cautious here. Some children will suggest things they are not capable of doing competently, such as cooking the evening meal. Other children will say they don't want to do anything. Don't be put off by this. Be prepared to insist that certain jobs are their responsibility, or suggest alternative things they can do. Constantly keep in mind each child's age and capabilities.

Finalise a job list for each child.

This involves writing down a final job list that will be included on the jobs chart. The child's responsibilities should be broken down into daily, weekly, and monthly jobs. Try to have the same number of items for each child. However, older children should be expected to take on more complex tasks than younger ones.

Prepare a large jobs chart.

A jobs chart similar to the one in figure 9 opposite can be used for keeping track of whether children complete their assigned jobs on time. A large whiteboard is useful for this purpose. The columns and headings can be written in permanent felt pens and the individual items for each child in pens that can be erased. An alternative is to use a large sheet of cardboard or a sheet generated from a home computer. This chart is also used as a reminder to children of what their responsibilities are, and as feedback on whether or not they have completed the tasks.

Involve your child in preparing the chart.

Many school-aged children love being involved in preparing charts like this. They can help with ruling columns, reading items from the draft list while you write them on the board, or writing them down themselves if they have neat handwriting.

Allocate a list of duties to each child.

Fill in the chart with jobs assigned to each family member. Some families prefer to have only the children's names on the chart. Others want the adults as well.

Select incentives for improved performance.

Children are more likely to cooperate if their efforts are acknowledged and recognised. There are several things that parents can do to motivate their children. These include providing praise and positive attention during or immediately following the completion of assigned tasks, and giving positive feedback at the end of the day (before bedtime) while you fill in the chart for that day. It is also possible to link the family roster into a pocket money system by assigning a monetary value to each item. Guidelines for establishing pocket money are detailed on page 216.

Figure 9: Family jobs chart

Month: _____ **April** _____

JOB	1	2	3	4	5	6	7	8	9	10	11	12	13	14	15	16	17	18	19	20	21	22	23	24	25	26	27	28	29	30	31
Mandy:																															
1 Set the dinner table	✓																														
2 Wash dishes																															
3	✓																														
4																															
Stephen:																															
1 Clear the dinner table	✓																														
2 Dry dishes	✓																														
3																															
4																															
David																															
1 Feed the dog	✓																														
2 Put away clean dishes	✓																														
3																															
4																															

List the jobs assigned to each family member and tick off the jobs completed each day
(N.B. Reusable form in Appendix 3)

Select consequences for failure to complete chores.

If the programme is linked to a pocket money system, those children who fail to do their assigned jobs simply do not get the amount specified for that job. Logical consequences can also be used, such as insisting that chores be completed before children are allowed out to play or to watch TV. Don't get trapped into allowing the child to do something if she promises to do her chores when she has finished. Children often manipulate parents into agreeing to this and then the child doesn't keep to the bargain.

Explain the incentives and consequences.

Let your children know what will happen if they complete their chores or fail to complete them. Then test the system for a week.

Remind your children of the rules before you start.

In particular, ask your child to describe what has to be done today.

Select times for doing daily chores that give the child some choice.

Generally homework should be done before chores are tackled. Give the child a specific time when the chores must be completed by but let the child decide when and how the tasks will be done.

Avoid hassling your child about starting the chores.

Give one reminder that chores need to be done by the specific time and then leave your child alone. Don't get trapped into giving repeated reminders or instructions to begin.

Attend to your child while he is busy.

Try to catch your child being good, and praise him during or immediately after completing individual tasks.

Help your child get started.

Children may initially need help in getting started, particularly if the job is a new one. Use 'ask, say, do' (see page 60) to help them learn the correct way of completing the job.

Provide back-up consequences at the agreed check time.

At the agreed time, quickly check which tasks have been completed and fill in the chart for each child on that day. It is important that children learn to complete each task satisfactorily. You should not reward sloppy or half-completed jobs. At the same time, don't expect a perfect performance. You will need to make a judgement here about whether the job is up to scratch.

Hold another family meeting to review progress.

At the end of the first week, hold another family meeting to review progress. This should involve giving children feedback on tasks they have completed regularly, asking for their opinions about how the first week has gone, and asking for their views on changes that might need to be made. You should also offer your own views on changes. For example, there may be certain jobs such as raking up leaves, vacuuming a swimming pool, or drying dishes, that can be rotated. It is often easier to rotate on a weekly basis rather than on alternate days to avoid the problem of children saying, 'I washed the dishes last night, it's Rosemary's turn tonight'.

Use cue cards as reminders.

Write down each child's daily and weekly chores on a large card and stick it on the child's bedroom wall. These cards can be useful in the early stages as an extra reminder.

Decide whether to phase out reminders, monitoring, and incentives.

Once children are in a good routine and are completing chores with a minimum of fuss, you will need to decide whether to phase out the jobs chart. Some large families find it very convenient to continue to use the chart and often do so for years. However, in smaller families, the chart can be phased out once the children know what to do. If you decide to phase out the chart, use the following strategy. Start off by reducing the amount of positive attention you give to the child while she is completing the chores, but continue to praise your child at the end of each day. Next, wait until two then three days pass before checking off the chart. Once this has been done, take down the chart altogether.

Increasing the number of chores.

As children progress through primary school, they become capable of learning more complex and responsible tasks. New tasks can be introduced and added to the new chart. When this occurs, simple daily chores that have become habits can be left off the chart.

It is only in this century that children have not been expected to work. Last century children as young as 5 worked in British coal mines for up to 12 hours a day, and were considered a vital part of the work force. Child labour laws were necessary to protect children from this kind of abuse. By contrast, many children in modern families contribute very little to the running of the family. The pendulum perhaps has swung too far. Common sense and balance should prevail. One 8-year-old girl I worked with was required to prepare the breakfast for a family of five, and to wake her mother for work with breakfast in bed at 8.30 a.m.. The child also made school lunches and did all the dishes on her own. This child was being abused in my view.

Always remember that chores should not be so time consuming that children's needs in other areas are neglected. They still need time for play, fun, hobbies, sport, and homework.

Pocket money

How soon should children get an allowance? Many parents start giving children a small regular allowance during a child's primary school years. The allowance given obviously depends on the family's financial circumstances. Some children earn as little as 20 cents, others are given $10 or more. From the age of 7 or 8 an allowance is generally a good idea. It gives children an opportunity to learn to save and manage small amounts of money. They can also learn the value of money and the cost of items they would like to buy, as well as make the connection between work and financial reward. Many problems over the money children receive from parents can be avoided with a properly planned allowance system. Some children think money grows on trees. They expect parents to have an unlimited supply, a myth supported by parents who give their children whatever they ask for. Many families start a pocket money system but don't operate it consistently. One week the child gets it, the next week they don't. Sometimes the allowance is in return for chores, at other times it's not. As they approach adolescence, many children complain about the amount they get compared with their friends, and so on. Sometimes parents refuse to give their child pocket money because they believe they will spend it all on rubbish.

Here are some ideas for setting up a pocket money system that is within a family's budget. It is often a good idea to start off a pocket money system with a savings plan for your child.

Decide on the amount you can afford.

Before speaking to your child about pocket money, chat to neighbours and friends about the going rate and the way other parents handle the issue. Work out approximately how much you already spend on each child on extras such as sweets, toys, gifts, outings, movies, and so on. Some of this money may be able to be used as pocket money. Look at your family budget realistically to decide what you can afford. It is not a good idea for young children to have access to large amounts of money. As a rough guide, a 7- or 8-year-old could earn between 50 cents and $2.00; an 8- to 9-year-old from $1 to $3.00; a 10- to 11-year-old from $2 to $4, and 12-year-olds up to $6 or $7. There are no hard and fast rules. The amount will depend on your means.

Decide how much should be spent by the child and how much banked.

A 50/50 split often works well. As your child is likely to be banking small amounts, it might be a good idea to establish a bonus system. For example, you might match every $5 your child saves if she is saving up for a new pair of skates.

Decide how much should be received automatically and how much 'earned'.

It is a good idea to give the child one-third to one-half of the allowance automatically, with the rest to be earned through doing chores and odd jobs. In essence, the child gets a bonus for helping out around the home.

Discuss the plan with your child.

Hold a discussion with your child to introduce the plan. Explain what you propose and what she is required to do to get money. Let your child know she may spend one-half or one-third of the money on whatever she likes and must bank the rest.

Decide on a regular pay day.

It is important that you stick to this. Make sure you always have enough small change or notes to pay the required amount. Every Friday night or Saturday morning is a good time.

Open a bank account with your child.

Many schools have a school banking facility. Get your child to fill out the relevant application forms under your guidance and open the account with a starting deposit.

Encourage your child to set savings goals.

Some children will immediately want to set themselves a savings goal, for example for a new bike, skateboard, record, or cassette, and this should be encouraged. Suggest but don't insist on a savings target. Some children just like the money to accumulate.

Keep track of chores completed towards pocket money.

Use a chart similar to the one in figure 10 opposite for keeping track of whether your child has completed the chores linked to earning pocket money. Not all chores should attract pocket money. Routine daily jobs should be left out. Weekend and other odd jobs are good for earning pocket money.

Let your child spend the money he has earned without too much interference.

If children ask for your opinion on what to buy, then give it. But let them make the decision. Let them spend some of their money on sweets if they wish. There may be some things you need to ban for children on special diets. Children should be encouraged to compare the prices of similar items in different shops so as to get value for money. Wise shopping comes with opportunities to make choices and with practice. Children's banking and shopping can be linked to your own shopping. Be prepared to allow children some time to do their shopping after or during the time you do your own.

Give children positive feedback for good purchasing.

Take an interest in what your child wants to buy. Offer praise and attention any time your child shows evidence of having shopped wisely. For example, if your child compares two similarly priced items and chooses the one that is more robust and likely to last longer, let her know why you think that was a good choice.

Avoid criticising your child's choices.

Don't get too upset if your child wants to buy something you consider a waste of money. She will become more skilled with practice.

Try to avoid letting large amounts of money accumulate in a child's money-box. Let the child bank even small amounts on a regular basis so that he can see the balance grow. An efficiently run pocket money system is an excellent way of giving children opportunities to become more independent and more skilled at making decisions to do with money. You should be prepared to adjust the allowance periodically because of inflation and the fact that

Figure 10: Pocket money chart

Month: _____ April _____

Chores to be done	Value	Week 1	Week 2	Week 3	Week 4
1 Hang out washing	40 cents	40 cents			
2 Clean up leaves	60 cents	—			
3 Sweep out garage	40 cents	40 cents			
4					
5					
Amount earned	$1.40	80 cents			

List the chores to be done and the value assigned to each task, then total the pocket money earned each week.

the child is getting older. Sometimes younger siblings will object to older siblings earning more money. Don't get trapped into feeling you have to treat each child the same way. However, be absolutely consistent so that when the younger child reaches the older child's age, he receives the equivalent amount.

Watching television

There has been much written both by scientists and in the mass media about the effects of television on children. It has been blamed for the increase in violence and juvenile crime, for family breakups, and for children's poor school performance. Many parents are concerned about the amount of violence children see on television cartoons and other shows.

There is little doubt that television does have a major impact on children. However, the connection is a complex one. The average 7- to 11-year-old watches 21 hours of television each week. This is an enormous slice of their time. In some families, watching the television is the only hobby the family has. The box is on from the time a child wakes in the morning until she retires at night.

Television has both positive and negative aspects. The good aspects include the fact that carefully selected programmes are both enjoyable and informative for children. Television can encourage fantasy and enable children to see people, animals, places, things, and events they may never actually experience. Shows such as 'Sesame Street' have gained such a good reputation because young children both enjoy them and learn from them. Television can also be used as a way of helping children relax and wind down after school or boisterous activity.

The negative aspects of television for children include the fact that there are still very few high quality productions designed especially for children. Many stations rely on filling children's TV time with violent cartoons or repeats of old comedies or soaps. Apart from the quality of programming, if children spend huge amounts of time watching television, other important activities can be neglected. These include homework, outdoor play, exercise, reading, and time for parents and children to communicate. Television watching is a passive activity. Activities that are interactive tend to be remembered more easily and therefore help learning. In other words, children often get more out of doing rather than simply watching.

The effects of television on children depend on a host of factors. These include how much they watch, whether their viewing habits are monitored by parents, and whether they have an opportunity to talk to their parents about confusing or upsetting programmes.

Television is neither good nor bad for children. It can be both under certain circumstances. It is important for parents to establish good television routines in the family. Here are some ideas about how to avoid problems, especially arguments over television watching.

Decide how many hours per week you will allow your child to watch TV.

This is probably one of the most important decisions you can make. In making this judgement, estimate how much your child watches at the moment. You may be staggered by the result. I would recommend a maximum of only one hour per day during the school week and a little longer on the weekend.

Tell your child about the plan.

Tell your child that from now on he can only watch programmes he has selected in advance from the TV guide.

Ask your child to select the programmes she wants to watch.

Go through the TV guide with your child and write down the shows she wants to watch. Some children may want to watch several programmes on a particular day. That is fine so long as the total weekly hours are not exceeded.

Explain the new ground rules for TV time.

These should include the following:
- only watch selected programmes;
- the television will be turned off for the rest of the day if there are any arguments over channels, or if the child turns on the TV at any other time;
- no TV before homework is completed;
- no boisterous play or fighting while watching TV.

Reach a compromise if children want to watch different programmes at the same time.

You may have to arbitrate here.

Keep a lookout for potentially interesting and suitable programmes for children

Be prepared to let children watch extra television if a particularly suitable programme such as a movie or educational programme is scheduled. These can be bonus extras you give to your child at your discretion.

If children break the rules, follow through with the planned consequences.

It is important that you break the habit children have of turning on television 'just to see what's on'. Any time this or one of the other rules is broken, cancel the child's viewing for that night. Ignore protests. If it happens again, unplug the television and remove it from the lounge room.

Reward children for complying with the rules.

If your child sticks to the rules, get a video or allow him to watch extra TV on the weekend as a treat.

Praise your child for participating in other activities.

Children will be less interested in TV if they receive attention and praise for selecting activities at times that were previously used for watching TV.

Control your child's access to other sets.

If there is more than one set in the house, you'll need to be especially watchful. It is much more difficult to enforce consistent rules if children have sets in their bedrooms. Consider selling such sets.

Sometimes parents contribute to problems over television because they themselves have become addicts. Some people use TV as company, or to provide background noise in much the same way that the radio used to be used. The early evening viewing time can be a particular problem if one of the parents likes to watch the news on arrival home from work. The programme will be easier to enforce if you watch most of your television after the children are in bed.

Many families who have made the decision to cut down on TV watching report some important changes in their family: parents start to talk to each other more, children get interested in hobbies and out-door activities, parents and children have more time for each other, children start to show an interest in reading, and the family computer starts getting used again. Children may also learn to amuse them-selves without having to be entertained all the time.

Sportsmanship

Primary school children are often expected to participate in activities that involve being a member of a team. Team games occur in physical education programmes and as part of organised school sports teams. Children may also join a club out of school hours, where they receive coaching in a variety of competitive sports such as soccer, rugby, hockey, netball, basketball, tennis, cricket, and so on. Many children find being a member of a team a very enjoyable experience. It is not only an opportunity to develop their physical coordination and receive regular exercise, but is also an opportunity to meet other children, make new friends, and to learn about teamwork and competition. Children's sporting activities are also a source of pleasure and pride for many parents, particularly if a child appears to have talent.

Such activities can also be a source of great frustration. As a coach of junior rugby I have often been aware of the pressures that parents can place on young children. It is not uncommon for families to experience tears and sore tummies on Saturday mornings before matches. Parents have been known to berate and abuse their children from the sidelines for dropped catches, missed tackles, not running hard enough, or appearing uninterested in the game. Winning often becomes the all-important goal for both parents and coaches and too much pressure from either source can create anxiety and other emotional problems in children. Parents may be unable to accept that their child dislikes, is not interested in, or has limited ability in a particular sport, especially if the parent was good at the sport as a child.

Other children are bad sports. For example, they gloat when they win, are ungracious in defeat, and might refuse to try a new activity if they think they can't do it. Some children will reluctantly join in with a lot of prodding from their parents but then refuse or complain bitterly about playing the game again. Coaches of children's sports have a big responsibility to ensure that children receive encouragement and proper instruction but still have fun while they are playing sport. This is not an easy task, particularly when coaches may be volunteers with little or no training in coaching techniques and have to deal with large numbers of children. They have to ensure that the activities are closely supervised and that children receive proper skill development to make sure the game is played safely. This is particularly important in contact sports where injuries can and do occur. Some children can also be quite disruptive and disobedient when participating in sporting activities, and are capable of ruining the enjoyment of other children because of their behaviour.

What can parents do to encourage children to participate in

sporting and other recreational activities and to develop sportsmanlike behaviour?

Spend time with your child to help her develop her coordination.

During the toddler and preschool years, be prepared to spend time
with your child playing games that involve developing coordination
and physical activity. There are a wide variety of activities that
promote children's muscle development and coordination. Hopping,
skipping, jumping, playing catch, rolling a ball to each other, throwing a ball, balancing games, taking walks, jogging, bushwalking,
backpacking, climbing, kicking a ball, and so on. Children often love
to play active games with their parents, particularly if the parent is
encouraging and avoids criticising their child for not being able to
master a skill. Parents who are active themselves through regular
exercise are more likely to develop active children. They learn a lot
through observation as well as practice. Remember to give lots of
praise and attention for small improvements in skill in these activities.

Be observant and take note of those activities your child is interested in or seems to enjoy.

Children differ a great deal in their coordination and a child who
appears poorly coordinated as a 6-year-old may catch up and be
particularly good at a sport as a 15-year-old. If children express an
interest in playing a particular sport or joining a team that their
friends belong to then be prepared to let them join, even if it is not a
sport you are particularly interested in. Children often develop interests in sports they play at school, have friends involved in, or that
their parents show an interest in. There is little doubt that children's
interests in particular sports can be influenced by parents, however it
is important for parents to avoid narrowing their child's choices too
soon. This can be done unintentionally when parents are critical of
specific sports, fail to show an interest in the child when he talks
about a sport, or tries to play it in games. Unless you feel the sport is
particularly dangerous or too expensive, have an open mind and
encourage experimentation so children can decide for themselves
what they would like to play.

Let children experience many different sports.

Parents should allow children to change their minds at the end of a
season about the sports they wish to play. If a child wants to play netball one year then change to tennis the next, let her do so. It is not a

good idea to allow children to withdraw from a sport once they have started a season unless you are concerned about how they are treated by the coach and the child is obviously distressed by the experience. The main reasons for encouraging children to continue until the end of the season are the expense involved in changing and the fact that some children learn quickly that if they kick up a fuss they will be allowed to avoid activities about which they initially lack confidence. The problem here is that the child might try the same tactic again. Confidence comes with practice and persistence, not by copping out.

Attend training sessions and games as often as possible.

It is a good idea for parents to attend training or practice sessions as often as possible, particularly the first few times. Children often approach new activities with some hesitation. This can be helped by knowing that their parent is there taking an interest. It also gives you an opportunity to see the coaching methods and approach employed. If the team's coach spends the whole time yelling and screaming at the kids, you might be better off finding another club. During training sessions and matches, watch your child closely and take particular note of what he does well. Remember that because your child is learning a sport, his performance should be compared with his previous efforts rather than with the efforts of other children. Specific comments after a game or practice will assist the child's motivation to improve further.

Offer to help.

Junior sport often suffers from a lack of parent support and involvement. Some parents act as taxi drivers for their children and leave all the rest of the work to other parents. If your schedule permits, take an active interest. Offer your help. Don't wait to be asked. Don't feel you have to be an expert in the sport to be of assistance. Also, don't be disappointed if your offer is declined, because at least you've made the effort. Your involvement can heighten your child's interests in the activity.

Encourage regular attendance and make sure your child is on time.

There is nothing more frustrating for coaches than to have children who simply don't turn up and don't notify them. If your child is ill or there is an emergency that prevents regular attendance, make sure you ring the coach or manager of your child's team. Don't give your child a bad name by always being 10 or 20 minutes late.

Avoid harassing your child during a game.

This is something many parents find very difficult to do. Comments from the sidelines during children's sport have to be heard to be believed. Grown men have been know to come to blows over refereeing decisions or the outcome of games. They abuse referees or opposition players, question decisions, and swear at their own child for not playing well. This type of behaviour provides a bad model for children and is usually motivated by an excessive emphasis on winning rather than on participation and enjoyment. There is absolutely no place for violent or abusive behaviour from parents during children's sport. This does not mean that parents should not enjoy the game, become excited, and cheer to offer support and encouragement. Many children, particularly when they first start organised sport, have no idea of the score or indeed who won, and usually it doesn't matter to them at all. This situation changes rapidly when children reach the age of 9 or 10.

Provide encouraging feedback at the end of the game.

Find something positive to say about the team's and your child's performance. Don't give negative feedback, leave that to the coach. If your child asks you for ideas about how the team's performance could be improved, offer your suggestions. Children respond better to one or two quite specific suggestions that you can demonstrate for them rather than a whole list of faults.

Dealing with poor sportsmanship.

Poor sportsmanship can come in many different forms, ranging from cheating to abusing opponents or referees, or displays of temper. Children who are bad sports are quite competitive and their parents may have observed similar behaviour at home during children's games. Sportsmanlike conduct should involve keeping to the rules of the game and acting in an appropriate manner whether you win, lose, or draw. If you notice poor behaviour during a game then, after the activity is over, describe what the child did wrong: 'Throwing your racket into the net is being a bad sport'. Describe what the child should have done instead: 'If you feel frustrated during the game, take a deep breath and count to 10'. Then provide an appropriate back-up consequence.

The consequence you select should be appropriate to the problem, as the following example illustrates. During a holiday at the beach, the Smith family was playing a game of cricket with two other families. There was an equal number of adults and children on each side. Robert, aged 7, was batting at one end and his mother was at the other. Robert swung and missed the first ball he received. The second ball bowled him middle stump. At that point he burst into tears and stormed off the pitch, throwing his cricket bat as he left. He refused to join the fielding team. It was a very embarrassing episode for the mother but she took the following decisive action. She immediately ran over to the child, reprimanded him for being a bad sport, took him back to the batting crease despite the struggle, and twice made him practise placing the bat down in the proper way. She then made him sit in time out on his own, off the pitch, for 2 minutes. As soon as the 2 minutes were over, she took him by the hand to take up his fielding position. The action was powerful and decisive. Robert quickly learned that temper outbursts would not work during cricket matches.

Many parents have very mixed feelings about competitive sport, particularly if their child shows talent. While a child's achievements are a source of pride and pleasure, parents often feel uncomfortable about the competitive aspects of sport. High achievers in many sports have to make tremendous sacrifices in normal family life. These include long hours of training and reduced opportunities to experience activities undertaken by other children of the same age. Children's sport can come to dominate a family's existence if parents let this happen, to the extent that every weekend is committed, families don't go on outings, and schoolwork and normal recreation are neglected. It is important to maintain a balance so children can still experience a full range of opportunities and experiences. No one activity should be allowed to take over completely, whether it is sport, music, schoolwork, watching television, or anything else.

Other parents become concerned about the competitive nature of sport itself. They feel that too much emphasis on winning, training, and competing, rather than on participation, can be harmful, particularly for young children. These are reasonable concerns, and parents and coaches of young children need to make sure children are protected from unnecessary emphasis on winning at all costs. Excellence does not necessarily mean beating the other person.

Many of the issues raised in relation to children's sport also apply to other activities, such as learning a musical instrument, speech and drama, and so on. Because sport is so highly prized in our society, it may lead parents to neglect children's interests and abilities in artistic, musical, and literary fields. Parents should allow children to pursue and develop these interests as they emerge, and provide as much encouragement and support as they would for sporting involvement. Too many parents label certain activities as 'sissy' or 'unladylike', and try to discourage their children's interest in them.

Bedwetting

Many children who are toilet trained during the day continue to wet their beds at night until the age of 7 or 8. Bedwetting, or nocturnal enuresis, is a condition where the child has not learned voluntary night-time control over his bladder and continues to wet after this age. Approximately 15 to 20 per cent of 4- and 5-year-olds, 5 per cent of 10-year-olds and 1 to 2 per cent of 15-year-olds wet the bed. In most cases there is no organic or physical cause for the bedwetting.

Nevertheless, enuretic children tend to have smaller bladder capacities than non-enuretic children. Bedwetting often seems to run in families and many bedwetters have one parent who wet the bed as a child, suggesting a strong genetic component. Many parents of bedwetters report that their children are very heavy sleepers and difficult to wake at night.

Children who continue to wet the bed throughout primary school are often very embarrassed by their problem. Sleeping over at other children's places or going on school camps creates considerable anxiety. Parents also become understandably anxious and worried about their child's wetting. Most family problems tend to be a consequence of the bedwetting rather than a cause, and once the child stops wetting the bed other problems often disappear. Children almost never wet the bed because they are lazy, stupid, sick, or defiant.

Some children wet the bed every night, while others wet once or twice a week but then experience periods of dryness for a week or longer. There is little evidence to show that bedwetting is related to allergies, disturbed family patterns, or psychiatric disturbance.

Bedwetting can be successfully treated in over 90 per cent of cases, although up to 40 per cent of children will relapse and require further treatment. There are several successful treatments, all of which require parental involvement. The most successful methods are the urine alarm device, dry bed training, and retention control training. In general, parents should seek professional advice to confirm the diagnosis and to help tackle the problem in the most appropriate manner. Here are some guidelines.

Consult your family doctor.

Your child should undergo a thorough medical examination to make sure there is no specific physical cause for the problem and to make the correct diagnosis.

Get a referral to a competent professional.

If your doctor suggests a referral to a paediatrician, psychologist, or psychiatrist, make sure you find out whether this person has specific interests, skills, and experience in dealing with enuresis, and ask what approach they take to treatment. Professional training does not guarantee that the person you are referred to has the necessary expertise to provide competent treatment for urinary incontinence problems. It is important that the person has specific experience and training in the use of behaviour modification techniques.

Make sure you ask questions.

Normally you and your child would take part in an intake interview, where the professional is interested in finding out as much as possible about the problem, the child's developmental history, and any other problems in the family. Such questions are important to ensure that the best possible treatment is offered.

Remember to ask questions yourself about the treatment proposed, its usual success rate with similar problems, how long it takes, what is involved, what specifically you will be required to do and, of course, the cost of the treatment.

Consider the treatment options.

The following are the most commonly used treatments for enuresis.

The urine alarm device, known as the 'bell and pad' device, is the most widely used form of treatment. A urine-sensitive foil pad connected to a buzzer or bell is placed on the child's bed. When the child wets, the urine completes a circuit and the alarm sounds, waking the child. The child is then expected to get up and complete their urination on the toilet. The basic idea behind this treatment is that if the bell or buzzer that wakes the child is repeatedly paired with the sensations associated with a full bladder, the child will eventually learn to wake up and inhibit urination. Over time, the child learns to wake up when his bladder is full instead of to the alarm. The alarm device is typically kept on the child's bed until 14 consecutive dry nights have been achieved.

This method has a good success rate, with more than 80 per cent of children stopping wetting. However, some children (approximately 30 per cent) relapse within the next few months, requiring a further period of treatment. This second treatment is usually successful.

Parents have an important role to play in this treatment. Be prepared for a few disturbed nights yourself as the alarm will often wake parents who need to make sure the child wakes up and goes to the toilet. You will also be asked to keep track of the child's dry nights using some kind of behaviour chart. Give praise and positive attention for successes.

Dry bed and cleanliness training is often used together with the urine alarm device. It involves the child repeatedly practising the correct toileting behaviour before retiring (lying in bed, waking up, and running to the toilet) and as an immediate consequence of wetting at night. The child is also expected to take complete responsibility for any accidents by removing dirty sheets, placing them in the washing machine, remaking the bed, resetting the alarm, and so on. Again, give praise and positive attention for successes. Parents sometimes find it difficult to get a half-awake child to go through these routines, and some children protest about being forced to do so. The advantage of the combined treatment, however, is that the child is taught proper cleanliness routines and is expected to take some responsibility for dealing with the problem. Dry bed training can also be a successful treatment and tends to have a lower relapse rate.

Bladder retention training is a technique that aims to eliminate bedwetting by increasing children's bladder capacity. Children are asked to drink fluids and to hold on for longer and longer periods during the day before they urinate. This strategy is intended to expand bladder capacity and so reduce the need for night-time urination. This procedure on its own is successful with less than 50 per cent of bedwetters, but is sometimes used together with the urine alarm device and dry bed training.

Some children respond to **drugs** to eliminate bedwetting. The most popular drug used in the treatment of bedwetting is imipramine hydrochloride, known by the brand name Tofranil, which is an antidepressant drug whose side effect is retention of urine. Drug treatment on its own is rarely an effective long-term cure, since the majority of children relapse as soon as they come off the medication.

Some children respond to fairly simple methods, such as using a star chart with a back-up reward for dry nights. However, if your child has a longstanding bedwetting problem and wetting occurs almost every night, this strategy is not likely to be as effective as other methods.

There is little evidence to show that other forms of therapy, such as family therapy, play therapy, or individual psychotherapy, are effective in eliminating bedwetting.

Various home remedies have been tried over the years, many of which are ineffective and some positively harmful. Parents who use severe punishment such as scolding or spanking for bedwetting often only make the child feel more anxious and inadequate. Some parents try to shame the child by hanging wet sheets out of her bedroom window. Other strategies, such as making the child sleep on her back, or trying to stop her sleeping on her back, or buying a hard mattress, are quite unsuccessful.

It is generally better to seek competent professional assistance with bedwetting, as modern treatment methods are usually quite successful.

Thumb and finger sucking

'Sarah, will you take your hand out of your mouth?' This is the exasperated plea of a parent who has just discovered her 7-year-old with her thumb in her mouth for the fourth time that morning, sucking furiously while her index finger is shoved up her right nostril. Thumb sucking is a very common behaviour in infants and young children and indeed can occur in a foetus in the womb. It occurs in almost all normal infants and then decreases throughout the pre-school years. About 10 per cent of 6- to 12-year-olds continue to suck their thumb or fingers. Thumb sucking, because it occurs so frequently and declines with age, is not a serious problem and not generally an indication of emotional or behavioural problems. However, it can become a source of friction and conflict between parents and children. In about 2 per cent of older children, the behaviour is clearly excessive and occurs whenever the child's hands are not

otherwise being used. It can occur both during the day and while the child is asleep.

There is little reason for parents of preschool children to be concerned about thumb sucking, although you might find the behaviour aesthetically displeasing, particularly when you have visitors. If the behaviour occurs very frequently, it can cause dental problems (severe malocclusion of the teeth) in older children that require treatment.

Thumb sucking in older children is often a habit they have developed and it is not generally a sign of emotional disturbance, although some disturbed youngsters may suck their thumb, fingers, hands, or arms.

Parents can reduce thumb sucking in several ways. One of the most effective is a technique known as habit reversal. If your child is sucking very frequently, or is developing buck teeth, or the thumb sucking is preventing your child from participating in other normal activities, then it is reasonable to help your child overcome this habit. Here are some guidelines.

Keep track of how often the behaviour occurs.

Instead of trying to note down every time your child sucks his thumb throughout the day, select a 1-hour time period where the behaviour occurs frequently. Use a behaviour diary similar to the one in figure 11 on page 234. Every 5 minutes, look at your child for 5 seconds and simply note down in the appropriate column whether or not he is sucking. Keep this record for a week. During this baseline period, continue to use your normal method of dealing with the problem. Your child should not know that you are monitoring his behaviour.

Hold a discussion with your child to introduce the programme.

After the one week baseline, explain to your child that you would like her to stop sucking her thumb. Tell her that you will help her learn to stop. Explain why you think it is important that she overcome the problem. You can mention the effects on teeth as well as aesthetic reasons such as it looks awful, is unattractive, unhygienic, and so on. Keep the explanation brief.

Explain the incentives for good performance.

Initially the child can earn a sticker on a chart for each 5 minutes without thumb sucking. The sticker can be whatever the child likes: a star, smiley face, a quickly drawn picture, or for older children, points

Figure 11: Baseline record of thumbsucking

Time	Date									
6 p.m.	10/6									
05 min	✓									
10 min										
15 min	✓									
20 min	✓									
25 min	✓									
30 min										
35 min	✓									
40 min										
45 min	✓									
50 min	✓									
55 min	✓									
60 min	✓									
Total	9									
%age	75									

Fill in the date and the time you begin monitoring, and place a tick in the appropriate box if thumbsucking is occuring at the time.

or ticks. Show the child a chart similar to the one in figure 12 on page 237. Explain that you will set a timer on the oven for 5 minutes and if she has not sucked she can earn a sticker. During the 1-hour period, a maximum of 12 stickers can be earned. If the child manages ten or better, a small back-up reward can be earned. Gradually increase the amount of time the child has to last before she can earn a sticker. This is explained later.

Suggest something the child can do during high-risk times.

The key is to find something else the child can do with his hands. Children who suck their thumbs a lot often do this when they are bored and are not meaningfully involved in activities. Try to find activities that involve the hands. If the child is watching television, which is often a high-risk time, he might interlock his fingers or clasp his hands together to prevent sucking whenever he feels the urge to put his hand near his mouth.

Introduce the child to habit reversal.

Each time you see your child sucking, she will be required to practise the correct behaviour repeatedly for a minute or so. When you observe your child sucking, say 'No, take your hand away from your mouth now. Do your exercises for 2 minutes.' The exercise required of the child is to repeatedly and slowly put the offending thumb to her mouth and to slowly lower her hand from the mouth, then interlock the fingers of one hand with the fingers of the other in her lap. The fingers should be interlocked tightly for 20 seconds. This exercise should be repeated five times. The parent should, if necessary, guide the child through the movements, ignoring protests. Once the exercise has finished, reset the clock for 5 minutes. In other words, each time your child sucks have her wait a further 5 minutes before she can earn a sticker. When you notice your child thumb sucking, speak matter of factly. Do not praise your child for doing the exercises.

Have a trial run with your child.

Demonstrate exactly what he will have to do if he sucks his thumb. Answer any questions your child may have. During the first few days, the programme should only operate during the selected 1-hour period until the child has mastered the goal of 60 minutes without sucking.

Remind the child of the rules.

Before you start, briefly remind the child of the rules.

Catch your child doing the right thing.

Offer encouraging comments frequently during the first hour while the child is engaged in an activity but not thumb sucking. 'That's 7 minutes now you've gone without sucking your thumb. Well done.' This helps focus the child's attention on her successes.

When sucking occurs, introduce the habit reversal procedure.

This must be done immediately, decisively, and every time the behaviour occurs.

Explain to your child that from now on she will have to last longer periods to earn back-up rewards.

Explain to your child that she must remember not to suck her thumb all day from now on. Divide the time your child is at home into 30-minute time blocks, using a chart similar to the one in figure 12 on page 237. If thumb sucking is also a problem at school, you might consider discussing the problem with the child's teacher with a view to setting up a home-school programme that also involves the teacher. If this is the case, refer to the guidelines for dealing with problems at school on pages 187–192. Continue the programme, using praise and rewards for the absence of thumb sucking and engagement in activities and habit reversal as a consequence for episodes of thumb sucking.

Phase the child off the programme

Once the child is able to go three days without thumb sucking, arrange a special treat such as taking him out for a meal or to a special activity in recognition of his efforts. After this, stop using the chart and praise the child occasionally but less and less frequently for solving his own problem.

Some children who suck their thumb during the day also suck in bed to help themselves get to sleep. Night-time thumb sucking can be dealt with by putting a bitter tasting substance on the thumb before retiring. On the first few nights, tell the child that after she is in bed and has fallen asleep you will check on her every 30 minutes until you go to bed. If she is not sucking when you come in, you will place a sticker on a chart in her bedroom. If the child lasts the whole night

Figure 12: Thumbsucking form for treatment monitoring

Name:_____ **Date:**_____ **Day:**_____

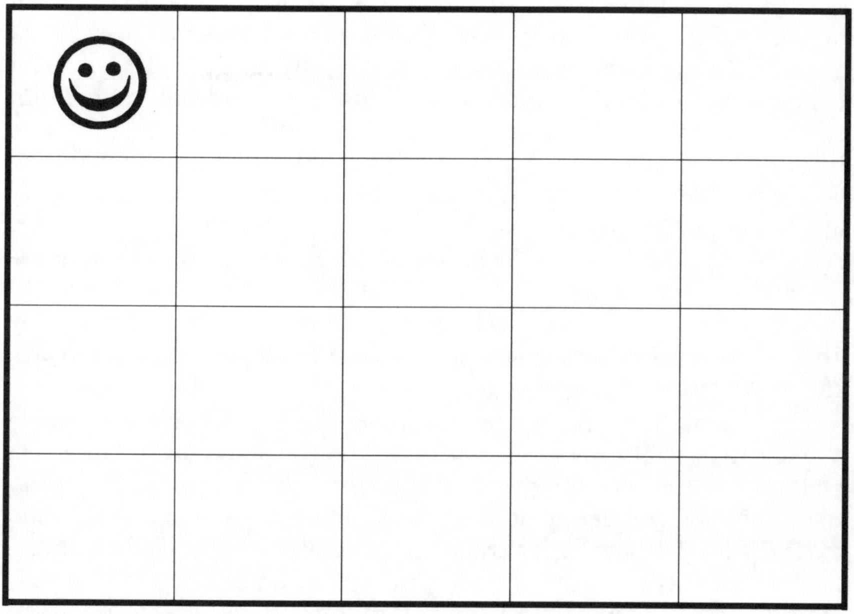

For each 30-minute interval in which thumbsucking does not occur, place a sticker or a smiley face in a square.

without sucking, a surprise treat can be put under her pillow in the morning.

Parents need to decide for themselves whether the time and effort involved in stopping a child from thumb sucking is worth it. As most children eventually grow out of the problem themselves, some parents may be prepared to endure the problem. However, if you do decide to try to reduce the problem then follow the programme guidelines carefully and consistently.

It is not a good idea to hassle, criticise, or keep giving instructions to children who thumb suck. Sometimes the extra attention they receive can make the problem worse. Furthermore, children can become quite frustrated and irritated when their attention is repeatedly but inconsistently drawn to the problem.

Bullying

Being bullied can be a traumatic experience for children and can seriously affect a child's attitude to school and academic progress. Bullying can range from minor teasing to threats of violence and actual assault. Children terrorised by a school bully may complain about feeling sick, and suffer abdominal pains before school; their sleep can be disturbed with nightmares, and bedwetting may be a problem. Bullying can take other forms, such as older children demanding younger children give them money, the stealing of a child's school lunch, being tripped up, pushed, made to stand at the back of a line, or being ridiculed or called names. Children with ginger hair, freckles, awkward gaits, big noses, ears that stick out, or who are members of a minority group, can be prime targets. Children who are shy and not very assertive or athletic, or are effeminate in mannerisms, can be teased and tormented.

Some of the worst bullying occurs when several children decide to pick on a child, making that child's life a nightmare. Parents of children on the receiving end of bullying are often extremely worried. They are frequently at a loss to know how to advise their child to deal with the problem, particularly when the child pleads with the parent not to contact the school. Children often fear reprisals if they are seen to have told tales or dobbed in the culprits. This is a particular problem with teenagers who are immature for their age. They may put up with months of bullying without telling a soul.

What should parents do if they discover their child has been bullied at school? Parents can sometimes help children handle minor teasing and bullying by helping them change the way they deal with the problem. Many children who are bullied make the problem worse by acting in ways that reward the culprit. For example, many bullies continue victimising particular children because the harassment pays off. The child reacts, becomes upset, cries, gives in, pays the money, gives the bully his lunch, and so on. These reactions often serve as rewards to a bully who is used to being able to manipulate others into submission. Often the behaviour at school is an extension of how the child behaves at home. Parents can help their child by using a two-pronged approach: coaching the child in better ways of reacting, and liaising with the school about the problem.

Some guidelines for helping children reduce bullying

If your child complains about being bullied, stop what you are doing, listen, and encourage him to describe exactly what has happened.

The best approach is to provide an attentive ear so as to encourage your child to describe what happened, whether it has happened before, and if so how often. Ask what the child did to deal with the problem. 'When he called you a sissy, what did you do?' Children will sometimes give vague answers, such as 'Nothing' or 'I tried to ignore him'. Prompt your child to elaborate and be more specific. 'When you say you did nothing, tell me exactly what you said or did.' Role playing can be useful here. 'OK I'm Bill, I come up and call you a sissy, and push you out of the line. What do you do?'

Avoid passing judgement, interrogation, over-reacting, or offering advice too soon.

Some parents immediately over-react, threatening to call the offending child's parents or the school immediately. This often backfires. Your child clams up or pleads with you not to say anything. Other parents immediately assume that it's all the other child's fault when their own child may be far from blameless. Don't act as a police interrogator. Children who are teased or bullied need to feel they can talk to you about the problem.

Ask the child what she has tried already to deal with the problem.

Sometimes children themselves have tried ways of dealing with the problem that could work if consistently employed. Typically, however, they try a tactic once or twice then give up because the bullying persists. Ask your child to describe exactly what happened when she tried each strategy. In other words, determine how successful the tactic was.

Summarise the problem as you understand it so far.

A summary draws together and highlights the key facts and issues involved and serves to focus the discussion. 'OK. So, since the beginning of term, Bill and Andrew have been teasing and bullying you at school by doing three things: calling you names, pushing in front of you when you lined up waiting to go into class, and threatening to belt you up after school. This has made you scared about going to school and you've been feeling sick in class. So far you've tried ignoring them but this seemed to make it worse, and once you told the teacher. Is that right?'

Acknowledge that a problem exists.

Let your child know that you think the bullying is definitely a problem and that you need to work out a solution together: 'This kind of stuff is just not on. We need to figure out a way of getting them to stop'.

Tell your child the possible reasons for the teasing or bullying.

Children are more likely to try a new way of handling the problem if they understand what is going on and are offered a plausible explanation as to why the problem continues. Many children will give very concrete reasons for bullying. 'Oh. He's just a bully,' or 'He's always like that. Everyone hates him,' or 'He's always getting into trouble.' Most children explain the problem in terms of the bully's negative personal characteristics. This rarely provides a basis for thinking of a way to deal with the problem. Sometimes it is helpful to give children some alternative ways of thinking about the problem. 'Let's try to think about why this happens. It sounds like Bill doesn't have too many friends. When he teases you, do any of the other kids laugh and join in?' 'Yes, I thought so. Maybe he does this to show the other kids how smart and tough he is. So one possibility is that he does it to get attention. Another one is that he picks on you because it works. He gets what he wants. Remember you said that last time when he pushed in front of you he got away with it? Maybe he's like a fisherman. You know, when you go fishing you put some bait on a hook and dangle it in the water to tempt the fish to bite. When a fish comes along, it takes the bait and is hooked. If the fish keep biting, the fisherman thinks he's pretty cool and keeps coming back to the same spot. But what happens when the fish stop biting?' 'Yes, that's right, the fisherman gives up. Maybe Bill is so used to getting a bite when he teases you that he keeps doing it. What do you reckon?'

Ask your child for his opinion on how best to deal with the problem.

The next step involves engaging your child in a problem-solving process. Many children are initially at a loss to know how to solve the problem and they may need help in generating ideas. Start by asking your child a fairly general question. 'So how do you want to handle this problem?' 'What else could you try if Bill teases you again?'

If the child says nothing or is unable to come up with a solution, suggest 'brainstorming' as a way of tackling the problem.

If the child appears stuck, get out a piece of paper and ask her to think of as many solutions to the problem as she can, no matter how crazy the ideas might sound. If your child suggests something, write it down and repeat it. Do not pass judgement on whether the idea is a good one or not. Just say 'OK that's one option. Let's think of a few more before you decide what to do.' If you think of other options, write them down after your child has finished. There are a number of things that a parent might suggest. These include teaching the child to ignore the teasing by yawning and walking away as soon as it occurs; encouraging the child to make friends with other children so she is not on her own during recess; teaching her to make assertive statements, and so on.

Review your list of possible solutions.

Once you have generated about eight to ten options, ask your child's opinion about each one. Put a tick beside those options that seem reasonable and cross out those that seem impractical or unlikely to work.

Help your child select a solution.

Practise the selected solution.

This involves role playing with your child exactly what he should do the next time that the problem arises. You should play the role of the problem child and your child should play himself. It can be introduced like this: 'Let's pretend I'm Bill and I come up to you and say, "Why don't you get lost, sissy." What should you say? You show me what you will do.' Provide feedback on the things you liked about what he did and then suggest things he might do differently. Keep practising and giving feedback until the child is able to carry out his plan reasonably well.

Consider other options.

If the bullying was serious and involved violence or threats you should also consider contacting the child's teacher about the problem. Some bullying stops as soon as the school becomes aware of the problem and the culprit is spoken to and monitored a bit more closely for a while. However, many children want to deal with the problem themselves. Respect these wishes unless the problem continues. Some children cannot carry out their plans because they lack the skills and confidence to confront their assailant. If this is the case, you could also consider getting your child into a social skills training group run by a professional therapist. Some parents immediately consider countering aggression with aggression, and send their child to karate, judo, or other self-defence classes. This strategy can backfire if the child has no real interest in these activities.

Keep track of how your child makes out.

For the first few weeks, ask your child each day about school and find out how her plan is going. Praise your child for employing her strategy, and note any signs that she is worrying less about the problem.

If the problem persists or escalates, arrange a conference with the child's teacher.

Discuss your concerns with the child's teacher, find out whether the school is aware of the problem, and talk about what can be done to overcome it. Follow up this discussion (if necessary) with a formal letter of complaint to the school about the incident. Be as clear and specific as possible and include details like the alleged dates, times, and children involved.

A conference with the offending child and his parents may be arranged by the school.

Handling children's fears

Fear is a normal emotional reaction to threatening or dangerous events. All human beings are afraid of something. Fear typically involves a subjective sense of anxiety, physiological arousal, which can include increased heart rate, blood pressure, and respiration rates, sweating, shaking, and hand tremors, and avoidance or escape from the feared object. When children are frightened of something, they may also shriek, scream, or run to their parents seeking comfort. Children's fears are much more common than was once thought. More than one-third of children between the ages of 2 and 14 experience fear that is intense enough to interfere with their daily lives.

There is an extremely wide range of things that children can be afraid of. The exact fear depends somewhat on the child's age.

Table 4 on page 244 includes a list of common fears experienced by children at different ages. You will notice that the specific fears experienced by children change with age.

When fear becomes intense, is clearly irrational in the sense that the amount of fear aroused does not match the objective danger, and significantly interferes with a child's normal activities, it is defined as a phobia.

Why do children develop fears and why do some fears persist? Some fears are learned through direct experience of the fear stimulus. One way this can occur is through **classical conditioning**. This involves children learning to associate a particular stimulus, such as the sight of a dog, with another stimulus, such as a dog barking or growling, that produces fear. For example, a child walking home from school might be confronted by a dog which approaches and starts barking loudly. This loud, sudden, unexpected noise may produce an automatic fear reaction, and the child may also learn to fear other stimuli that preceded or were associated with the original frightening experience or event, that is the sight of a large dog, or walking past a particular house. The fear of a specific dog might be transferred to other dogs, even if they are some distance away. Whenever he sees a dog the child may cling, shake, hide, or in some other way try to avoid the feared object. This process of **avoiding** a feared object prevents the child from confronting his fear and thereby overcoming it.

Fears can also be developed through **observation and imitation**. For example, if a child observes a parent or older sibling scream and shriek at the sight of a spider or cockroach, the child may also learn to fear the same object. Many children learn to fear precisely the same things their parents are afraid of.

A third way fear can develop is through **directly rewarding a fear response**. For example, if a child displays fear in a particular situation, such as when her bedroom light is turned out at night, and the parent gives the child a lot of attention and reassurance, or spends time soothing, stroking or calming the child while leaving the light on, the child may be directly rewarded for her fear reaction or, more accurately, for not confronting the basis of her fear.

It is believed that the capacity to develop fear is partly inherited. Children appear to differ from birth in how easily fears can be conditioned or learned. Children who from very early in life react with distress to sudden changes, noises, strangers, or other sudden

Table 4: Common fears across age groups

	Age groups				
8-10 years		**11-13 years**		**14-16 years**	
Item description	% reporting this fear	Item description	% reporting this fear	Item description	% reporting this fear
Nuclear war	68	Nuclear war	80	Nuclear war	69
Being hit by a car	72	Not being able to breathe	62	Not being able to breathe	55
Not being able to breathe	68	Being hit by a car or truck	62	Bombing attacks —being invaded	53
Bombing attacks —being invaded	65	Bombing attacks —being invaded	62	Being hit by a car or truck	50
Earthquakes	62	Earthquakes	51	Fire — getting burned	48
Falling from high places	58	Fire — getting burned	51	Falling from high places	42
A burglar breaking into our house	56	A burglar breaking into our house	47	A burglar breaking into our house	39
Fire — getting burned	52	Falling from high places	46	Snakes	39
Being sent to the principal	47	Snakes	40	Spiders	36
Getting lost in a strange place	46	Death or dead people	39	Earthquakes	35

Adapted from N.J. King et al (1989). 'Fears of children and adolescents: A cross-section Australian study using the Revised Fear Survey Schedule for Children'. *Journal of Child Psychology and Psychiatry, 30,* 775-784. Pergamon Press. Reproduced by permission.

stimulation, appear to learn fear reactions more quickly than more placid infants.

How can parents help their children overcome a fear? Children are most likely to be successful when they confront the source of their fear, while at the same time learning a new way of handling their anxiety. The key to overcoming fear is to help your child face the situation that provokes distress. Here are some guidelines.

Avoid modelling fearful reactions.

Since children learn a great deal through observation, it is important to keep your own anxieties and irrational fears in check. This means avoiding becoming highly emotional or agitated when you confront things that make you feel uncomfortable. Indeed, some parents find that acting bravely when they are with their child in a situation of threat is a very powerful way of confronting their own fear.

Model active coping rather than avoidance.

Be prepared to talk to your child about situations where you have felt awkward, embarrassed, or fearful, and tell him how you overcame your fear. Many adults have experienced anxiety in social situations that involve meeting new people and it may be helpful to discuss how you dealt with this problem if your child is experiencing similar problems.

Praise your child for tackling or confronting situations that were previously avoided.

Praise is a very effective strategy for helping children tackle and confront feared situations. If your child has been very reluctant to invite other children home to play then one day makes the effort to do so, offer praise and encouragement. However, be careful not to go overboard as you might embarrass your child by drawing too much attention to her efforts.

Give your child something to do when confronting feared situations.

Teach your child active coping strategies to handle the feared situation. For example, if your child becomes uptight before tests or exams, teaching her simple relaxation techniques can be useful. Much of the research on the treatment of fear shows that when individuals have some specific active coping strategy for confronting fear, their anxiety is reduced.

Remain calm when your child is upset.

If your child is obviously becoming upset after having seen, touched, or heard something he is afraid of, do your best to remain cheerful, relaxed, and in control. You will only make the situation worse if you allow your child's distress to affect your own actions.

Be firm but positive.

Sometimes children must tackle things they are afraid of despite this fear, for example going to the dentist, receiving an injection, or starting a new school. At these times do not allow your child to manipulate you into letting her avoid the situation. The child should be made to confront the situation, despite having some anxiety.

Talk to your child about situations of genuine threat or danger.

There are some situations that pose a genuine risk to children, such as riding bicycles on the road, crossing a busy street, open fires, being approached by strangers, and poisonous snakes or spiders. Parents can often help children learn to cope with these situations by discussing them and laying down clear, specific ground rules.

Enlist the help of other children.

Children often cope better with new and potentially frightening experiences if they are with other children of the same age. For example, if a child is anxious about starting school, a trip to the local school on a weekend with a child who already attends the school can be useful. The other child can tell your child about the school.

Deciding whether to seek professional help.

If your child develops a specific fear or is troubled generally by anxiety, you need to decide whether the fear reaction is sufficiently intense to justify seeking expert help. Generally speaking, if your child is genuinely phobic, that is the fear significantly interferes with her daily activities, or has a large number of specific fears, then it is worth seeking professional help. This help can be obtained by getting a referral to a clinical psychologist or psychiatrist who specialises in the management of anxiety problems. Generally speaking, treatments that involve children in actively learning to confront and deal with their anxieties are more effective than passive methods where a lot of talk takes place but little else happens.

Stomach pains

A surprisingly large number of children suffer from recurring aches and pains of one kind or another. One of the most common of these complaints is the infamous stomach ache. It is known medically as recurrent abdominal pain (RAP). Pain that is severe enough to interfere with a child's usual activities occurs in 10 to 15 per cent of school-aged children. In the vast majority of cases (90 to 95 per cent), medical investigation fails to show any specific organic cause that can explain the pain. Many children eventually grow out of the pain, although up to a third may experience pain for several years. Children suffering from RAP can experience considerable disruption to their normal lives, with sometimes quite intense episodes of distress. Parents often wonder whether the pain is 'real' or put on, particularly when no physical cause can be found. In the vast majority of cases children do indeed experience pain. It is rarely in their heads.

The cause of recurring stomach aches is not known. There are lots of theories but no one knows for sure why some children develop these problems and others do not. Some researchers think the pain is a symptom of psychological distress, particularly anxiety, conflict in the family, or the parents' marital problems, however there is little firm evidence to support this. In fact much of the evidence shows that most children with RAP are psychologically quite normal. Some researchers believe such children may have some ill-defined physiological disturbance that makes them vulnerable to abdominal distress.

More recently, researchers have looked at the possibility that children may learn pain behaviours within the family. It is important to remember that pain is a subjective experience. Individuals' sensitivity to painful stimulation, their tolerance of pain and how they act when in pain are influenced by a whole variety of factors. For example, one child will accidentally hit his thumb with a hammer, then wince, hold back tears, perhaps yell, but continue with the task despite the injury. Another child might literally scream the house down, bellowing and sobbing with such intensity that his parents are convinced he must have broken his leg.

The things children do and say when in pain are referred to as 'pain behaviours'. It is through these behaviours, such as complaining, bracing, guarded movement, lying down, resting, taking medication, and so on that children communicate to others the amount and type of distress they are experiencing. Like other forms of behaviour, pain behaviours can be learned. Persistent pain can begin after a period of stomach upset or other illness where the child has associated being sick with attention, sympathy, and care.

Complaining of pain often leads to lots of attention. It can also lead to sympathy, back and shoulder rubs, reassurance, cuddles, being allowed to stay home from school, not having to do the dishes, being offered painkillers and so on. This kind of response from parents is quite normal and appropriate for dealing with acute pain. However, it is not always helpful for a child with chronic pain problems. The attention leads the child to complain more, not less.

Children also learn about pain through observation. Many children with recurring tummy pains have parents who themselves have a chronic pain problem (particularly headaches) or chronic illness. Children can learn a great deal through observation. If they see their own parent frequently complaining of pain, lying down and resting, not being able to complete normal activities including housework, or getting attention and sympathy from other family members, they are more likely to experience pain. Many parents of children with recurring pain can accidentally make the problem worse by giving too much attention when they complain, letting them off routine chores and activities such as going to school, or worrying and talking a great deal about the pain.

When children experience persistent pain, they have only a limited number of strategies to deal with it. They may tell Mum or Dad they feel sick and the parent might, in turn, tell the child to lie down and rest, give him a painkiller, or take their child to the doctor. Some children will try other tacks such as trying not to think about the pain, distracting themselves with another activity, placing a hot water bottle on their stomach, and so on.

More commonly, children complain and expect their parents to take their pain away. This of course is quite normal and is quite appropriate if the child has a virus infection, has injured himself, or is generally unwell. However, it is not always the best way for a child to deal with a chronic pain problem.

There are several things parents can do to help children with persistent pain learn to manage or cope with their pain. In many cases the pain will disappear. It is important for your child to be under medical supervision if you attempt any of the strategies discussed below.

Take your child to your doctor for a thorough medical examination.

It is very important for parents of children who suffer from persistent pain to have the problem thoroughly assessed medically. Some children have a specific physical problem that is causing the pain. The doctor should take a detailed history of the problem and examine your child thoroughly. He or she may also order laboratory tests or refer you to a paediatrician who specialises in gastrointestinal problems (a gastroenterologist). Physical causes for recurring pain do occur, including constipation, worms, hernia, appendicitis, spinal cord tumour, and lactose malabsorption. These need to be checked out and treated.

You might also be asked whether there are any other problems in the family or at school, as for a minority of these children the pain is a symptom of stress or other emotional or behavioural problems.

If the medical investigation shows that there is no medical cause for the pain, which is often the case, many doctors will advise you of that fact, which is often quite reassuring. You may be told not to worry and that the child will eventually grow out of the problem. Some doctors may also give you specific suggestions about not fussing over the child and advise you to concentrate your attention on times when your child is well.

Discuss the problem with your child.

Do not tell your child that she is imagining her pain or that its 'in her head'. If your doctor did not discuss the problem with the child, then explain to her that she is not seriously ill, that while the pain is uncomfortable it will eventually pass, and that she must learn to cope with the problem herself.

Offer to help your child learn a new way of dealing with the pain.

Explain that this will involve three things: keeping a pain diary, practising some special exercises to reduce the pain, and being provided with some incentives for having fewer and fewer pain complaints.

Introduce your child to the pain diary.

Figure 13 on page 250 is an example of the kind of pain diary your child should complete three times a day. The diary is a 10 cm line in the shape of a thermometer, with one end corresponding to 'no pain at all' and the other to 'really bad pain'. The child marks the point on

Figure 13: Pain diary

Name:_____ **Date:**_____

Rate your level of pain today by marking on the thermometer how bad the pain is.

7.00 a.m.

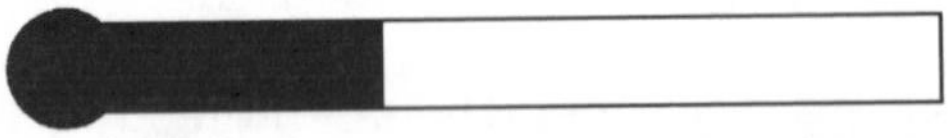

no pain at all   really bad pain

3.30 p.m.

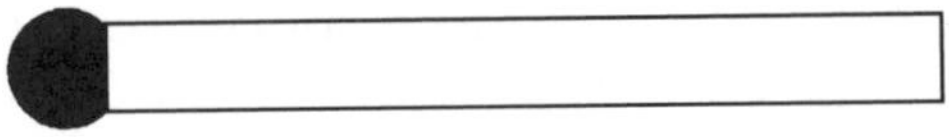

no pain at all   really bad pain

7.30 p.m.

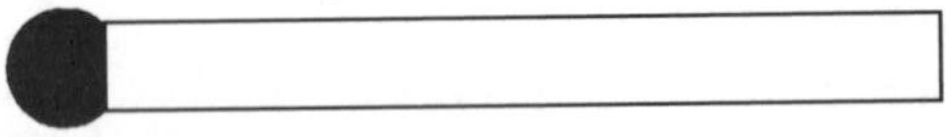

no pain at all   really bad pain

the line that corresponds to how much pain she is experiencing at the specific time. It is important that the ratings be done at the same time each day. This record is used throughout the programme to monitor your child's progress.

The diary should be kept in a convenient place, such as in the kitchen, so that it serves as a reminder to fill in the record.

You should also keep an independent record of your child's pain behaviour similar to the one in figure 14 on page 00. This record breaks each day into one hour time blocks. If any of the behaviours occur during the hour, simply put a tick in the appropriate column. Don't bother to record every instance during the hour, just note whether the behaviour occurred at all.

Help your child learn some coping skills to deal with the pain.

Explain that from now on you want your child to try some new ways of dealing with the pain. There are several things that children can do when they are in pain. These include using deep breathing and relaxation techniques, changing what they say to themselves when in pain, diverting their attention, and using imagery. These are explained below. The best way to teach children these skills is to practise the skills with them until they learn to use them correctly. Rather than insisting that the child use these skills, turn the exercise into an experiment. This involves suggesting that the child tries each one then decides for himself which ones work best for him.

Relaxation techniques

There are many different ways of learning to relax. We have found a method developed by Dr Tom Ollendick very helpful with school-aged children who have pain problems. Rather than trying to teach your child the technique yourself, you might be able to find a commercially produced audiotape that is suitable, however most of these are not developed specifically for children. You could also consider taking your child to a psychologist or other professional who offers relaxation training. If you tackle the task yourself, make a good quality audiocassette recording of your own voice as you read the list of instructions below. It is very important to use a soothing, relaxing, calming tone of voice when making the recording. Perhaps a friend would be willing to help you here. The full list of instructions is given in Appendix 2.

Relaxation training works best when your child practises it regularly, say once or twice a day for about 15 to 20 minutes. Do the exercise with your child the first few times and offer praise for completing the practice session.

It often takes several practice sessions before a child learns to relax completely. Once the child has mastered the basic technique he should be encouraged to practise relaxing as soon as he feels a pain starting.

Positive thinking

This involves teaching children things that they can say to themselves when they are in pain, as an alternative to complaining. Some children in pain think a lot of negative thoughts, such as 'This is never going to go away.' 'Gosh this hurts.' 'Why is this happening to me?' 'What have I done to deserve this?' 'I hate this. I can't bear it.' These

Figure 14: Pain observation record

Name:_____ Day:_____ Date:_____

Time	PC	RA	CR	VP	NVPB	RST	NI	Other
7–8 a.m.	✓	✓	✓			✓		
8–9 a.m.								
9–10 a.m.								
10–11 a.m.								
11–12 p.m.								
12–1 p.m.								
1–2 p.m.								
2–3 p.m.								
3–4 p.m.								
4–5 p.m.								
5–6 p.m.								
6–7 p.m.								
7–8 p.m.								

Instruction sheet for parent's pain observation record (Figure 14)

During the day, your child may exhibit behaviours as a result of being in pain. These pain behaviours could include any of the following:

Pain complaint (PC): This includes any instance of intelligible vocal protests about pain, for example 'I've got a sore tummy.' It does not include whining, crying, or other protests that do not mention or refer directly to the experience of pain.

Requests of assistance (RA): This includes any requests for help or assistance as a consequence of being in pain, such as request for medication, or for help to perform or complete a task.

Crying (CR): This category includes any crying due to the child being in pain.

Vocal protest (VP): This category includes any instance of intelligible vocal protests, displays of temper, or oppositional behaviour such as refusing to comply with a request.

Non-verbal pain behaviours (NVPB): This category refers to any of the following:

Guarding — abnormally stiff, interrupted, or rigid movement while moving from one position to another.
Bracing — a stationary position in which a limb supports another part of the body for a few seconds.
Rubbing — rubbing or holding of the areas affected by the pain for a few seconds.
Grimacing — obvious facial expression of pain such as narrowed eyes, tightened lips, corners of mouth pulled back.
Sighing — any obvious exaggerated exhalation of breath accompanied by shoulders rising then falling.

Resting (RST): This category includes resting on the bed other than at bedtime, or lying down anywhere else in the house without being engaged in an activity.

Non-interaction (NI): This category describes an absence of interactions with objects or persons.

Each time you observe any of these behaviours occuring during successive 1-hour intervals, please place a tick in the appropriate column or columns on the recording sheet.

sort of thoughts often make the pain seem worse. Positive thinking involves substituting different thoughts to deal with pain. Here are some examples of things children can be encouraged to say to themselves.

When they have no pain. 'I feel great. That's two days now.' 'It's working, I have not had a bad pain all morning.' 'Keep cool, stay relaxed, and you'll beat it.'

When the pain starts. 'Stay cool. Don't get uptight.' 'Think positive.' 'Where is my pain?' 'Take a deep breath. Count back from ten.' 'What do I do next?' 'Hang in there. This will pass.' 'Just relax. Focus on deep slow breaths.' 'OK, find something to look at.' 'Just keep on going with what I'm doing.'

When the pain improves. 'Well done, I'm beating this.' 'Good work. It's starting to go.' 'I can't wait to tell mum about this.'

When the pain worsens. 'Move slowly. This will pass.' 'It'll be over soon.' 'Keep trying one of my strategies.'

Figure 15 opposite shows a summary of a self-coping strategy we have used to teach children with RAP to challenge and confront their pain.

Deal with pain complaints by prompting your child to use self-coping strategies.

This involves changing the way you as a parent deal with complaints like 'Mummy, my tummy hurts,' or 'Daddy, I feel sick.' When your child approaches, suggest he tries one of his strategies. 'OK. Now's the time. Remember what we talked about. Why don't you try one of the exercises I showed you?'

If the child complies, offer praise and encouragement for getting started.

'That's the boy Dean, you're dealing with it yourself.'

If the child continues to complain or refuses to practise, suggest a specific exercise to try.

Become more specific in your suggestion. 'How about listening to the relaxation tape first to see if that helps?'

If complaining continues, describe the problem then withdraw all attention.

Let the child know that complaining simply does not help. 'Talking about it will not help your pain. It's over to you.' Walk away, ignoring all further protests.

Figure 15: Self-coping strategy for dealing with pain

Step 1   **Notice**

A   Notice where the pain is.

B   Tell myself to take a deep breath.

C   Ask myself: What do I have to do next?

Step 2   **Check**

A   Is my pain 1, 2, 3, or 4? (1 = a little pain, 2 = slight pain, 3 = fairly bad pain, 4 = really bad pain.)

B   Watch what happens to my pain now.

Step 3   **Relax**

A   Look closely at something nearby.

B   Relax my muscles.

C   Is my pain 1, 2, 3, or 4?

D   Check to see if the pain has eased

Step 4   **Reward**

A   Say to myself: I am doing well.

B   Remind myself that the pain will go away as I am in control.

C   If I have no more pain then??? leave out the next step.

Step 5   **Imagine**

A   Imagine eating the rest of my pain away.

B   Is my pain 1, 2, 3, or 4?

Step 6   **Repeat**

A   Repeat steps 2, 3, 4, and 5 as needed.

If your child acts as though she is in pain but doesn't complain to you, then ignore her completely.

If you see your child bracing her stomach, walking in a guarded way, or grimacing, ignore this behaviour completely.

Do not give your child any medication to relieve pain unless it is under medical supervision.

There is little evidence to show that analgesics (painkillers) are effective in relieving recurrent abdominal pain in the long run.

Give your child plenty of attention when she is well.

The idea here is to praise frequently and give positive attention to your child when she does not complain of pain and is engaged in normal activities.

Establish some incentives for 'well' behaviour.

Use a chart similar to the one in Figure 16 on page 257 to reward your child for pain-free days. Each day the child goes without any pain he can earn a sticker, star, smiley face, or points. Start off by setting a goal such as three pain-free days for a back-up reward such as a special treat, or activity. Gradually increase the requirement to four, five, six and seven days before the reward can be earned. Review the chart before bedtime each night and offer praise and encouragement for the child's efforts.

Closely monitor your child's symptoms.

Make sure you don't treat all pain complaints in this way. Children with RAP also get influenza, measles, mumps, and viruses, and have accidents. These problems need prompt medical attention and different remedies. You need to distinguish between these kinds of complaints and RAP.

Fostering independence

As children move towards puberty, there can be increasing conflict with parents over desires to become more independent. They may wish to have more privacy, spend more time with friends, talk on the telephone, listen to loud music, and express their opinions more forcefully. Their appearance starts to become more important to them

Figure 16: Self-coping strategy for dealing with pain—record form

Name: _____ Month beginning: _____

Week: _____ Date: _____

	Mon	Tues	Wed	Thurs	Fri	Sat	Sun
Morning (7.00 a.m.– Midday)	—						
Afternoon (Midday–5.00 p.m.)	🙂						
Evening (5.00 p.m.– 10.00 p.m.)	🙂						
Total	2						

Place a sticker, a smiley face, or agreed points in the appropriate box for each time period without pain.

and arguments may develop over hairstyles, use of make-up, and the style of clothing they wish to wear. Most of these changes are quite normal and should not generally be viewed as problems. They need not become a major source of friction in a family if they are handled sensibly.

Some parents experience major traumas with teenagers because they have not prepared themselves or their children adequately for the task of taking increased responsibility. The groundwork for preparing children for adolescence should be laid during the later primary school years. This involves gradually allowing children more freedom to make their own decisions in some areas while keeping firm control in others. Children at this age are generally capable of contributing to family decisions if given the opportunity. Children still need rules to be enforced consistently but at the same time they need to be encouraged to express their opinions and views in appropriate ways. Older children often want to listen to and participate in adult conversation occasionally. They should not be excluded. Here are some ideas for encouraging children to become responsibly independent.

Give children more responsible tasks.

Children learn to act responsibly through practice and experience. There are numerous ways parents can gradually encourage more responsible behaviour. For example, a child may be given the job of being the 'light checker' or family conservationist, whose job it is to turn out lights that are not being used thereby conserving electricity. Children can be involved in responsible chores such as helping clean the pool, planning activities for children who will be visiting, and helping serve and entertain adult guests. The best way to tell whether a child is ready for increased responsibility is to look for signs that they are interested. For example, they may ask to help or enquire how a particular task is done. The key is to take it slowly. Don't over-burden your child too soon.

Give praise and positive attention for successful completion of responsible tasks.

Children deserve praise and recognition when they rise to the occasion and undertake new responsibilities, particularly in the early stages. Offer a specific comment on the parts of the task the child did well, even if they needed your help for some aspects of it.

Pay particular attention to responsible conduct that occurs without prompting or reminders.

When children take the initiative and act responsibly of their own accord, praise and positive attention will encourage them to do so more often. If your child acts responsibly during a crisis, for example if a child is hurt in the playground, remembers what to do if she gets lost in a department store, volunteers to stand for election at school, initiates a plan to start a school newsletter, helps with deliveries for a community voluntary organisation, and so on, these efforts should be met with your approval.

Help your child learn the skills involved in carrying out responsible tasks.

Children often need help in carrying out responsible tasks. Some children will offer to take on things they are not ready for or tasks that are a little too ambitious. Suggesting a more modest plan may be necessary to prevent your child becoming discouraged. One or two quite specific suggestions are better than a lecture or numerous ideas on how to carry out the task.

Ask children for their opinion about issues affecting the family or their own future.

Another aspect of becoming more independent involves children learning appropriate ways to express their ideas and opinions about matters that interest them. Parents can play an important role here by asking children for their opinion on events at school, items of news or current events. 'Brian, what do you think about...?' Children initially may have very little to say or may respond with 'I don't know,' or 'What do you think, Dad?' As children move towards their late primary school years and sense that you are genuinely interested in their opinions, listen to them and take them into account in deciding important family matters. This way they often become better able to express their views more clearly, logically, and concisely.

Do not feel you have to agree with what the child says. It is OK for family members to have differences of opinion, providing they are expressed constructively.

Allow children to make more decisions for themselves.

Another important part of becoming less dependent on parents involves children learning to make decisions. Good decision-making involves identifying alternative courses of action, weighing them up, and choosing which course to pursue. Preadolescent children often find this a difficult task because they find it hard to take into account all relevant pieces of information. For example, they tend to see things from their own perspective, that is, 'How it affects me.' Despite this limitation, children are quite capable of making some decisions for themselves, and the more practice they get the better they become.

The fact of the matter is that children are often confronted with dilemmas or choices before they are ready to make them. For example, many children have their first cigarette before reaching high school, and many teenage girls have sex and some get pregnant before they are legally able to consent.

Children should be encouraged to make simple choices first, such as how to spend their pocket money, who to invite to their birthday party, what gift to choose as a birthday present, which chores to complete in what order, which homework tasks to tackle first. There are many other decisions that parents try to influence, and quite rightly so, until their children reach adolescence, for example when the children should be indoors, where they go after school and who with, what clothes they are allowed to wear, what television programmes they are permitted to watch, what time they go to bed, when they are allowed to date, and which school they attend. In each of these areas it is irresponsible to expect children to be capable of making informed decisions.

How much freedom and choice children should be allowed and at what age is a controversial topic. There are no hard and fast rules here because children of the same age can differ quite considerably in maturity and capabilities. Giving children free reign too soon can be just as damaging and irresponsible as being overly controlling and not allowing a child any choice at all. In general, it is better to introduce more and more opportunities for decision making over a period of years, rather than to wait until a child reaches a specific age when he gets all his freedoms at once. By approaching the task gradually and slowly, children have time to get used to the increased responsibility and trust and become more skilled at making responsible choices. Throughout this process, parents should be prepared to restrict then reinstate freedoms at a later time should the child act irresponsibly.

Helping children solve their own problems

One of the most important life skills young people can learn is the capacity to solve problems for themselves. Throughout their lives they will need this ability if they are to have successful, productive, and happy lives. Problems children are capable of solving come in many shapes and forms. They range from dealing with conflicts with siblings and peers, to handling disappointments and frustrations, to applying knowledge to work out the solution to a mental task. The skill can be developed in children through a combination of practice, observation, learning a few basic skills, and feedback.

Some parents actively discourage their children from becoming independent problem solvers by trying to solve all their child's problems for them. This can be done in quite subtle ways when parents deal with children's questions about dilemmas they confront, and by always giving them the answer to the problem rather than the tools they need to solve the problem for themselves.

Not all children are ready to learn problem-solving skills at the same time, and some will progress slowly. It takes many years for individuals to become skilled problem solvers. The sooner they start the better. Here are some guidelines.

Create opportunities for children to observe family problem solving.

The basics of effective problem solving are best introduced by letting children experience the process. Calling a family meeting to discuss an issue or dilemma can be a useful introduction. Initially start on a problem that is relatively straightforward and not too emotionally charged, for example deciding on where to spend a summer holiday.

Encourage children's participation in and constructive contributions to problem-solving discussions.

When the child expresses an opinion on a possible course of action or solution to a problem, use encouraging comments. 'That's a good idea.' 'Yes that's one possibility. Can you think of any more?'

Prompt children to come up with their own solutions.

Children who run into problems over homework or conflicts with friends often want their parents to solve the problem for them. When this happens, prompt the child to express her own view on how the problem might be resolved. 'Is there anything else you might say to Mandy when she tries to copy your work in class?'

Teach the child the basics of problem solving.

The basic steps in problem solving are defining the problem clearly, generating alternative solutions to the problem ('brainstorming'), weighing up the alternatives, choosing the best solution, implementing the solution, and evaluating the outcome. When your child asks you to solve a problem he is capable of dealing with himself, remind him of each step one at a time. Get out a piece of paper. Ask your child to write down each heading.

Put the responsibility back on to your child. For example, you might say, 'I know this is important to you, but I can't solve the problem for you. Let's do some brainstorming and see what we can come up with. OK?'

PART III

Positive Parenting: Tackling the Task

CHAPTER 7

Putting a Plan
Into Action

This chapter deals with how to tackle the task of putting into action the parenting advice covered in earlier chapters. The best way to ensure that your plan for solving a particular family problem is successful is to take the time to prepare both your child and yourself in advance so that you can carry it out consistently. No strategy will work if you rush into it, without properly considering what will be involved. You will quickly become discouraged and will more than likely give up. Follow the steps below.

Choosing where to begin

This is often the hardest step, particularly if your child has several problems that need to be worked on. Most of the strategies for dealing with specific problems work best when you work on trying to improve the positive aspects of your relationship with your child at the same time. It is generally better to begin with a problem that you are likely to be able to solve. This does not mean choosing a trivial or unimportant issue. Select one or two problem areas to work on.

Check to make sure that the changes you would like to make in your child's behaviour are reasonable. Ask yourself these questions. Do you want to change your child's behaviour for your own convenience, or would your child genuinely benefit from the change?

Carefully read the guidelines dealing with your child's specific problem to make sure you understand what is required and that you have the time, energy, and commitment to follow the plan consistently.

Do not tackle a problem on your own if you feel it requires professional help. For those problems that may have a physical cause contact your family physician for advice.

Taking a baseline and keeping track

A **baseline record** is a measure of how often the problem behaviour occurs over a specific time, usually 7 to 10 days. There are two main types of records that many parents find useful: a frequency record and a duration record.

A **frequency record** involves counting the number of times a specific behaviour occurs during the day and recording this information on a chart or tally sheet. Alternatively, you might be interested in how long a behaviour lasts. An example of a frequency record appears in figure 17 on page 267. Mrs Jameson used this record to get a clear idea of how frequently Daniel, her 8-year-old, threw temper tantrums each day.

You will notice that each time Daniel screamed, shouted or threw himself on the ground, his mother wrote down the time it occurred, where the child was, what happened just before the outburst, and what she did about it. This type of information is often very revealing for parents. You might find that the behaviour is occurring much more frequently than you thought, or that in fact it occurs fairly infrequently. Some parents may decide that the problem is not really a problem at all. You can also get an idea of the times of the day, activities, or other events that seem to trigger outbursts. Finally you can see for yourself how consistently you deal with the problem. In Mrs Jameson's case it was clear that in the week concerned she tried six different methods of handling the problem. The other important purpose of a baseline is that it enables you to evaluate whether your parenting plan is working or not.

A **duration record** involves simply timing how long a behaviour lasts. This is of interest for recording behaviours such as how long a child cries after being put to bed, how long it takes a child to get ready for school, how long a child spends on her homework or chores. An example of a duration record appears in figure 18 on page 269. The Bedford family used this record to assess how long their daughter Mary cried when put into her cot at night.

Another useful way of recording how often a behaviour occurs, especially when it occurs often, say, more than several times an hour, is a **time sample record** like the one in figure 19 on page 270. Simply divide the child's day into time periods — 60, 30, 15 minutes — and place an X in the box corresponding to the time interval when the behaviour occurred.

Information from both of these records is easier to interpret if the data are presented as a simple graph like the one in figure 20 on page 271. To plot the data, simply locate the column corresponding to the day concerned, move up the column until you reach the number of times the behaviour occurred, and place a circle or cross on the graph at that point. After a few days of recording simply join the lines with a ruler.

Working out a parenting plan

The next step is to select the parenting guidelines appropriate to the problem at hand. Read each step carefully. It is often helpful to

Figure 17: Frequency record

Date: 9/10

Problem event	When and where did it occurr	What occurred prior to the event	What occurred following the event	Other comments
Shouting	7.30 a.m. TV room	Told to get dressed for school.	Let him watch TV a little longer.	
Crying	8.00 a.m. TV room	TV turned off, told to get dressed.	Made him go and get dressed.	Rotten morning.
Hitting fists on floor	8.05 a.m. bedroom	Sent to room.	Ignored him.	

List the problem behaviours, when and where they occurred, and what happened before and after the event.
(N.B. Reusable form in Appendix 3)

Figure 18: Duration record

Date	Successive episodes																									Total
	1	2	3	4	5	6	7	8	9	10	11	12	13	14	15	16	17	18	19	20	21	22	23	24	25	
14/11	30 mins	25 mins	32 mins	10 mins	15 mins																					1 hr 52 mins

For each separate occurrence of the target behaviour, record how long it lasted in seconds, minutes, or hours. Total the times at the end of each day.

Figure 19: Time sample record

Child's name: _____   Starting date:_____

Target
Behaviour_____

Time of day
Thirty minute intervals

	M	T	W	T	F	S	S	M	T	W	T	F	S	S	M	T	W	T	F	S	S
7.00–7.30	X	X		X	X	X	X														
7.30–8.00	X		X		X		X														
8.00–8.30	X	X	X	X	X	X	X														
8.30–9.00																					
9.00–9.30																					
9.30–10.00																					
10.00–10.30																					
10.30–11.00																					
11.00–11.30																					
11.30–12.00					X	X	X														
12.00–12.30	X	X		X	X	X	X														
12.30–1.00	X	X	X	X	X		X														
1.00–1.30			X				X														
1.30–2.00																					
2.00–2.30					X																
2.30–3.00																					
3.00–3.30																					
3.30–4.00	X		X	X	X		X														
4.00–4.30	X	X		X	X	X															
4.30–5.00	X	X	X	X	X	X	X														
5.00–5.30	X	X	X	X	X																
5.30–6.00	X	X	X	X	X	X	X														
6.00–6.30	X	X	X	X		X															
6.30–7.00	X	X	X	X	X	X	X														
7.00–7.30																					
7.30–8.00																					
8.00–8.30																					
8.30–9.00																					
9.00–9.30																					
9.30–10.00																					

M T W T F S S   M T W T F S S   M T W T F S S

Successive days

☐ Behaviour did not occur   ☒ Behaviour occurred at least once

(N.B. Reusable form in Appendix 3)

summarise the steps in a checklist like the one in figure 21 on page 273. This will serve as a quick reminder of what you need to do. For the first few weeks of the programme, or until you have learned what to do, note down for each step whether you carried it out or not. Just record 'yes', 'no', or 'not applicable' (which indicates that the step was not appropriate on that occasion). Simply add up the yeses, divide by the number of nos, and multiply by 100 to get a measure of how accurately you carried out the plan. You should be aiming for 100 per cent accuracy.

Putting a plan into action

Perhaps the most important ingredient in successful efforts to change children's behaviour is laying the groundwork properly. Take particular note of the sections in the guides that tell you the advance preparations you need to make, particularly those involving discussing the problem and the plan with your child. Once this has been done, put the plan into action for an adequate trial period. A trial period can last 7 to 10 days. At the end of the trial period, if good progress is being made and things have been working smoothly, you need to decide whether to continue as is or to make minor changes in your plan.

Monitoring progress and trouble shooting

During the early phases of a new parenting plan you will need to monitor your child's progress closely. Keep your baseline record going and continue to graph the information so that you can properly assess whether the desired results are being achieved. If you are experiencing problems, first check to make sure that you have been following the suggested guidelines accurately. If you have been following them accurately but your partner has not, you will need to discuss the issue with him or her and try to reach agreement on how best to deal with the problem.

Tackling other problems

Once you have successfully tackled one problem, you may decide to deal with other problems. The main guide here is not to tackle too

Figure 20: Behaviour graph

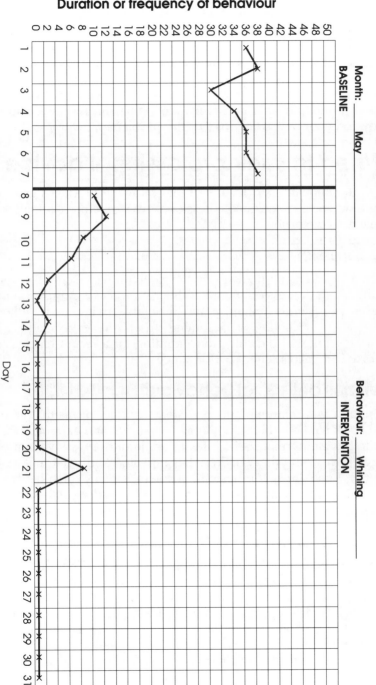

Month: _____ May _____

Behaviour: _____ Whining _____

BASELINE

INTERVENTION

Duration or frequency of behaviour

Day

Plot the number of times the behaviour occurs each day by placing a cross or circle in the appropriate column, then join up the marks for each day.

N.B. Reusable form in Appendix 3

271

much at once. Changing children's behaviour, and indeed your own, is often most successful when the task is tackled gradually. If you rush into making too many changes at once, your child may feel overwhelmed and gains achieved in one area may be compromised. Many of the principles and ideas can be successfully employed in dealing with problems not specifically discussed in this book. If you have found the advice useful then by all means be creative and develop your own solutions to other problems.

When to seek professional advice

If your child suffers from any of the following problems give serious consideration to seeking professional advice before deciding how to deal with the problem.

Depression

Some children, particularly in the later primary school years, may suffer from depression. Some of the symptoms of depression include being persistently unhappy and miserable, withdrawn, sullen, not sleeping well, crying or becoming upset very easily, talking about harming oneself, difficulty concentrating, or a recent change for the worse in a child's school performance.

Serious antisocial behaviour

Children with extreme and persistent conduct problems often need professional help. If your child has persistent and extreme difficulties in following normal social rules or adult authority, is violent or very aggressive with other children, has repeated and persistent rage outbursts, lights fires, is repeatedly insolent, cheeky, or rude, has been truanting from school, or stealing, then consider professional assistance.

Unusual or bizarre behaviour

A small number of children engage in behaviour that is clearly unusual compared to that of their peer group. These include hallucinations, such as hearing voices that no one else can hear; bizarre beliefs or delusions, for example believing that they are on a special mission from god; obsessions, such as recurring distressing thoughts over which they have no control; or compulsions such as rituals which they have to perform in order to avoid considerable anxiety.

Figure 21: Parenting checklist

Situation: Fighting over toys

Steps to be completed	Date:								
	Time:								
1 Gain child's attention.									
2 Give a terminating instructions.									
3 Describe the correct behaviour (what the child should do).									
4 Wait five seconds.									
5 Repeat the instructions once if necessary.									
6 Speak up and praise if the child obeys the request.									
7 If the problem continues, describe what is wrong and introduce an immediate natural consequence (eg. remove the troublesome toy); explain why you are doing it.									
8 If the child disobeys or throws a tantrum, describe what he or she has done wrong again and take the child immediately to quiet time.									
9 If the problem continues, put the child in time out immediately with a brief explanation.									
10 Remove the child from time out when he or she has been quiet for the assigned time.									
Number of Steps Completed:									

Whenever this situation occurs, record yes, no, or n.a. (not applicable) for each of the steps.
(N.B. Reusable form in Appendix 3)

Traumatic experiences

If your child has had an extremely distressing experience such as witnessing a violent crime, or a death of a parent or sibling, or has been in an accident or a natural disaster, she may suffer from a condition called post-traumatic stress. Symptoms include having vivid and distressing flashbacks to the event, recurring nightmares, marked anxiety, depression, and recurring thoughts about the distressing event.

Persistent anxiety or fear

Consider referral to a specialist for any child who generally appears nervous, anxious, panicky, or fearful in many different situations.

These are just a few examples of behaviours that are outside the normal range of problems experienced in most families. *If in doubt and the problem does not go away, then get an independent professional opinion.*

Conclusion

In the preceding pages we have covered a wide range of parenting issues and problems relating to promoting children's development and dealing with children's behaviour. Some of you may feel that many of the things you are doing as parents contribute to your child's difficulty. In my experience this is rarely the case. The vast majority of parents I have worked with are doing a great many positive and effective things with their children; they care for their children and want to do things that are in their best interests. The solutions to many common difficulties often involve relatively minor changes or adjustments to the things that parents are already doing. For example, praising good behaviour a little more often, using a different discipline tactic a little more consistently, or simply observing your children more closely so that you become more aware of what they are doing, can produce dramatic and lasting improvements in some children's behaviour.

The basic message in this book is an optimistic one. The vast majority of children's behaviour and adjustment difficulties can be resolved by parents and children working together towards a common end. Many serious problems can be substantially improved so that a child does not have to endure a life of misery and unhappiness. More minor problems, which are often part of children's normal development, can be tackled in a straightforward way using commonsense parenting. Remember, all children whine, complain, protest, have disagreements with their parents, and become upset at times. The way we deal with these issues does, however, influence whether the problems continue, worsen, or improve as the child grows older.

In concluding I hope you have found the information on parenting in this book useful in undertaking the complex task of raising a well-adjusted youngster.

Further Reading

For general readers:

Dodson, F. and Alexander, A. (1986). *Your child: Birth to age 6*. New York: Simon & Schuster.

Forgatch, M. and Patterson, G.R. (1989). *Parent and adolescent: Living together: Part Two, Family problem solving*. Eugene, Oregon: Castalia Publishing Co.

Sloane, H.N.C. (1988). *The good kid book: How to solve the 16 most common behaviour problems*. Champaign, Illinois: Research Press.

White, B.L. (1975). *The first three years of life*. Englewood Cliffs, New Jersey: Prentice-Hall Inc.

For professional readers:

Patterson, G.R. (1982). *Coercive family processes*. Eugene, Oregon: Castalia Publishing Co.

Sanders, M.R., & Dadds, M.R. (1992), *Behavioural Family Intervention*. New York: Pergamon Press.

APPENDIX I

Dietary guidelines for children

It is necessary to have a variety of foods in the diet to promote growth, health and well-being. Daily selection of foods from the five food groups helps to ensure the provision of a nutritionally adequate diet.

The five food groups

Food group	Minimum number of servings for young children	Key nutrients	Some foods to choose
Breads, cereal, rice, pasta	4 1 serving = 1 slice bread = 1/2 cup cooked pasta/rice	Carbohydrate Thiamine Iron Niacin	Wholegrain/white bread, cereal, pasta, rice, muffins, crackers, bagels
Fruit and vegetables	4 1 serving = 1 fruit = 1/2 cup vegetables	Vitamin A Vitamin C	Apple, applesauce, apricots, banana, cantaloupe, fruit juices, pear, plum, broccoli, carrots, capsicum, cauliflower, corn, green beans, peas, potato, tomato, zucchini
Meat, poultry, fish, and meat alternatives	2 1 serving = 90g meat = 120g fish = 1 egg = 3/4 cup pulses = 1/4 cup nuts*	Protein Niacin Iron Thiamine	Beef, veal, pork ham, lamb, chicken, turkey, fish, soya beans, chick peas, lentils, peanut butter, eggs, nuts*
Milk, yoghurt, cheese	3 1 serving = 250ml milk = 1 cup yoghurt = 30g hard cheese	Calcium Riboflavin Protein	Milk,+ yoghurt,+ hard cheeses,+ cottage cheese,+ puddings, custard
Fats & oils	1 1 serving = 1 tablespoon oil = 30g butter or margarine	Vitamin A Vitamin D Vitamin E	Vegetable oils (canola, olive, safflower), margarine (Pufa), butter

* Not to be given to children under 5.
+ Low fat varieties not to be used under 2 years of age.
Pufa = high in polyunsaturated fatty acids.

Sample Menus

Example menus for 18 months – 3 years	Example menus for 3 – 5 years
Breakfast Cereal - 1 Weetbix or 1/2 cup porridge and milk Toast - 1/2 slice with butter or margarine (Pufa), peanut paste, vegemite, honey, jam Milk - 250ml whole milk, to drink	**Breakfast** Cereal - 1 1/2 Weetbix or 3/4 cup porridge and milk Toast - 1/2-1 slice with butter or margarine (Pufa) with 1 egg scrambled, boiled or poached Milk - 150ml whole milk, to drink
Mid-morning Milk or juice and/or piece fruit, cracker	**Mid-morning** Milk or juice, and/or 1 banana, 1 apple
Lunch Sandwich - 1 slice bread with butter or margarine (Pufa) with cheese, peanut paste - 1/3 cup yoghurt and/or fruit	**Lunch** Sandwich = 1–2 slices bread with butter or margarine (Pufa) with cheese, peanut paste, cottage cheese and tomato - 1/3 cup yoghurt, 1/3 cup custard and/or fruit
Mid-afternoon Milk or juice and/or 1/2 banana	**Mid-afternoon** Milk or juice, and/or 1/2 slice fruit cake
Tea - Minced or chopped meat, flaked or crumbed fish or vegetarian dish including pulses - 1 small boiled or mashed potato and 1/3 cup vegetables - Milk to drink	**Tea** - Small crumbed and grilled leg of chicken or 1 grilled sausage or 1/2 cup savoury mince or fish fillet in sauce - 1 small baked potato or 1/2 cup pasta and 1/3 cup vegetables or a small salad with carrot and celery sticks - 1/3 cup ice cream and/or fruit
Supper Milk to drink	**Supper** Milk to drink

Example menus for 5 - 8 years	Example menus for 8 - teen years
Breakfast Cereal – 1 1/3 Weetbix, 3/4 cup porridge, 3/4 cup cornflakes and milk Toast – 1 slice with butter or margarine (Pufa), 1 slice cheese, 1/4 cup baked beans, 1 egg Milk and or juice to drink	**Breakfast** Cereal – 2 Weetbix, 1 cup porridge, 1 cup cornflakes and milk Toast – 1 slice with butter or margarine (Pufa), cheese, 1/2 cup baked beans, 1 egg, etc Milk and/or juice, tea, coffee
Mid-morning Milk or juice and/or 1 fruit	**Mid-morning** Juice and 1 fruit
Lunch Sandwich – 2 slices bread with butter or margarine (Pufa) with 1 slice ham, cheese, peanut paste, chopped egg, meat paste Small salad or raw carrot, tomato, celery – 1 Fruit or 2 tablespoons dried fruit and/or 1/2 carton yoghurt	**Lunch** Sandwich or roll (wholemeal or grain) with butter or margarine (Pufa) with ham, cheese, cottage cheese, peanut paste, meat paste, egg etc Plus salad with carrot, celery, capsicum Plus fresh fruit, dried fruit, nuts or cheese
Mid-afternoon Milk or juice and/or 2 crackers with cottage cheese	**Mid-afternoon** Fruit or sandwich or crackers and low fat cheese Milk to drink
Tea – Meat, meat rissole/burger grilled, fillet of fish – 2 small potatoes boiled, mashed, baked or 3/4 cup pasta/rice – 1/2 cup vegetables or a salad OR – Made up dish, e.g. pizza, fish pie, cottage pie, pasta and meat sauce, lasagne etc – Fruit and 1/2 cup custard or 1/2 cup yoghurt or 2 scoops frozen yoghurt	**Tea** – Meat, fish, vegetarian dish – 2-3 small potatoes boiled, mashed, baked, roasted or 3/4 cup pasta or rice – 1/2 cup of vegetables (include at least 2 types) OR made up dish, e.g. fish pie, lasagne, etc - Fruit pie plus 1/2 cup custard or 2 scoops ice cream or 3/4 cup yoghurt - Milk to drink
Supper Milk or cocoa to drink	**Supper** Milk, cocoa, etc Older children may enjoy a bowl of cereal or toast or a sandwich snack

Prepared with the assistance of Ms Clare Wall, Research Dietitian, Children's Nutrition Research Centre, Royal Children's Hospital and Department of Child Health, University of Queensland.

APPENDIX 2

Relaxation training

Rationale

Sometimes we all feel kind of tense or nervous. When you feel nervous your muscles get all tight and tense and it is hard to pay attention to what you are supposed to be doing. For example, some people feel nervous before they take a test or feel tense when they are meeting someone new. Can you give some examples of when you have felt tense? [allow children to respond] We're going to learn how to make ourselves feel nice and relaxed instead of tight and tense. We'll learn how to tell when our muscles feel tense and how to make them feel relaxed. [If any muscles are sore on a particular day and tensing them hurts, be sure to stop the child tensing those muscles and just relax them.]

Hands and arms

Pretend you have a whole lemon in your left hand. Now squeeze it hard. Try to squeeze all the juice out. Feel the tightness in your hand and arm as you squeeze. Now drop the lemon. Notice how your muscles feel when they are relaxed. Take another lemon and squeeze it. Try to squeeze this one harder than you did the first one. That's right. Real hard. Now drop your lemon and relax. See how much better your hand and arm feel when they are relaxed. Once again, take a lemon in your left hand and squeeze all the juice out. Don't leave a single drop. Squeeze hard. Good. Now relax and let the lemon fall from your hand. [Repeat the process for the right hand and arm.]

Arms and shoulders

Pretend you are a furry, lazy cat. You want to stretch. Stretch your arms out in front of you. Raise them up high over your head. Way back. Feel the pull in your shoulders. Stretch higher. Now just let your arms drop back to your side. OK, kitten, stretch again. Stretch your arms out in front of you. Raise them over your head. Pull them back, way back. Pull hard. Now let them drop quickly. Good. Notice how your shoulders feel more relaxed. This time let's have a great big stretch. Try to touch the ceiling. Stretch your arms way out in front of you. Notice the tension and pull in your arms and shoulders. Hold tight now. Great. Let them drop very quickly and feel how good it is to be relaxed. It feels good and warm and lazy.

Shoulders and neck

Now pretend you are a turtle. You're sitting out on a rock by a nice, peaceful pond, just relaxing in the warm sun. It feels nice and warm and safe here. Oh-oh! You sense danger. Pull your head into your house. Try to pull your shoulders up to your ears and push your head down into your shoulders. Hold in tight. It isn't easy to be a turtle in a shell. The danger is past now. You can come out into the warm sunshine, and, once again, you can relax and feel the warm sunshine. Watch out now! More danger. Hurry, pull your head back into your house and hold it tight. You have to be closed in tight to protect yourself. OK, you can relax now. Bring your head out and let your shoulders relax. Notice how much better it feels to be relaxed than to be all tight. One more time now. Danger! Pull your head in. Push your shoulders way up to your ears and hold tight. Don't let even a tiny piece of your head show outside your shell. Hold it. Feel the tenseness in your neck and shoulders. OK. You can come out now. It's safe again. Relax and feel comfortable in your safety. There's no more danger. Nothing to worry about. Nothing to be afraid of. You feel good.

Jaw

You have a giant jawbreaker bubblegum in your mouth. It's very hard to chew. Bite down on it. Hard! Let your neck muscles help you. Now relax. Just let your jaw drop. OK, let's tackle that jawbreaker again now. Bite down. Hard! Try to squeeze it out between your teeth. That's good. You're really tearing that gum up. Now relax again. Just let your jaw drop off your face. It feels so good just to let go and not have to fight that bubble gum. OK, one more time. We're really going to tear if up this time. Bite down. Hard as you can. Harder. Oh, you're really working hard. Good. Now relax. Try to relax your whole body. You've beaten the bubble gum. Let yourself go as loose as you can.

Face and nose

Here comes a pesky old fly. He has landed on your nose. Try to get him off without using your hands. That's right, wrinkle up your nose. Make as many wrinkles in your nose as you can. Scrunch your nose up real hard. Good. You've chased him away. Now you can relax your nose. Oops, here he comes back again. Shoo him off. Wrinkle it up hard. Hold it just as tight as you can. OK, he flew away. You can relax your face. Notice that when you scrunch up your nose that your cheeks and your mouth and your forehead and your eyes all help you, they get tight, too. So when you relax your nose, your whole face relaxes too, and that feels good. Oh-oh! This time that old fly has come back, but this time he's on your forehead. Make lots of wrinkles. Try to catch him between all those wrinkles. Hold it tight, now. OK, you can let go. He's gone for good. Now you can just relax. Let your face go smooth, no wrinkles anywhere. Your face feels nice and smooth and relaxed.

Stomach

Hey! Here comes a cute baby elephant. But he's not watching where he's going. He doesn't see you lying there in the grass, and he's about to step on your stomach. Don't move. You don't have time to get out of the way. Just get ready for him. Make your stomach very hard. Tighten up your stomach muscles real tight. Hold it. It looks like he is going the other way. You can relax now. Let your stomach go soft. Let it be as relaxed as you can. That feels so much better. Oops, he's coming this way again. Get ready. Tighten up your stomach. Real hard. If he steps on you when your stomach is hard, it won't hurt. Make your stomach into a rock. OK, he's moving away again. You can relax now. Kind of settle down, get comfortable, and relax. Notice the difference between a tight stomach and a relaxed one. That's how we want it to feel: nice and loose and relaxed. You won't believe this, but this time he's really coming your way and not turning around. He's headed straight for you. Tighten up. Tighten hard. Here he comes. This is really it. You've got to hold on tight. He's stepping on you. He's stepped over you. Now he's gone for good. You can relax completely. You're safe. Everything is OK, and you can feel nice and relaxed.

Legs and feet

Now pretend that you are standing barefoot in a big, fat mud puddle. Squish your toes down deep into the mud. Try to get your feet down to the bottom of the mud puddle. You'll probably need your legs to help you push. Push down, spread your toes apart, and feel the mud squish up between your toes. Now step out of the mud puddle. Relax your feet. Let your toes go loose and feel how nice that is. It feels good to be relaxed. Back into the mud puddle. Squish your toes down. Let your leg muscles help you push your feet down. Push your feet. Hard! Try to squeeze that mud puddle dry. OK, come back out now. Relax your feet, relax your legs, relax your toes. It feels so good to be relaxed. No tenseness anywhere. You feel kind of warm and tingly.

From T.H. Ollendick. Relaxation training instructions. Department of Psychology, Virginia Polytechnic and State University. Reproduced by permission from the author.

Reusable forms of key figures

Family job chart

Instructions: List the jobs assigned to each family member and tick off the jobs completed each day.

Month: _____

Date

	1	2	3	4	5	6	7	8	9	10	11	12	13	14	15	16	17	18	19	20	21	22	23	24	25	26	27	28	29	30	31

Frequency record

Instructions: List the problem behaviours, when and where they occurred, and what happened before and after the event.

Date:

Problem event	When and where did it occur	What occurred prior to the event	What occurred following the event	Other comments

Time sample record

Child's name: _____   **Starting date:** _____

KEY: ☐ Behaviour did not occur   ☒ Behaviour occured at least once   **Target Behaviour:**_____

Time of day / Thirty minute intervals																				
7.00–7.30																				
7.30–8.00																				
8.00–8.30																				
8.30–9.00																				
9.00–9.30																				
9.30–10.00																				
10.00–10.30																				
10.30–11.00																				
11.00–11.30																				
11.30–12.00																				
12.00–12.30																				
12.30–1.00																				
1.00–1.30																				
1.30–2.00																				
2.00–2.30																				
2.30–3.00																				
3.00–3.30																				
3.30–4.00																				
4.00–4.30																				
4.30–5.00																				
5.00–5.30																				
5.30–6.00																				
6.00–6.30																				
6.30–7.00																				
7.00–7.30																				
7.30–8.00																				
8.00–8.30																				
8.30–9.00																				
9.00–9.30																				
9.30–10.00																				

Successive days

Instructions: Place a cross in the box for any time period during which the target behaviour occurred.

Behaviour graph

Month: _____

Behaviour: _____

Instructions: Plot the number of times the behaviour occurs each day by placing a cross or circle in the appropriate column, then join up the marks for each day.

Duration or frequency of behaviour

BASELINE

INTERVENTION

Day

Parenting checklist

Situation:

Instructions: Whenever this situation occurs, record yes, no, or n.a. (not applicable) for each of the steps.

Steps to be completed	Date:													
	Time:													
1														
2														
3														
4														
5														
6														
7														
8														
9														
10														
Number of Steps Completed:														

Index